A
Rush
to
Judgment

A
Rush
to Roger
E. Salhany
Judgment

The Unfair Trial of Louis Riel

DUNDURN
TORONTO

Publisher: Scott Fraser | Editor: Laurie Miller
Cover designer: Sophie Paas-Lang
Cover image: Library and Archives Canada, R5768-2-5-F.
Printer: Webcom, a division of Marquis Book Printing Inc.

Library and Archives Canada Cataloguing in Publication

Title: A rush to judgment : the unfair trial of Louis Riel / Roger E. Salhany.
Names: Salhany, Roger E., author.
Description: Includes bibliographical references and index.
Identifiers: Canadiana (print) 20190196130 | Canadiana (ebook) 20190196157 | ISBN 9781459746091 (softcover) | ISBN 9781459746107 (PDF) | ISBN 9781459746114 (EPUB)
Subjects: LCSH: Riel, Louis, 1844-1885—Trials, litigation, etc. | LCSH: Trials (Treason)—Canada—History—19th century. | LCSH: Riel Rebellion, 1885.
Classification: LCC KE228.R54 S22 2019 | DDC 345.71/0231—dc23

We acknowledge the support of the Canada Council for the Arts and the Ontario Arts Council for our publishing program. We also acknowledge the financial support of the Government of Ontario, through the Ontario Book Publishing Tax Credit and Ontario Creates, and the Government of Canada.

VISIT US AT

dundurn.com | @dundurnpress | dundurnpress | dundurnpress

Dundurn
3 Church Street, Suite 500
Toronto, Ontario, Canada
M5E 1M2

You shall inherit hours which are replaced,
The earth won back, the trustier human ways
From history recovered, on them based
An amplitude of noble life.

— John Pudney, "The Dead"

Over and above the question whether the evidence supports the conviction is the question whether the trial is being conducted by an unprejudiced Judge who understands the limits of the judicial function and understands his sworn duty to conduct the case within the limits of its issues.

— Mr. Justice Bora Laskin in dissent in *Regina v. Bevacqua and Palmieri*, January 22, 1970

Contents

1	Introduction	1
2	The Early Years	13
3	The Rebellion	31
4	The Players	53
5	The Evidence of Treason	81
6	The Defence of Insanity	135
7	The Speech by the Defence	179
8	Riel's Speech from the Dock	201
9	The Speech by the Crown	223
10	The Judge's Charge to the Jury	239
11	The Verdict of the Jury	255
12	The Appeals	261
13	The Medical Commission	275
14	The Aftermath	283
	Appendix	299
	Notes	313
	Bibliography	318
	Image Credits	322
	Index	323

CHAPTER 1

Introduction

At ten o'clock sharp on Tuesday, July 28, 1885, the trial of Louis David Riel for treason against Her Majesty Queen Victoria began in a small, makeshift courtroom on the ground floor of a rented two-storey brick building in downtown Regina. The province of Saskatchewan had not yet been created and Regina was a small prairie town in the North-West Territories.[1] Although criminal trials at the time were usually conducted at the barracks of the North-West Mounted Police, the barracks were considered too cramped for a trial of this importance. Journalists from all parts of Canada and prominent local citizens had gathered to witness the trial. To accommodate everyone, including the lawyers, the jury and the various court officials, the offices of a land company had been rented.

That day was a typically hot and dusty dry summer day on the Prairies. Reporters, lawyers, and officials had arrived in Regina from around the world to watch the biggest trial in Canadian history. All of the participants in the trial and the spectators were packed into the sweltering fifty-foot by twenty-foot airless room. The trial lasted five days, ending in the late afternoon of Saturday, August 1, 1885. At 2:15 p.m. on that day, Judge Hugh Richardson, after a long charge to the jury, which he had begun on the previous day, sent the jury of six men out to the jury room to deliberate. After only an hour, they returned with their verdict. Francis Cosgrove, the foreman, rose to announce it.

"Guilty."

But Cosgrove was not finished. He had a message for the judge from his fellow jurors: "Your Honor, I have been asked by my brother jurors to recommend the prisoner to the mercy of the Crown."

The law required Judge Richardson to ask Riel if he had anything to say as to why the sentence of the court — death by hanging, which was the only sentence for treason — should not be pronounced upon him.

Louis Riel had a great deal to say. "Yes, your Honor ..." — but before he could speak, one of his lawyers, Charles Fitzpatrick, interrupted Riel to ask the judge to note the objections Riel's lawyers had already made at the beginning of the trial to the jurisdiction of the court to try Riel. The judge said that he would do so. Riel then asked, "Can I speak now?"

"Oh yes," Richardson replied.

Riel knew that it would be the last time that he would ever be able to speak in a public forum to the people of Canada. He was anxious to justify to them why he had led his Métis people against the government in a rebellion that had just been crushed by the Canadian Army. He had sent letters to the prime minister, Sir John A. Macdonald, asking for a trial before the Supreme Court of Canada so that he could explain to the Canadian public his reasons for the Métis rebellion, but his letters had gone unanswered. Now, if he was going to die, he wanted to die with honour and dignity. He began, "Your Honors, gentlemen of the jury," but was interrupted by Judge Richardson, who reminded him that "there is no jury now, they are discharged."

Riel responded with an unusual comment: "Well, they have passed away before." Riel, who had studied law, must have known that the jury had been discharged after they had rendered their verdict. His answer is puzzling.

Instead of inquiring what Riel had meant, Judge Richardson, anxious to bring an end to the trial and deliver the sentence, simply agreed: "Yes, they have passed away."

Riel quickly responded: "But at the same time I consider them yet still there, still in their seats."

It was unlikely that Riel was speaking about the jury of six men that had just found him guilty of treason. He was probably speaking about the jury of Canadian citizens to whom he had sought to justify his actions from the first day the trial began. He had addressed the jury in the courtroom the day before, when the judge had finally allowed him to speak from the prisoner's dock for the first time during his trial. In a long, rambling address, he had denounced his lawyers' attempts to paint him as a lunatic who did not appreciate the nature of his actions. Although the law in 1885 did not allow an accused to give evidence as a sworn witness from the witness box, the judge had allowed him to speak to the jury as an unsworn witness from the prisoner's dock. It would be eight more years before Canadian law would abolish this ancient and illogical obstacle that prevented an accused from answering his accusers.

The jury had rendered its verdict and had found him guilty of treason. Only the court of appeal of the province or the Judicial Committee of the Privy Council in England could reverse the verdict. If that failed, it would be up to the Canadian government whether to honour the jury's recommendation of mercy and to commute the death sentence to one of life imprisonment.

Riel went on to address the court for the next three hours, attempting to justify his life of revolution, but no one really listened. When he had finished, Judge Richardson pronounced the sentence he was required to impose under the law:

> For me, I have only one duty to perform, that is, to tell you what the sentence of law is upon you. I have, as I must, given time to enable your case to be heard. All I can suggest or advise you is to prepare to meet your end, that is all the advice or suggestion I can give you. It is now my painful duty to pass the sentence of the court upon you, and that is, that you be taken now from here to the guard-room at Regina, which is the gaol and place from whence you came, that you be kept there until the 18th of September next, and that on the 18th of September next you be taken to the place appointed

for your execution, and there be hanged by the neck till
you are dead, and may God have mercy on your soul.

Riel's face betrayed no reaction to the sentence. He knew that there
was only one sentence that could be imposed once the jury found him
guilty. Riel, however, was not hanged on "the 18th of September next," as
ordered by the judge. There was still the right to appeal the jury's verdict.

Although he had been tried in the North-West Territories and not in
Manitoba, the appeal had to be heard by the Manitoba Court of Appeal
because the Canadian government had not created an appeal court for
the North-West Territories. On September 8, his appeal was heard by
a three-member court composed of Mr. Justice Taylor and Mr. Justice
Killam, presided over by Chief Justice Wallbridge. It did not take them
long to reach their decision. Although each judge delivered his own separate opinion the next day, all three concurred in dismissing Riel's appeal.

The execution of the sentence was postponed again while Riel's lawyers travelled to London, England, to apply for leave to appeal to the
Judicial Committee of the Privy Council. Although the Supreme Court
of Canada had been created in 1875, the Judicial Committee consisting of British Law Lords was still the final court of appeal for legal dis-
putes arising out of the British colonies. It would take another sixty-four
years for the Supreme Court to become truly supreme. Riel's lawyers
had decided to bypass the Supreme Court since its influence at the time
was modest and go directly to the Judicial Committee. However, the
right of appeal was not automatic; the Judicial Committee had first to
grant leave before they would even hear the appeal. The application for
leave to appeal was argued on October 21, 1885, before six British Law
Lords. They were not sympathetic to Riel's lawyers' arguments. The following day, Lord Halsbury, chancellor of England, delivered the Judicial
Committee's ruling: Riel was denied leave to appeal the verdict.

The question now was whether the government of Canada, led by
Prime Minister Sir John A. Macdonald, would exercise the prerogative
of mercy recommended by the jury and order that the sentence of death
be commuted to life imprisonment. Macdonald wanted Riel, who had
been a thorn in his side since the Manitoba rebellion fifteen years earlier,

removed from the political scene forever so that he could get on with his goal of building a railroad to British Columbia and settling the west. He wanted no further obstruction from disgruntled Métis and First Nations peoples. But he also knew that if Riel was truly insane as his lawyers and psychiatrists — and others — had claimed at his trial, it would have been inhumane to execute him. His government did not wish to be accused, particularly by French Quebec, of hanging a man who was not responsible under the law for his actions.

Macdonald was not prepared to run that risk. On October 31, 1885, he decided to appoint two medical men to examine Riel. Unfortunately, neither was a psychiatrist — the only medical specialists qualified to determine whether Riel was truly legally insane. The first, Dr. Michael Lavell, was warden of Kingston Penitentiary; the second, Dr. F.X. Valade, a French Canadian civil servant, was the official analyst of the Department of Inland Revenue. In his formal letters of appointment to the two men, Macdonald made it abundantly clear what he wanted:

> I need scarcely point out to you that the Enquiry is not as to whether Riel is subject to illusions or delusions, *but whether he is so bereft of his reason as not to know right from wrong and is not an accountable being.* (italics added)

In another private letter written to Dr. Lavell on the same day, Macdonald decided to impose a more stringent test:

> A man may have his mind so unhinged as to warrant two medical men to certify his insanity so as to send him to an asylum for curative purpose and *yet be open to the penalties of the law for a breach of such law.* (italics added)

Doctors Lavell and Valade promptly boarded separate trains for Regina, arriving on November 7, and immediately began their investigation. Posing as a newspaperman, Lavell had a chat with Riel and sent a telegram to the prime minister.

I have the honour to report that having given conscientious consideration to the case of Louis Riel, now
confined here under sentence of death, and fully appreciating the trust committed to me, and the consequences involved, I am of the opinion that the said
Louis Riel, though holding and expressing foolish and
peculiar views as to religion and general government,
is an accountable being capable of distinguishing right
from wrong.

Dr. Valade's official report, which he sent the next day, read:

Sir, after having examined carefully Riel in private conversation with him and by testimony of persons who
took care of him, I have come to the conclusion that
he suffers from hallucination on political and religious
subjects, but on other points I believe him to be quite
sensible and able to distinguish right from wrong.

But his own thirty-four pages of rough notes seem to reflect a different conclusion:

He was not fit to perceive the crime of High Treason of
which he had been guilty; and that when I examined
him, he could not, in my humble opinion, distinguish
between right and wrong on political questions.

* * *

On Wednesday, November 11, Macdonald's cabinet met to consider the
reports of the two doctors. Macdonald now had the official report that he
needed to convince the members of what he had decided. After some de-
liberation by the cabinet, the petition for clemency was denied. Warned
by one member of his cabinet that the execution of Riel would foment

trouble in Quebec, he is famously quoted as saying, "He shall hang though every dog in Quebec bark in his favour." The next day, a special messenger carrying the governor general's warrant for execution left Ottawa, arriving in Regina on Sunday evening, November 15. Colonel Irvine came directly to Riel's cell to inform him that the execution would be carried out at eight o'clock the next morning.

Riel did not sleep after receiving the news. There was little, very little time left, little time to inform his wife, Marguerite; his mother; and his brothers and sister, who had all believed his assurances that he would be reprieved. There was time only to write to his mother and his wife.

Riel had broken with the Catholic Church during the rebellion, espousing religious doctrines radical to the church. At his trial, he had explained:

> I wish to leave Rome aside, inasmuch as it is the cause of division between Catholics and Protestants. I did not wish to force my views … If I have any influence in the new world it is to help in that way and even if it takes 200 years to become practical … so my children's children will shake hands with the Protestants of the new world in a friendly manner. I do not wish those evils which exist in Europe to be continued, as much as I can influence it, among the half-breeds. I do not wish that to be repeated in America.

However, he had reconciled with the Catholic Church after his trial and had assigned Father Alexis André as his spiritual adviser. On August 5, the Feast Day of Our Lady of the Snows, he had written to Father Fourmond from his Regina cell.

> Jesus, Mary, and Joseph, Save Me!
> Father Vital Fourmond, my director of conscience —
> Archbishop Bourget said to me: "God, who has always guided and assisted you until the present hour will not

abandon you in your most profound sorrows. Because he has given you a mission which you must accomplish to the full."

My director of conscience tells me that my misfortunes and missteps come from not having understood my mission correctly. The religious principle which gave me so much confidence in the words of Archbishop Bourget now logically induces me to have the same confidence in the interpretation of those words approved by my spiritual director.

Renouncing, then, all my personal interpretations I have assigned to my mission and which are not approved by my confessor and director, I submit to the Catholic, Apostolic and Roman Church in making the following declaration:

> My father, my confessor, my director of conscience, forgive please all of my sins and the punishment due for my sins; all of my faults and the consequences of my faults; all of my offenses and all that resulted from my offenses — be they against God, against religion, against society, against my neighbor, against myself.

Your poor penitent, Louis Riel

* * *

At seven o'clock that evening, Riel ate a light supper of eggs and milk. During the evening and long hours of the next morning, he and Father André prayed together. After midnight, he wrote his last letters to Marguerite, asking her to look after the children; and to his mother, bidding her farewell. At 5:00 a.m. Riel prayed final mass with Father André. The sacrament of extreme unction followed two hours later. Although the execution was scheduled to take place at 8:00 a.m., Sheriff S.E.

Chapleau (brother of Joseph-Adolphe Chapleau, secretary of state for the Dominion of Canada and minister for the militia in Macdonald's cabinet, who had been involved in the reprieve proceedings) did not arrive at the appointed time. Fifteen minutes later, Deputy Sheriff Gibson arrived in his place to lead Riel from his prison cell to the gallows that had been erected the night before.

Riel was dressed in a black coat, woollen shirt and collar, grey tweed trousers, and moccasins. Father Charles McWilliams, an old school friend of Riel who had joined him at the end, and Father André conducted the services in French while Riel repeated his responses in a clear, firm, and unbroken voice.

The law required that a jury be empanelled to pronounce the cause of death after a condemned person had been hanged. A jury consisting of foreman Frederick Champness, jurymen William P. McCormick, John Dawson, William D. Firstbrook, David Gillespie, and W. Bedford Jones were sworn to witness the execution. Present as well to witness the execution were Dr. Augustus Jukes, a mounted police surgeon who had testified against Riel; Dr. Henry Dodd, coroner for the North-West Mounted Police; and a guard of twenty North-West Mounted Police officers under the command of Inspector White-Fraser.

At 8:30 a.m. on Monday, November 16, 1885, a cold, clear Regina morning, Father McWilliams preceded Riel up the ladder and led him across the scaffold to an empty noose hung from a beam. The hangman, Jack Henderson, of Winnipeg, who had been held a prisoner by Riel at Fort Garry in 1870 and who had sworn revenge against Riel for the death of his friend Thomas Scott, stepped forward to bind his arms and adjust the noose. Riel then spoke to Fathers André and McWilliams and reaffirmed his belief in God. "I believe and trust in Him. Sacred Heart of Jesus, have mercy upon me." André, after explaining to Riel that the end was at hand, asked him if he was at peace with men. Riel answered, "Yes." The next question was "Do you forgive all your enemies?" Riel answered, "Yes," and shook hands with Dr. Jukes and thanked him in English. He then continued: "*Jesu, Marie, Joseph, assister moi en ce dernier moment.*"

Deputy Sheriff Gibson asked Riel if he had anything to say. Riel, who had wanted to make a speech from the gallows but had been persuaded by Father André to devote himself to spiritual matters, replied, "No," and was given two minutes to pray. As Father McWilliams then began to lead Riel and Father André in the Lord's Prayer, Father André began to cry and was calmed by Riel. "Courage, *père*." Henderson then placed the hood on his head and the noose around his neck. When they reached the words "lead me not into temptation," the trapdoor opened and Riel quickly passed into eternity. Although his neck was broken by the fall, death was not instantaneous. Louis Riel's pulse ceased four minutes after the trapdoor fell. During that time the rope around his neck slowly strangled and choked him to death, but he had probably suffered little pain. He had shown tremendous courage and had remained erect and calm until the very end.

After a half hour, the body was cut down and put into a plain wooden coffin that had been placed beside the scaffold. Dr. Jukes, who conducted the post-mortem, wrote:

> The execution was most cleverly performed. From the moment he fell, judging from the nature of the injuries received, he must have been entirely without sensation. The neck was entirely dislocated from the bone of the two upper joints of vertebrae, thus paralysing all the lower portion of the body. He could have felt no pain whatsoever. The circulation ceased in four minutes. An unusually short time. No death could be more merciful.

The coroner and a jury of six men were then required by law to view the body, and they found the features much distorted. The coroner Henry Dodd, as was the legal custom, asked the jury to determine the cause of Riel's death. Although one of the jurors had become upset by the distorted features and had to retire, a verdict that Riel had died by a legal hanging was delivered by the jurors and recorded by Dodd. Dodd cut hair off Riel's head and face and removed parts of his clothing, as mementos.

Riel had wanted to be buried at Saint Boniface in Manitoba where his father and friends had been buried. It took three weeks before the federal government finally gave its consent to transfer his body to his grandmother's home in Saint Boniface. A funeral mass was celebrated before hundreds of mourners on December 12 and Riel was buried beside his father, a simple stone marking his grave. In 1891, a monument was erected to mark the gravesite.

Although a hundred and thirty years have passed since Riel's execution, there are still strong public feelings — for and against — the legality and fairness of his trial, and particularly the necessity of his execution. Numerous books, poems, plays, and articles about Riel, particularly in the last thirty years, have kindled and fuelled the controversy. Some have argued that critics fail to remember that the trial of Riel was conducted in a different time — albeit only 130 years ago — and under different circumstances. In 1885, the rules of criminal procedure and evidence, and the attitudes of Canadians toward the trial of a person accused of a crime, particularly of treason, were different than they are today. The Canadian west was still a frontier struggling to find itself amidst waves of British and European immigration disrupting the lives of the Indigenous Peoples — the Plains, the Woodland, and the Cree of Saskatchewan; and the French and Scottish Métis — who had carved out and settled the west, resenting the fact that their efforts had not been recognized by the Canadian government. It was also a country threatened by American domination, fighting for its life under threats of annexation by its southern neighbour.

Louis David Riel's important role in the development of western Canada cannot be simply swept aside by branding him a notorious and traitorous western renegade, as many in Protestant Ontario portrayed him at the time, and still regard him today. As Manitoba's father of Confederation, his contribution to Canada's historical development is no less important than Sir John A. Macdonald's. A man of letters, five volumes of his papers demonstrate his eloquence as a writer and poet. He is commemorated by a residential street named after him in Winnipeg, and a statutory holiday, Louis Riel Day, is celebrated on the third Monday of every February throughout Manitoba. Today, he is regarded by many as a heroic freedom fighter who stood up for his people in the face of racial bigotry and government indifference. Canadians cannot ignore the several private member's bills over the last thirty years seeking to revoke his conviction for treason. It is important that his trial be revisited and examined closely to assess whether there was any miscarriage of justice in his conviction or his sentence.

CHAPTER 2

The Early Years

S ome historians measure the fairness of a prosecution by the state
of one of its citizens, particularly for a crime as serious as treason,
against the time and place that gave birth to the trial. The time here was
the last half of the 19th century. The place was western Canada. The
principal player in this drama, Louis David Riel, was born on October
22, 1844, at Saint Boniface, across the river from Lower Fort Garry, the
present site of the city of Winnipeg. The area at the time was known as
the Red River Settlement, taking its name from the confluence of the
Red and Assiniboine Rivers. The settlement was nominally administered by the Hudson's Bay Company (HBC), and inhabited largely by
Indigenous Peoples and the Métis, a mixed ethnic group involving Cree,
Stoney, Ojibwa, Saulteaux, French Canadian, Scottish, and English an-
cestral heritages.

This was the crossroads of canoe routes travelled by Indigenous
Peoples before the arrival of the Europeans. In the early 1700s, in spite of
the arrival of the HBC, French traders travelled the area to trade with the
Indigenous Peoples for the coveted furs, especially beaver pelts for the in-
creasingly popular beaver felt hats that were in fashion in Europe. Many
traders married Indigenous women and eventually joined the North
West Company (NWC), a Montreal-based company formed in 1779 to

compete with the HBC. The children of their marriages were known as Métis (persons of mixed European and Indigenous ancestry).

In the early 17th century, the French had a de facto monopoly on the Canadian fur trade with their colony of New France. When two French traders, Pierre-Esprit Radisson and Médard des Groseilliers, were unable to persuade the French governor, the Marquis d'Argenson, to allow them to set up a trading post on the Hudson Bay to reduce the cost of moving furs overland, the two travelled to London, England, in 1665, where they met and received the sponsorship of Prince Rupert, the cousin of King Charles II. In 1668, two ships left England to explore possible trade into Hudson Bay and landed in James Bay, where the first fort was founded and named after the sponsor of the expedition, Prince Rupert. On May 2, 1670, King Charles II decided to grant a royal charter to the Hudson's Bay Company, giving it a monopoly over the fur trade in the region drained by all rivers and streams flowing into Hudson Bay in northern Canada, and complete control of the territory. The area became known as "Rupert's Land," after Prince Rupert, whom Charles appointed the first governor of the company. Nine posts were established between 1668 and 1717. In 1684, York Factory became the main post because of its convenient access to the vast interior waterway systems of the Saskatchewan and Red Rivers. Complete physical and legal control over this vast territory — 7.7 million square miles — had been given to the HBC in the charter granted by Charles II.

With the signing of the Treaty of Utrecht in 1713, France relinquished to England all claims to its colonies in North America, and Hudson Bay became a British possession. In 1779, the North West Company was founded in Montreal and began competing with the HBC for furs, much to the annoyance of the HBC, who were under the impression that they had a monopoly. While the HBC was distinctly English in its culture and flavour, the NWC was a mix of French, Scottish, and Indigenous cultures. By 1784, the NWC had begun to make serious inroads into the HBC's profits. The result was a series of conflicts between the two companies, including a deadly encounter known as the Battle of Seven Oaks on June 19, 1816. Finally, the British government decided to put an end to the often-violent competition, and in 1821 forced the two companies to merge. A total of 175 posts, 68 of them the HBC's, were reduced to 52, both for efficiency and because many were redundant and inherently unprofitable now that the rivalry was over. The HBC maintained a monopoly on the fur trade thereafter until the mid-19th century.

In the middle of the 19th century, the legislative power of the Dominion of Canada ended at the western end of the Great Lakes, while at the other end of the country lay the British colony of British Columbia. In between was Rupert's Land, which included what is today northern Quebec, Ontario north of the Laurentian watershed, all of Manitoba, most of Saskatchewan, southern Alberta, and a portion of the North-West Territories. While British traders waited at their posts for the Indigenous Peoples to bring their furs to them to trade, the French traders had built a chain of trading posts from the Great Lakes to the Rocky Mountains. As trade expanded, so did intermarriage of European men and Inuit and other Indigenous women, mainly Cree, Ojibwa, or Saulteaux. These marriages were commonly referred to as *marriage à la façon du pays*, or "marriage according to the custom of the country." The children often grew up primarily in their mothers' cultures, but were often also introduced to Catholic and indigenous belief systems, and to both cultures. However, as more Métis became part of communities with a fur-trapping tradition, they created a new, distinct, Indigenous People in North America, the Indigenous women becoming the link between cultures.

By the end of the 18th century, a population of Métis had appeared that considerably outnumbered the white population. Although the HBC initially attempted to suppress these "country marriages," the effectiveness of these unions in establishing trade networks, along with the successful use of intermarriage by the rival NWC, convinced the HBC that the success of the fur trade relied on intermarriage. It modified its policy.

At the heart of the Métis culture lay the buffalo hunt. Large herds of buffalo populated the Prairies and were hunted in summer for meat and to make pemmican: dried, lean buffalo meat, pounded into shreds, then mixed with berries and melted fat. It was imperishable and, on long trips, an essential staple for the voyageurs, traders, and buffalo hunters who had no time to hunt, fish, or cook elaborate meals while on the trail. The success of the fur trade depended entirely upon a good supply of pemmican. As the Métis' fur trade expanded, they organized more expeditions for buffalo each summer to ensure an adequate supply of pemmican for the fur-harvest season. The men hunted while the women skinned the buffalo and hung up the meat to dry.

The Métis' ability to supply pemmican to the NWC became essential as the NWC trade extended to the Athabasca and beyond. The Métis also began to look upon themselves as members of an independent group of Indigenous People, entitled to a property in the soil, to a flag of their own, and to protection from the British government. A unique Métis language, Michif, also developed. However, the HBC governor began to antagonize the Métis by forbidding the export and sale of pemmican to anyone but local HBC forts. Hunting buffalo from horseback was soon banned, too, and economic sanctions were levied against Métis families who provisioned the NWC with pemmican. Those decrees resulted in escalating raids on rival fur trade forts by HBC and NWC officers.

By the 1850s, the government of Canada wanted to acquire Rupert's Land and the North-Western Territory, along with British Columbia, to fulfill its dream of having a country that stretched from sea to sea to sea. It was hoped that a railway could be built linking the eastern provinces to the lands of the west. Western expansion by Canada's southern neighbours threatened a takeover of the North-Western Territory, and even of Vancouver Island and British Columbia. However, in the 1830s and 1840s, manifest destiny arose; the Americans' belief that the United States was preordained to expand from the Atlantic coast to the Pacific coast, including all the lands north of the 49th parallel. "To overspread the continent allotted by Providence for the free development of our yearly multiplying millions," as magazine editor John L. O'Sullivan expressed it in 1845 in his *Democratic Review*. "Manifest destiny" became a rallying cry for expansionists in the Democratic Party during the Tyler and Polk administrations, and "manifest destiny" became the cry of United States' settlers seeking land in the west to promote further U.S. territorial expansion north across the 49th parallel. At the same time, the HBC was anxious to be released from its responsibility of governing Rupert's Land. The growing population there was becoming difficult to control, and the HBC turned to England for help.

Section 146 of the British North America (BNA) Act 1867, passed by the British Parliament, welded the provinces of Quebec, Ontario, Nova Scotia, and New Brunswick into the Dominion of Canada, and authorized Newfoundland, Prince Edward Island, and British Columbia to be admitted into the Canadian confederation when their legislatures agreed to it. The same section of the BNA also gave the Parliament of Canada the right to incorporate Rupert's Land and the North-Western Territory into Canada when the federal government was prepared to take on that responsibility. Section 146 simply required an address from the houses of the Parliament of Canada, and from the respective provincial or colonial legislatures, and the approval of Queen Victoria's government in Britain. This meant that the residents of Newfoundland, Prince Edward Island, and British Columbia, through their legislatures, had a right to negotiate the terms of their union with Canada. On the other hand, the residents of Rupert's Land and the North-Western Territory had no such rights. Since Rupert's Land was owned and administered by the Hudson's Bay Company, the consent of the residents was not required, nor did the government of Canada even consider that they should be consulted. It was this refusal to consult with the population, particularly the Métis, the largest population in the North-Western Territory, that would eventually cause conflict between the Canadian government and the residents of the territories when Rupert's Land was transferred to the Dominion of Canada.

By the end of 1867, the government decided that Canada was ready to bring the western part of the country under its jurisdiction and control. All that was necessary was for the government of Canada to request the British government give their consent and transfer the land. The request was made, and the HBC agreed to transfer the land back to the British government for the sum of £300,000 and one-twentieth of the fertile lands to be opened for settlement. On July 31, 1868, the

British Parliament passed the Rupert's Land Act, consenting to the formal transfer of the North-West Territory to the Dominion of Canada, to take place on December 1, 1869. Without consulting the twelve thousand residents of the new territory, the Canadian government appointed William McDougall, its minister of public works, as the new lieutenant governor for the eastern portion of the territory, which was to be called the province of Manitoba.

Thomas Douglas, the fifth earl of Selkirk, was born in Scotland to a wealthy family. As seventh son of the fourth earl, he did not expect to inherit his father's estate and studied law. When he unexpectedly did inherit the Selkirk title and estates in 1799, he decided to use his money and political connections to purchase land and settle poor Scottish farmers who had suffered forced displacement during the Highland Clearances. Since the mid-18th century, thousands of Scottish highlanders had been forced to abandon land their families had farmed for many generations, by hereditary, aristocratic landowners who sought greater economic gain from new agricultural processes. In the clearances, large numbers of Scottish highlanders were forced into very poor coastal villages or the newly industrialized cities as workers in the mills and factories. Others immigrated to the new world, looking for opportunities to rebuild their lives where they would be free from the exploitation of the ruling elites.

An experienced farmer, Douglas envisioned agricultural colonies in British North America, and undertook to transplant groups of those highlanders who had lost their lands to the aristocrats' extensive flocks of sheep. In 1803, he had planted a colony in Prince Edward Island, and another in Baldoon, Upper Canada, the following year. In 1811, he decided to settle a colony in the western interior of Rupert's Land. Douglas asked the British government for a land grant in the Red River valley, which was part of Rupert's Land. Initially, the government refused, because of the HBC's fur-trading monopoly on that land. Determined to succeed, Douglas, together with Sir Alexander Mackenzie, bought enough shares in HBC to gain control of the company, and persuaded the directors that an agricultural settlement would lower the company's costs because local farmers would produce goods that until then had been transported into the territory at great expense. On May 30, 1811, the HBC granted Douglas the territory of Assiniboia, an area of 116,000 square miles, in the heart of the fur country, upon condition that he would recruit two hundred servants for the company annually for ten years, and develop an agricultural colony that would supply food for the fur trade posts. He also agreed that the settlers would not be allowed to participate in the fur trade. The result was the end of the economic dominance by the fur trade, and the demographic and social transformation of western Canada.

The NWC, trading in furs in the interior, was naturally opposed to an agricultural colony in Rupert's Land, foreseeing that such a settlement would strike at the very existence of their fur trade operations. Starting in 1812, three groups of settlers arrived over the next four years. There were clashes between NWC traders on the one hand, and the colonists and their HBC supporters on the other. At the heart of the conflict was the Pemmican Proclamation, issued in 1814 by Miles Macdonell, governor of the new Red River Colony, prohibiting the export of pemmican from the colony for the next year. Meant to guarantee adequate supplies of pemmican for the Hudson's Bay colony itself, the proclamation was viewed by the NWC as a ploy to monopolize the foodstuff, which was equally important to them and to the NWC. The local Métis refused to acknowledge the authority of the Red River Settlement, and the NWC accused the HBC of unfairly monopolizing the fur trade by this edict. The Métis, who made a living selling pemmican to the NWC traders, responded by arresting Macdonell and burning the settlement. In 1815, after several conflicts, and suffering from "severe emotional instability," Macdonell resigned as governor of the Red River Colony and was replaced by Robert Semple, an American businessman with no previous experience in the fur trade.

In 1816 a band of mostly Métis working for the NWC seized a supply of pemmican from the HBC and headed out to sell it to NWC traders. On June 19, 1816, they encountered Semple and a group of HBC men and settlers north of Fort Douglas along the Red River at a location known as Seven Oaks to the settlers, and la Grenouillère (Frog

Plain) to the Métis. The NWC sent a French Canadian, François-Firmin Boucher, to speak to Semple's men. Boucher and Semple argued and a gunfight ensued when Semple's men tried to arrest Boucher and seize his horse. Although there was some dispute as to who fired the first shot, W.B. Coltman, the royal commissioner appointed to investigate the incident, concluded "next to certainty" that it was one of Semple's men. The Métis, who outnumbered Semple's forces by nearly three to one, ended up killing twenty-one men, including Governor Semple, while suffering only one fatality. The next day the settlers, demoralized from the losses, gathered their belongings and headed northward, leaving the Métis in command of the settlement. Douglas and his men retaliated by seizing Fort William, a trading post belonging to the NWC.

Although the Métis were exonerated by Coltman, Douglas attempted to prosecute several members of the NWC for murder and kept Boucher in prison for nearly two years without specific charges. All trials eventually ended in acquittals, and the remaining charges were dropped. Members of the NWC counter-sued Douglas for the unlawful occupation of Fort William and Douglas spent much of his fortune defending himself. His health and influence in decline, Douglas died in 1820. The HBC and the NWC, the two companies involved, merged in 1821.

Louis David Riel was born on October 22, 1844, in the Red River Colony, to Jean-Louis Riel and Julie Lagimodière. His grandfather Jean-Baptiste Riel, who was born in Berthierville in Lower Canada, had joined the NWC as a voyageur at the age of fifteen and had gone west to pursue the fur trade. There he met and fell in love with Marguerite Boucher, a Métis, the daughter of Louis Boucher and Marie-Joseph Leblanc, a Chipewyan. It was from his father's parents that Louis Riel was to later claim his Métis background, although it was only one-eighth.

Louis Riel's father, Jean-Louis, was born on June 7, 1817, during the worst confrontations between the HBC and the NWC. The eldest of seven children, Jean-Louis was only five when his father, Jean-Baptiste, lost his job with the NWC after it merged with the HBC and decided to move his family back to Berthierville. As young Jean-Louis approached the age of twenty, he, like Jean-Baptiste before him, decided to pursue the fur trade. He joined the HBC, and returned to the Red River area. However, two years later he went back to Lower Canada to enter the priesthood. Then, a year later, he decided to return to the Red River Settlement with the expectation of becoming a schoolteacher. When this prospect failed, he decided to go into business for himself as a miller.

Most of the Métis were descendants of NWC traders before the amalgamation with the HBC, and they chafed under the HBC now. Their leaders, which included Jean-Louis, appealed to a growing sense of Métis identity and nationalism, arguing that by right of their historical exploration and trade, the Métis should not be subject to the HBC's restrictive trade policies. Jean-Louis soon gained prominence in the community by organizing a group that supported Guillaume Sayer, a Métis imprisoned for challenging the HBC's historical trade monopoly.

Sayer was accused of illegal fur-trading, and was brought to trial in Upper Fort Garry on May 17, 1849, by the Court of Assiniboia. Backed by Jean-Louis and fellow Métis, Sayer was allowed to pick his jury. Nevertheless, he was still found guilty, although the jury did recommend mercy, based on Sayer's belief that what he had done was legal. When the judge imposed no fine or punishment, the HBC realized that it could no longer use the courts to enforce its monopoly on the settlers of Red River. In 1868, Rupert's Land was bought by the government of Canada and became part of the newly formed Dominion. Two years later, in 1870, the HBC trade monopoly was finally abolished, and trade in the region was opened to any entrepreneur. Agitations by Jean-Louis's group had effectively ended the monopoly, and the name Riel was well known in the Red River area.

Jean-Louis, after coming back to the Red River Settlement, had fallen in love with Julie Lagimodière, the youngest daughter of his neighbours Jean-Baptiste Lagimodière, a voyageur and buffalo hunter, and Marie-Anne Gaboury. Marie-Anne had married Jean-Baptiste in

Lower Canada in 1806 and the couple had travelled west together. She was the first white woman to move to the Red River Settlement with her husband. By the early 1840s, the Lagimodière family had become one of the most highly respected and prosperous families in the French-Métis community. When Marie-Anne Lagimodière died at the age of ninety-five in 1875, she had become known as the matriarch of Saint Boniface.

Young Julie Lagimodière had wanted only to be a nun but gave into to her parent's wishes and married Jean-Louis Riel in the chapel of Saint Boniface Church on January 24, 1844. Louis David Riel, their eldest child, was born almost nine months later, on October 22. His parents were to have ten more children. Louis, the apple of his mother's eye, was soon instilled with all of his mother's religious fervour, and Julie prayed that her son would serve God as she had once longed to do. His first lessons were learned at home. When he was old enough, he was sent to schools run by the Grey Sisters and the Christian Brothers at Saint Boniface. An excellent student, he came to the attention of Alexandre Taché, the suffragan bishop of Saint Boniface, who was eagerly promoting the priesthood for talented young Métis.

As a youngster, growing up on the east side of the Red River, Louis witnessed the Red River ox carts that lumbered slowly across the prairie, watched the Métis preparing for the buffalo hunts, and revelled in the music of the Métis dances. By the time he reached his teens and his First Communion, it was clear that his education in the Red River would soon end. Bishop Taché had plans for Louis and other young Métis men who had promise. Determined that their education should be furthered so that they could return to the Red River and help their people, Taché sent Louis, who was then thirteen, and two other boys to Lower Canada in 1858 to study for the priesthood at the Petit Séminaire of the Collège de Montréal, under the Sulpicians. Louis was soon noted as a fine scholar of languages, science, and philosophy, though he was also known for frequent and unpredictable moodiness.

In February 1864, Louis received news that his father had died. It threw him into a fit of despondency. He realized that the restrictive life of a priest was not for him and, since he was now the head of the family, he knew he could hardly support them on a priest's salary. In 1865, Louis left the college and took a job in Montreal as a clerk in a law office, planning to become a lawyer. He also fell deeply in love with Marie Guernon, the daughter of his next-door neighbour. Even though Marie's father was a simple carpenter and labourer while Louis was highly educated for his day, the young suitor's Métis background made him an unacceptable choice for her family. Louis and Marie, however, continued to see each other without her parents' knowledge, and even signed a marriage contract. But her parents forbade the marriage, and Marie eventually acceded to their wishes. Louis, devastated by the rejection, returned to the Red River and was reunited with his family in Saint Boniface in July of 1868, just one year after the four provinces — Nova Scotia, New Brunswick, Ontario, and Quebec — had been united in Confederation.

Louis Riel's father had been a leader in forcing free trade on a reluctant HBC, and this, coupled with Riel's eastern education, particularly in law, singled him out as a natural leader of the Métis, even though he was only twenty-five. In the ten years of his absence from the Red River, a great deal had changed. A wave of Anglo Protestant immigrants had swept into the area from Ontario and the United States, raising fears among the Métis that they were coming "pour piller notre pays" (to plunder our country). The priests, who had built a French-speaking Catholic community on the banks of the Red River, feared that the influx of immigrants would destroy their work. Both Métis and priests feared that a way of life was disappearing. Two other disasters also hit the Red River Settlement in 1868, the year that Louis returned. An army of grasshoppers that spring had stripped every plant of its green foliage, and the buffalo hunt had been a complete failure.

The Métis of the Red River Settlement were concerned that the new government imposed on them by Canada, without consultation, would neglect their rights. They decided that they should oppose the takeover. They quickly turned to the newly arrived Louis Riel for assistance and leadership. Under his leadership, a National Committee, whose goal was to oppose annexation by Canada, was organized, with Louis as its secretary. Opposing them was John Christian Schultz, an Ontarian by birth and the owner of a newspaper in the Red River Settlement called the *Nor'Wester*, and Charles Mair, another Ontarian, who had founded the Canada First movement. Their goal was to push for annexation by Canada and encourage immigration of English-speaking settlers from Ontario.

When a party of surveyors was sent out by the federal government to survey the settlement as if it were already part of Canada, the National Committee decided to take action and halted the surveys. The newly appointed lieutenant governor, William McDougall, and his party of officials, who had to travel through the United States to reach the settlement (there was no road or railway from Ontario to the Red River Settlement at the time), were met at the American border and prevented from entering the Red River.

Riel, with the support of his community, worked toward establishing a provisional government. Schultz, posing as a defender of law and order, worked toward the overthrow of the provisional government. In early December 1869 he and others of the Canada First party barricaded themselves in his buildings, ostensibly to guard supplies of government pork stored there. On December 7 Riel surrounded the buildings with overwhelming force and arrested about forty-five men and three women. Schultz escaped and made his way to Kildonan (Winnipeg), where he attempted to persuade the settlers there to join with a group of volunteers from Portage la Prairie in an attempt to rescue the prisoners and to overthrow Riel's provisional government. Then Schultz, realizing that the Métis were searching for him, decided to travel on to Toronto.

To avoid a civil war between the Métis and the Canada First movement, which had begun to organize armed resistance against Riel's National Committee, the federal government decided to postpone the transfer of Rupert's Land, and Lieutenant Governor McDougall was ordered to return to Canada.

Riel issued a Declaration of the People of Rupert's Land and the Northwest. When Riel and his followers created a provisional government and Riel became its head on December 23, Canada decided to send special commissioners of goodwill to meet with him. One of them, Donald Smith, the chief commissioner of the Hudson's Bay Company, was later to achieve fame as the prime financial backer of the Canadian Pacific Railway (CPR).

Three delegates were chosen by Riel's provisional government to go to Ottawa to negotiate the entry of the Red River into Confederation. Meanwhile, the Canada First prisoners who had been arrested by Riel's Métis were released. However, when they used their freedom to try to enlist an army in the special parishes to move on the provisional government in Fort Garry, they were surrounded by a contingent of Métis horsemen and disarmed. This second attempt to march on the provisional government was considered serious enough by the council to require a court martial. Although their leader, John Schultz, had escaped to Toronto, two of the men who had led the uprising, Major Charles Boulton and Thomas Scott, a surveyor, were tried, found guilty, and sentenced to death. Pleas to save Boulton were successful and he was pardoned. But Scott, who had nothing but contempt for the Métis, stayed quarrelsome. Attempts by Donald Smith, the "good will" special commissioner from Canada, to save Scott were denied by Riel, who felt that it was necessary to demonstrate to Canadians that the Métis were to be taken seriously. Scott was executed by a firing squad on March 4, 1870. Although the court martial had been conducted by Ambroise-Dydime Lépine, an associate of Riel, it was Riel who was soon denounced in Ontario as Scott's murderer. The denunciation was led by the Orange Lodge, of which Scott had been a member.

Bishop Alexandre Taché of Saint Boniface arrived in the Red River four days after Scott's execution, carrying a copy of a federal proclamation granting amnesty for all actions carried out by the provisional government up to the time of its signature, and persuading Riel to free any remaining prisoners. The three delegates the provisional government sent to Ottawa had also been able to obtain an agreement, later embodied in the Manitoba Act, which provided for a land grant of 1,400,000 acres for the Métis and bilingual government institutions and services for the new province. The Manitoba Act was passed on May 12, 1870, and the transfer was set for July 15. This time, Adams G. Archibald from Nova Scotia was named lieutenant governor of the new province.

In the summer of 1870, however, Canada sent a military force to the province of Manitoba, under the command of Colonel Garnet Wolseley. Riel, fearing for his safety, decided to flee to the United States. But when the military force was disbanded the following summer, Archibald had to appeal to Riel and Lépine to raise a force to defend the settlement against a threatened Fenian raid from the United States. Riel and Lépine were able to raise an army of three hundred Métis riflemen to defend the colony, although United States troops dispersed the Fenians before they were able to cross the border.

Although Riel was regarded as a hero in Quebec, a defender of the French culture and the Roman Catholic faith in Manitoba, he was denounced in Ontario as Scott's murderer. A price of $5,000 was placed on his head. Prime Minister Macdonald, anxious to avoid a political confrontation between Ontario and Quebec, persuaded Riel in 1872 to go to the United States again. In 1873, Riel decided to return and enter the federal political arena. He was elected member of Parliament for Provencher in Manitoba in a by-election. However, when he attempted to take his seat in Parliament in Ottawa, he was expelled by its members, when they voted in favour of a motion by the Ontario Orange leader, Mackenzie Bowell.

In 1873, the Conservatives under Macdonald, tainted by the railway scandal, were swept from office by the Liberals under Alexander Mackenzie. Riel was again elected as a member of Parliament in the general election, but this time did not try to take his seat. In the meantime, Ambroise-Dydime Lépine had been arrested and tried for the murder of Thomas Scott and convicted by a mixed French and English jury. Although public sentiment in Quebec was that the Métis resistance had been justified and its leaders should be given clemency, Orange Ontario was equally adamant that Scott's execution was nothing more than murder and that the leaders responsible for it should be punished. The federal government was now in a dilemma, from which it was, thankfully, rescued by the governor general, Lord Dufferin. Influenced by the fact that Riel and Lépine had raised a Métis army to confront the Fenian threat, Lord Dufferin in 1875 commuted Lépine's sentence to two years' imprisonment with loss of his civil rights, and banished Riel from "Her Majesty's Dominions" for five years.

The strain of events was too much for Riel, who suffered a nervous breakdown. He saw his first vision on December 18, 1874: a spirit appeared, telling him he had a vision to fulfill. The spirit called him by his full name, and from that time he began to sign his full name: Louis David Riel. That vision was supported by Bishop Ignace Bourget, whose letters to Riel promised that "God, who has always led you and assisted you up to the present time, will not abandon you in the darkest hours of your life. For he has given you a mission which you must fulfill in all respects." In his diary, Riel wrote: "The Spirit of God penetrated my brain as soon as I fell asleep ... The Spirit of God affects us where He wishes, and to the extent that suits Him." Riel, overwhelmed, began a lengthy period of convalescence in a mental asylum at Longue Pointe and Beauport, Quebec. He stayed for the next twenty months.

Released in January 1878, with two more years of his exile still to serve, Riel set out for the United States, eventually arriving in Montana. There he went to live in a Métis settlement on the Sun River, where he met and married a Métis, Marguerite Monet Bellehumeur, and took out American citizenship. A little over a year later, on May 4, 1882, Marguerite gave birth to a son, Jean, and on September 17, 1883, a daughter, Marie-Angélique. To support his family, Riel tried unsuccessfully to eke out a living roaming the plains with the Métis, hunting and trading, but he abandoned that in May 1883 and accepted a position as a schoolteacher at St. Peter's Mission on the Sun River. There he taught young Métis and First Nations children, got involved in the American Métis movement fighting for their rights, and soon became known by the United States government as an agitator.

* * *

Although the Métis of Manitoba had achieved many of their demands, their resistance had caused a great deal of hostility between the
Métis and the English-speaking Protestants of Ontario. Now English-
speaking settlers began to arrive in large numbers in the new province
and Francophones soon found themselves outnumbered. Often white
settlers simply occupied their lands while the Métis were off hunting on
the southern plains over the U.S. border. When the land grants eventually arrived, land speculators quickly bought them up. The Métis, who
had lost their leaders and their way of life, now felt like strangers in
their own province. Many decided to move farther west into the valley
of the South Saskatchewan River, with the English-speaking Métis to
the north and the French Métis to the south, while others moved to
settlements near Fort Edmonton farther west. The Parish of St. Laurent
and the village of Batoche, which had been built by a trader named
Xavier Batoche on the east side of the South Saskatchewan River about
halfway between Prince Albert and Saskatoon, soon became the centre
of the new Métis settlement, and of Métis discontent. There, as in the
Red River, they laid out their farms in narrow, ribbon-like strips with a
river frontage on the Saskatchewan of ten to twenty chains (two hundred to four hundred yards). It has been estimated that over two-thirds
of the six thousand people of mixed blood who lived in Manitoba left.

Both the Métis and the Indigenous Peoples around Batoche soon
began experiencing the same problems with the Canadian government
that they had in Manitoba. The government had learned little from
the Red River scandal. Settlers began pouring into the territory, Métis
rights were no longer being respected, and their lands were threatened. When British Columbia joined Confederation in 1871, it was
on condition that Ottawa build a railway across the west within ten
years. To fulfill that obligation, the Canadian government had to hur-
ry to obtain the necessary western lands so that the railway could
be built. Unfortunately, Indigenous Peoples were in the way and had
to be pressured to sign treaties, turning over their rights to almost
the entire western plains to Ottawa in return for a promise of food,

education, medical help, and other kinds of support. They did not understand that they were now also expected to keep to their reserves and be farmers.

By the early 1880s, the buffalo, which were the main source of food for both Indigenous and Métis people, had disappeared almost entirely because of over-hunting and human encroachment on their habitat. When the Métis asked to be given clear title to the lands they had been occupying and farming along the Saskatchewan River, the government temporized. They were told that the homestead regulations required them to register with Ottawa the lands they had been farming for generations, and then wait three years for their title. Then the Dominion land surveyors arrived. They began laying out an Eastern-style grid system of survey, ignoring the Métis' linear lots that stretched back from the river. Land speculation companies bought up huge tracts of land in anticipation of the coming railway. The Indigenous Peoples, denied by treaty and by loss of the buffalo from being able to look after themselves in their traditional way, were now forced to sit and face slow starvation as winter approached. Instead of helping, the government cut back on rations — to encourage them to become self-supporting.

Seven hundred miles to the southwest, in the tiny settlement of St. Peter's Mission in the Sun River country of Montana, Louis Riel had built a new life for himself, with Marie Bellehumeur and their children. But he had not forgotten either his people or the personal wrongs that he felt he had been made to suffer by the politicians. It was at St. Peter's Mission that Gabriel Dumont, a tough buffalo hunter and the leader of the Métis at St. Laurent; his brother-in-law, Moise Ouellette, also a leader of a Métis clan; James Isbister, a Métis farmer from Prince Albert; and Michel Dumas found him in the hot summer of June 1884 after the long trip from St. Laurent. Their goal was to persuade him to return to Canada, take up their cause, and help them obtain their legal rights in the Saskatchewan valley since the Canadian government had now decided to bring the lands west of Manitoba under its control.

The Louis Riel that the four Métis met that day had changed physically and emotionally in the nearly ten years since his banishment from Canada. He had put on weight, and now sported a beard and moustache that almost covered his mouth. Although he had been a brilliant but erratic man of thirty when he left for the United States, the last ten years had weighted him heavily with his failure to improve the lot of his beloved Métis countrymen. To preserve the nomadic life that his people lived, trading and hunting, they had been forced to move farther west and to seek refuge in North Saskatchewan or in Montana. He realized now that politicians were not to be trusted. And his visions had continued as he brooded about the injustice that he had been forced to suffer. He had been in contact with the Métis along the Saskatchewan and had received word a few days before their arrival that the delegation was coming. He was sure that the culmination of his mission to lead his Métis people and create a Métis and Indigenous nation had finally arrived.

In the spring of 1884, a seven-point list of grievances had been prepared by the French Métis and some of the English Métis in meetings in the Prince Albert–Batoche area. The list demanded that the Métis settlers be given title to the lands they then occupied; that the districts of Saskatchewan, Assiniboia, and Alberta be granted provincial status; that laws be passed to encourage the nomadic Indigenous Peoples and Métis to settle on the land; and that the Indigenous Peoples be better treated. The men showed Louis the list. He had three options: he could advise the settlers from his home in Montana; he could take the petition to Ottawa and present it to the government personally; or he could return to lead the Métis of St. Laurent in their political movement. It took Louis little time to choose the last option: he would return to the North-West Territories to represent the settlers.

CHAPTER 3

The Rebellion

In 1869, when the United States drove its first transcontinental train to San Francisco, it had a population of forty million, with three-quarters of a million living on the Pacific coast and another six million living between the Mississippi and the mountains. By contrast, Canada's entire population in 1881 was only a tenth of that number, with a little over sixty-five thousand in Manitoba and thirty-six thousand in British Columbia. At the time of Confederation in 1867, British Columbia had three options for survival: to continue as a British colony, to be annexed by the United States, or to join the newly formed Dominion of Canada. Annexation by the United States made the most economic sense, since British Columbia was economically a satellite of San Francisco, whose population in the 1860s exceeded sixty thousand. Most of the residents of British Columbia lived in Victoria on Vancouver Island and depended on the mail service through San Francisco. The opening of the American transcontinental railroad had made it possible to travel by ship from Victoria to San Francisco, then by train to Ottawa in just twenty-four days. American secretary of state William H. Seward was in favour of incorporating the entire northwest Pacific coast for the long-term commercial advantages to the United States in terms of Pacific trade. He believed that the people of British Columbia wanted annexation and that

Britain would accept this in exchange for the United States' dropping its 1869 claims against Britain for damages — called the *Alabama* Claims — for the American Civil War attacks upon Union merchant ships by Confederate Navy raiders that were built in British shipyards. However, the United States was so focused on reconstruction after the war that few Americans picked up on Seward's grand dream to expand manifest destiny to include the entire Pacific northwest.

By the late 1860s, an economic depression after the collapse of the gold rushes, and a desire for responsible and representative government led to pressure for British Columbia to join the Canadian Confederation. Among the many inducements, Canada promised to take on British Columbia's debt, and to build a rail link from Montreal to the Pacific coast in ten years. British Columbia accepted, and on July 20, 1871, joined Confederation as Canada's sixth province. The promised railway would connect not only the Pacific coast to the Eastern provinces but would also connect the Prairies to both. Although driven from power in 1871 by scandal and the election of a Liberal government opposed to a railway, Sir John A. Macdonald's government was returned to power in 1878 and the last spike of the Canadian Pacific Railway was driven in Craigellachie on November 7, 1885, fulfilling Macdonald's promise to British Columbia.

The complaints of the Métis who met Louis Riel at St. Peter's Mission in Montana on June 4, 1884, were the same as those that had precipitated the Red River Rebellion. When the Métis realized that the Canadian government was not prepared to honour the guarantees they had promised Riel's provisional government in Manitoba, they decided to look westward to the Saskatchewan country as a place to make a fresh start. In 1872, they established a settlement along the South Saskatchewan River that would stretch from Saint-Louis de Langevin in the north to La Coulée-des-Tourond (Fish Creek) in the south, spanning the Carlton Trail, the main trade route between Fort Garry and Fort Edmonton. In 1873, Xavier Letendre dit Batoche built a ferry where the Carlton Trail crossed the South Saskatchewan River. There the Métis laid out their farms in their usual long river-lot fashion, cultivating a small portion of the land, and hoping that they could live as they had lived before — freighting goods by canoe, trading, farming, and hunting the buffalo. Soon a little village began to flourish on the banks of the river and by 1885 the community of Batoche numbered about five hundred people.

By the late 1870s, the new life the Métis had made for themselves along the South Saskatchewan River began to crumble. The buffalo had quickly dwindled in numbers and had vanished by the end of the 1870s. Although in 1878 the government had surveyed some of the traditional river-lot farms of the Métis already at Batoche, Métis who arrived later had to settle on lands surveyed in the eastern Canadian square-township system without water access. There were also difficulties with acquiring "legal" land titles and obtaining scrip (a certificate that could be exchanged for a land grant or money). Since the Métis had no Crown grants or land titles, speculators began to claim title to their land. Even some of land grants to the Canadian Pacific Railway included land that the Métis were living on.

The Métis were not the only people unhappy with their treatment by the federal government. The Indigenous Peoples had not received the food, farm equipment, and farming assistance that they had been promised when they signed their land away in treaties. As the railway and white settlers soon followed, the Métis found themselves outnumbered. And even white settlers became angry and disillusioned with Prime Minister Macdonald's national policy of railway development and protective tariffs. Although there had been good crops up to 1881, a series of disastrous harvests followed, and what produce the farmers had been able to save could not be transported to market. Farmers also had to pay higher prices for eastern-Canadian manufactured farm implements because of the high tariffs that the government placed on what would have been cheaper American equipment.

The federal government's decision to build the Canadian Pacific Railway along a southern route through Regina instead of a northern route through Prince Albert also aggravated the situation. A railway through the northern route would have brought construction jobs to the

Métis, easing their financial burden. Instead, with the buffalo gone, and the Cree starving, the refusal of the Canadian government, which had taken over control of the North-West Territories, to respond to the complaints of the Métis and the requests of Indigenous Peoples for assistance lit a spark of rebellion.

Petitions and letters sent by Métis leaders to the Canadian government starting in 1878 were routinely ignored. Métis leaders, such as Gabriel Dumont, Maxime Lépine, Moise Ouellette, Pierre Parenteau Sr., and Charles Nolin, had held meetings and had drafted petitions to draw the government's attention to the situation. Although there were demands for representation in the North-West Territorial Council and for more government jobs, their main demands were for grants of the lands they already occupied. On May 6, 1884, the South Branch Métis met and passed resolutions specifying grievances. In a petition drawn up at the meeting and sent to Prime Minister Macdonald, Gabriel Dumont and the Métis of Saint-Antoine de Padoue claimed exemption from the township survey system of mile-square lots that threatened to disrupt their long, narrow river lots. In an editorial on May 10, the *Prince Albert Times* newspaper taunted the Dominion Government as "a greedy, grasping, overbearing bully," noting that "where they get the information which induces them to believe the people are likely to submit much longer, we do not know; but we can answer them that they need not look for their friends among the Canadians, half breeds, or Indians, as they are likely soon to be made aware of in a manner at once startling and unpleasant." The Métis believed that they, along with the "Indians," were the original owners of Rupert's Land, which they had settled long before Canada had become a nation, and that their aboriginal title had to be extinguished in the North-West Territories in the same way that their aboriginal title had been extinguished by the land grants in Manitoba. They believed that they were entitled to free patents for the lands that they were now occupying. Finally, in desperation, on May 18 they decided to send those three men to Louis Riel, the Métis leader in Manitoba in 1870, to lead his people again.

* * *

The coming of the Canadian Pacific Railway had changed the face of the North-West Territories as its branches spread like tentacles opening up good farmland to settlers. The buffalo had been killed in large numbers and the great herds were now a memory. The Indigenous Peoples, with the buffalo gone, saw farmers and ranchers taking over lands that had once been theirs and did not realize that the treaties that they had signed meant that they had sold their land forever and were expected to live and survive by farming themselves. Many bands had signed treaties with the government giving up their rights to the land in return for promises of food and help, and did not understand that they were now expected to stay on their reservation unless given a permit to leave it.

Once treaties were signed, the attitude of the Department of Indian Affairs toward the Indigenous Peoples became a policy of folly. Permits to leave the reservation were suddenly cancelled; staff and rations were reduced. There was a decree that rations were to be issued only in return for work. This penny-pinching policy was exacerbated by a severe winter in 1883–84, resulting in a confrontation at the Crooked Lake Reserve in February 1884 between twenty-five young Cree and the assistant commissioner for Indian Affairs.[1] By June 1884, large groups of Cree were gathering to decide what to do. The inability of the federal government to understand the danger of their policy toward the Indigenous Peoples was tinder that a spark could turn into a war. It was in this atmosphere that Louis Riel decided to accept the Métis' invitation.

Although Louis had built a life for himself in the United States during his seven years in exile, he had never abandoned the belief that he was a divinely inspired prophet with a mission from God to help his people. He had made a promise to God that he would fulfill that mission and interpreted the arrival of Gabriel Dumont and the St. Laurent delegation as a signal that his time had come. Packing all of his belongings together, he set out on June 10 with his wife, Marguerite, and his children for the border, arriving at Fish Creek on June 27, where he was greeted by fifty wagonloads of his people. The next day they arrived at the Métis village of Batoche, where he and his family were to stay with his cousin Charles Nolin for the next four months. Nolin, who had been a former member of the Manitoba Legislature, had been described by Sergeant Harry Keenan, the resident North-West Mounted Police officer as "the most dangerous of the half-breeds for the reason that he is strongly in favour of tampering with the Indians." Nolin was to eventually break with Riel and to figure as an important witness for the Crown against him at his trial. Not only the French Métis but also the English Métis soon heard of Louis's arrival and welcomed him. Although each had different complaints, Louis did not have to convince the two groups that they should work together.

Before Louis's arrival, some of the Indigenous people had begun to talk about uprising. Big Bear, Chief of the Cree Nation, who had been one of the last to sign a treaty with the Canadian government, now refused to withdraw to the reserve assigned to him. The Cree began to gather and talk about a great Indigenous confederacy. Big Bear decided to organize a Thirst Dance on Poundmaker's reserve to discuss the worsening situation of the Indigenous people. By the middle of June 1884, over two thousand people from various bands had gathered to discuss the promises in Treaty 6 that Canada would provide food in time of famine. Now the crops had failed, and the buffalo had disappeared. Many Indigenous people were dying from starvation and needed the promised food and support. When John Craig, their farming instructor, stubbornly refused to dispense rations during the Thirst Dance, he was assaulted. The Thirst Dance celebration was disrupted when the North-West Mounted Police arrived to make arrests. To prevent bloodshed, Poundmaker and Big Bear intervened between the Indigenous people and the ninety-man police force. Craig finally decided to distribute food, and the situation was defused.

Riel arrived at La Coulée-des-Tourond (Fish Creek) on July 5, and was greeted with excitement. The Métis groups along the Saskatchewan were rallying to his leadership. On July 8, he gave his first speech at Batoche, then another on July 11, and he met with and spoke to the

English-speaking settlers. On July 19, he spoke again to an enthusiastic group of English-speaking and Métis settlers at Prince Albert.

Although there had been some resistance to Riel's return, that resistance lessened when it became apparent that his speeches were always moderate in tone. Conciliatory speeches followed in other parts of the district. A series of meetings was conducted with the settlers, to hear and discuss their complaints. These complaints were collected and contained in a petition sent to Ottawa on December 16 for consideration by the government of John A. Macdonald, who had now returned to power. The petition requested representation in the government of the North-West Territories, land grants for the Métis, and better treatment for the Indigenous Peoples.

On January 28, the prime minister, by order-in-council, authorized the creation of a three-person commission to review and settle "half-breed" claims in Manitoba and the North-West Territories.

However, instead of replying directly to the petition, the government advised Charles Nolin by telegram that a federal commission would be appointed to look into the Métis' complaints; Lieutenant Governor Dewdney was also advised, but the Métis were not.

When nothing was heard from the government for over three weeks, Riel decided to call a meeting of his followers at Batoche on February 24. Superintendent Gagnon of the North-West Mounted Police at Prince Albert tried to attend the meeting but was turned back by fifty or sixty of Riel's followers. At the meeting, Riel revealed that he was intending to return to Montana, because he felt that his involvement in the Manitoba uprising in the 1870s was only hurting his followers' cause with the government now. Whether his announcement was a true expression of his intention, or simply an attempt to shore up what he felt was flagging support, will never be known. What did happen was that his followers would not hear of it and told him that their priests, who were siding with the government, had abandoned them. Louis, they said, was the only person who could champion their cause. Another meeting on March 2 at Prince Albert went the same way.

By early March of 1885, the Métis' patience had begun to wear thin. There was talk of unilateral action by armed rebellion. After all, it had worked in the Red River Settlement and representative government had been granted there by Ottawa. By the middle of March, events were moving quickly. However, white settlers, who originally had been with the Métis cause, decided that they wanted nothing to do whatsoever with any appeal to arms, and told Riel so on March 10, in writing. On March 13, Superintendent Leif Crozier of the North-West Mounted Police sent a telegraph to Ottawa advising of the worsening situation at Batoche, stating that the "half-breed rebellion [was] liable to break out at any moment. If half-breeds rise, Indians will join them."

Relying on a rumour from Lawrence Clarke,[2] chief factor of the HBC in the Saskatchewan District, on his way back from Winnipeg, that many soldiers were on their way to arrest Riel and Dumont and that they were "sending five hundred men behind me, who will answer your petition with lead," Riel and his followers seized several government offices on March 18, and cut the telegraph lines to Prince Albert. The following day, a provisional government was formed, as had been done in the Red River District, and twenty men were named to serve on the governmental council. Gabriel Dumont became the head of the army and Pierre Parenteau, an old Red River settler, was appointed president of the council. Since Louis was considered the acknowledged leader of the movement, it was not felt necessary to elect him to any post.

Charles Nolin, who earlier, along with Gabriel Dumont, had been in favour of an all-out war against the whites, was also named to the council but now refused to join it. The Catholic clergy also condemned armed rebellion, and Father Fourmand preached that anyone who took part in the uprising could no longer call himself a Catholic. Louis, angry that he was not receiving the support of the Catholic clergy, decided to turn against them, refused to enter any church, and began to talk to God directly. He told his followers that God was directing him to go ahead. In the meantime, Nolin had been enlisted by the clergy to oppose the movement and had agreed to try to split the Métis, but on March 19 he was arrested by Dumont's men and put on trial for treason. To save his life, he agreed to join the movement.

Two days later, Louis sent a message to Crozier demanding that he surrender Fort Carlton, otherwise the Métis would attack the fort "when tomorrow, the Lord's day, is over, and to commence without delay a war of extermination upon all those who have shown themselves hostile to our rights." All members of the Exovedate — a name Louis invented for his provisional government from the Latin *ex*, "out of," and *ovile*, "the fold or flock" — signed the message. He began using it when referring to himself in decisions made by the council to show that he was merely one of the group. Crozier decided not to respond, but to wait for the arrival of his superior, Commissioner Acheson Irvine. The next day, the English Métis of St. Catherine's and the Ridge voted to remain neutral in the event of armed conflict. The threat to attack Fort Carlton on that Monday never materialized.

On March 23, the prime minister, after receiving an urgent telegram from Lieutenant Governor Edgar Dewdney, ordered mobilization of troops in every province of Canada and gave orders to Canadian major general of militia Frederick Middleton to march west from Ottawa with all due speed. At 2:30 a.m. that same day Commissioner Irvine set out from Prince Albert with eighty-three police and twenty-five civilian volunteers to bolster the defences at Fort Carlton. But before the relief column from Prince Albert arrived, HBC factor Clarke urged Superintendent Crozier to attack the Métis at Duck Lake, allegedly by challenging him, "What! Are we to be turned back by a parcel of half-breeds? Now is the time, Crozier, to show if you have any sand in you."

DUCK LAKE — THURSDAY, MARCH 26, 1885

The village of Duck Lake, a community of white and Métis farmers, lay between Fort Carlton, to the northwest on the south bank of the North Saskatchewan River, and Batoche, to the southeast on the east side of the South Saskatchewan River. On Wednesday, March 25, while waiting for Crozier's reply to Riel's demand that Crozier surrender Fort Carlton or the Métis would attack it, the council sent Gabriel Dumont and a force of two dozen men to Duck Lake to establish a base there. On March 26, Crozier decided to send a contingent of fifteen Mounties and seven militia with sleighs under the command of Sergeant Alex Stewart to collect the arms and ammunition from the general store run by Hillyard

Mitchell at Duck Lake before they were commandeered by Dumont. As an advance party of Stewart's men approached Duck Lake, they were intercepted by Dumont and his force of Métis and a verbal brawl ensued, with each side threatening the other. Riel had told Dumont not to shoot unless the Métis were fired upon. Stewart and his men decided to return to Fort Carlton.

In the meantime, Stewart had sent one of his scouts back to Fort Carlton to tell Crozier that Dumont had already seized Mitchell's store. The scout, however, was unaware that Dumont had allowed the Mounties to return to Fort Carlton with their sleighs. Without waiting for the arrival of Commissioner Irvine, who was only a few miles from Fort Carlton, Crozier decided to act. With fifty mounted policemen and an equal number of volunteers that he had mustered from Prince Albert weeks before to beef up Fort Carlton, Crozier decided to take his men and a seven-pounder cannon down the Carlton Trail to Duck Lake to try to retake Mitchell's store.

When Riel, who was in Batoche, learned that Colonel Irvine was approaching Fort Carlton, he gathered a force of 120 Métis and Indigenous people and started for Duck Lake to join Gabriel Dumont. No sooner had Dumont returned to Duck Lake after his confrontation with Stewart than he learned from Albert Monkman that a large force led by Crozier was coming toward them. Dumont decided to stop them, and led a squad of two dozen men back down the Carlton Trail to meet Crozier. Crozier, alerted that there were some Métis approaching, halted his men in the middle of a large clearing and drew up his sleighs across the road. The mounted policemen were lined up on his left and the Prince Albert volunteers on his right.

Arriving at the edge of the clearing, Dumont saw the police in position and dismounted. Instead of firing on Crozier and his men, Dumont decided to parley, and sent out Assiyiwan, an elderly headman from the reserve, and Isadore Dumont, his older brother, holding a blanket high, to meet with Crozier and his interpreter, Joe McKay. Before the parley could get under way, however, Assiyiwan suddenly lunged forward and attempted to take away McKay's rifle. McKay dropped the rifle, pulled out his pistol, and shot Assiyiwan, killing him. Whatever precipitated the confrontation between Assiyiwan and McKay is unknown. Crozier ordered his men to open fire. Isadore Dumont, caught in the crossfire, was immediately killed. The Métis returned fire. The battle of Duck Lake had begun.

Charles Nolin, who had been one of the early agitators, swung his cutter around and raced back to Duck Lake as soon as the first shots were fired. The battle went well for the Métis, who had the police and the Prince Albert volunteers trapped in a hollow and were able to fire from above. Riel, arriving at the battle on horseback and carrying only a cross, rode back and forth rallying his men and exhorting them to hold steady. Although Riel was miraculously unharmed, Gabriel Dumont was not so lucky. As he urged his men on, a bullet creased his head, forcing him to sit out the rest of the battle.

Superintendent Crozier had assumed that the Métis would retreat when his cannon began firing. In the excitement, however, his men put the first shell into the cannon before they put in the gunpowder and the cannon could not fire. More rebels started to arrive, and taking up positions around the perimeter of the woods. The superiority that the police and volunteers initially enjoyed soon disappeared, and their attempts to advance through the snow were prevented by rifle fire from the Métis, who began to encircle the flanks of the police. Crozier, realizing that there was no cover for his men to extend his flanks, ordered them to withdraw to the sleighs. Within thirty minutes of the first shot, Crozier realized that the battle was lost and ordered his troops to retreat. The bodies of three of his men who had been killed were loaded into the sleighs, but other dead Prince Albert volunteers had to be abandoned. The government forces had lost a total of twelve men. Riel ordered the Métis and Indigenous people not to follow the retreating police and volunteers as their sleighs sped off down the trail to Fort Carlton. Instead, the Métis retrieved the bodies of five of their comrades who had been killed and returned to Duck Lake, where they sent word to Crozier to come and recover his dead.

When Crozier arrived at Fort Carlton, he found Irvine with the reinforcements from Prince Albert. Irvine soon realized that Fort Carlton, which was surrounded by wooded hills, was vulnerable to attack, and ordered an evacuation of the police and volunteers to Prince Albert.

Although the trail to Prince Albert would lead his men through a densely wooded area, where they could easily come under attack, Irvine decided to take the chance. Dumont, told by his scouts that the police and volunteers were abandoning Fort Carlton, wanted to prepare an ambush but Riel would not agree to it. The police and volunteers were allowed to travel safely to Prince Albert. Four days later, funerals were held as both sides mourned their dead.

In the meantime, Charles Nolin, who had fled the battle at Duck Lake when the first shots were fired, showed up in Prince Albert seeking sanctuary, and was arrested and thrown in jail. After hostilities were over, he made a deal with the Crown to testify against Riel in exchange for his freedom and was never prosecuted for his own role in the rebellion.

Finally, the government decided to order a special commission to look into the grievances. It had taken eight years and the death of seventeen men to move the government to action.

The victory at Duck Lake had convinced the Métis and the Indigenous people that they could win a war against Ottawa. Riel capitalized on his victory by writing to the English-speaking Métis, exhorting them to rise up, face the enemy, and take Fort Pitt and Battleford. Although they were also told to stir up the "Indian" population, the English-speaking Métis were not prepared to take up arms and get involved in rebellion. All they would do was express their sympathy with the French Métis fight to achieve their legal rights.

Some of the Indigenous people, however, had been impressed with the Métis victory. Big Bear and Poundmaker were convinced that it was better to join Riel than to side with the federal government that had disrupted their lives and left their people starving. Chief Crowfoot, however, realized that the white people, with their superior numbers, could not be defeated. Although he was unhappy with his people's treatment by the government, he decided to stay out of the fight, and convinced his people not to join forces with Riel.

Any hope for eventual victory by the Métis was futile. Although rebellion in the Red River Settlement fifteen years earlier had caused the government to give into their demands, this time it was different. This time there had been open warfare, men had been killed, and the mood of Ontario was openly hostile. More importantly, there was now a railway to bring troops west quickly to put down any rebellion. The call for eastern volunteers brought eight thousand men forward to join a force to crush Riel and his rebels.

Major General Frederick Dobson Middleton, an Irishman and career officer in the British Army, had been given command of the Canadian militia in 1884. On March 23, he had been sent off to Winnipeg within a few hours after news had reached Ottawa that Riel had set up a provisional government. Within twenty-four hours of the Duck Lake uprising on the 26, he had ordered one part of the militia force in Winnipeg toward Battleford, which was now surrounded by Indigenous people, and dispatched the other toward Batoche, where Riel and his forces were stationed.

In the meantime, the commission appointed by the federal government to look into the complaints of the Métis finally arrived in Regina. Riel believed that they would be sent to Batoche to negotiate with him but, to his disappointment, they did not arrive. He now realized that the federal government had no intention of negotiating with him and planned to end the uprising with force, if necessary. Gabriel Dumont also realized that open warfare against a much larger and better-supplied army would only result in a quick defeat of the Métis. Only an estimated 250 to 300 Métis of approximately 1,500 in the region had rallied to the defence of Batoche. Dumont, experienced in plains warfare, urged Riel to immediately launch guerrilla attacks to harass the government forces and make them lose heart. A mobile force could easily raid the advancing forces and then quickly slip away to safety. This strategy, he argued, would demoralize Middleton's soldiers, who had no experience fighting such a campaign, and would prolong the conflict, forcing the government to negotiate. Riel, however, disagreed. God had told him to wait until the soldiers attacked the Métis at Batoche and, with divine intervention, they would win. Dumont now realized that Riel could not be persuaded to change his mind, but, as a faithful disciple of Riel, all he could do was grudgingly follow Riel's orders and wait to be attacked. It was exactly what General Middleton wanted — a battle which his superior numbers would certainly win.

FISH CREEK — APRIL 24, 1885

A few days after the Battle of Duck Lake, a series of confrontations be-tween small groups of Indigenous Peoples and white settlers ended with the death of some settlers. Big Bear's men had captured Fort Pitt on the North Saskatchewan River and there was now genuine fear that there would be a general uprising. Although this was exactly what Gabriel Dumont wanted, Riel was opposed to using the Indigenous Peoples because he felt he could not control them.

Middleton had dispatched one force to search for Big Bear; another to liberate the citizens of Battleford, who were surrounded by several res-ervations; and decided that he would lead a force numbering eight hun-dred to attack Batoche. Among his officers was Major Charles Boulton, who had been condemned to death fifteen years earlier by Riel's Manitoba provisional government and later reprieved. Middleton's plan for Batoche was to march north toward Clarke's Crossing, some forty-five miles south of Batoche on the South Saskatchewan River, and there divide his men into two forces, each to advance on one side of the river. On April 6, his force started out from Fort Qu'Appelle toward Batoche.

In the meantime, Riel and Dumont could do nothing but wait for the arrival of Middleton's army. On Friday, April 17, Métis and Indigenous scouts brought news that Middleton's forces had reached Clarke's Crossing and that Middleton was preparing to ferry half of his men to the west bank of the river. Dumont wanted to raid the camp with men on horseback on several nights and harass the soldiers, but Riel would not agree. He still believed that the federal commission would arrive and resolve the dispute. On Thursday, April 23, the scouts ad-vised Dumont that Middleton was ten miles south of Batoche and had camped at McIntosh's farm. Dumont realized that if they had any chance of stopping Middleton's army, they had to do it now. At last, he was able to persuade Riel to allow him to go on the attack.

Dumont decided to lay an ambush for Middleton's forces at Fish Creek, a small stream that ran westerly across the prairie, twelve miles south of Batoche. He knew that to get to Batoche, Middleton and his soldiers would have to cross Fish Creek. The road to Fish Creek from the south required Middleton to lead his men across an open stretch of prairie and, once that was crossed, to travel down a steep ravine that was heavily wooded and filled with dense underbrush to reach the creek. After crossing the creek, Middleton's men would have to climb up the bank to reach the plateau on the other side.

That afternoon, Dumont led a force of two hundred men and boys, armed with shotguns, ancient muzzleloader rifles, and a few Winchester repeating rifles, toward Fish Creek. Unlike Middleton, they had no cannon. After camping overnight at the farm of Roger Goulet (one of the commissioners), Dumont decided to send fifty men back with Riel to defend Batoche. He then led his remaining force of just over 150 men south to about three miles north of Fish Creek.

Early Friday morning, April 24, Dumont positioned his men on the north bank of the creek and then rode south with several scouts to reconnoitre where he expected Middleton's army would arrive just before noon. Returning to his troops, he decided to position his men on both sides of the creek. On the south side, he spread out some of his men in the dense underbrush and placed some of his best marksmen along the trail leading to the creek. His plan was to wait until Middleton's army had passed them on their way down to the creek, then ambush them from the rear. His men on the north side of the creek would cut off any soldiers who were able to escape in that direction.

If the trap had succeeded, Middleton's army would have been caught in a crossfire and would have suffered heavy casualties. However, some of the younger boys in Dumont's party rode their horses across the road leading to the creek, leaving fresh hoofprints. When Middleton's advance party of army scouts were a few hundred yards from the ambush, they noticed the hoofprints and stopped. Then they suddenly spotted Dumont's men, and the scouts began to fire. The planned ambush had failed.

Riel, in Batoche, could hear the sound of guns firing and Middleton's cannon booming. All day long he stood praying with the Métis women, holding his arms high so that his body formed a cross. When he eventually began to tire, the people held up his arms for him. And, although Middleton's soldiers outnumbered the Métis, Middleton decided to withdraw his men from Fish Creek due to the high number of casualties they had suffered, while only five Métis had been killed. Riel ordered four days of fasting and prayer to ask God for assistance in the final battle that he knew would be coming.

Defeat for the Métis was now only a matter of time. Outnumbered by Middleton's army, who also had better weapons and ammunition, the Métis decided to make their last stand at Batoche, their stronghold. For two weeks, Middleton kept his men in camp getting ready for the final battle and waiting for the *Northcote*, a Hudson's Bay steamer, to come down the South Saskatchewan River with supplies and reinforcements. On Thursday, May 7, he finally ordered his army of eight hundred to start moving toward Batoche to meet the Métis force that now numbered only 150.

BATOCHE — SATURDAY, MAY 9, 1885

Gabriel Dumont believed that there was only one way that his men could defeat Middleton's army and that was by guerrilla tactics — hit and run, at night, and when the enemy least expected it. However, Riel had forbidden him to employ such tactics, still believing that the delegates from the commission would eventually arrive to settle the dispute amicably. When they didn't arrive, Dumont, knowing it was now too late for guerrilla tactics, realized his men would have to fight from a defensive position. Batoche would have to be turned into a defensive stronghold.

The main part of the village of Batoche lay on the Carlton Trail on the east side of the South Saskatchewan River some seventy-five feet below a high bank and a plateau still farther east. To get to the Walters and Baker store, on the west side of the river, where a few other dwellings were located, one had to take the ferry across the river. Dumont decided to build rifle pits along the crest of the bank on the east side, which was heavily wooded and would camouflage his men. The snipers in the concealed rifle pits would be able to fire down on Middleton's soldiers if they tried to assault the village from the river. Rifle pits were also built on the north side of an old riverbank that lay immediately to the south of the village. Also to the south of the village were the Catholic church and rectory, and farther south still, the farm of Adolph Caron.

Middleton started his advance on Batoche from the south on May 7 with his eight hundred soldiers, his cannons, and a Gatling gun. The Gatling gun, invented by Dr. Richard Gatling in 1861, was a hand-driven, crank-operated, six-barrelled weapon capable of firing twelve hundred rounds per minute. Gatling created his gun during the American Civil War, sincerely believing that his invention would end the war by reducing the size of armies needed, and thus the number of deaths by combat and disease.[3] Lieutenant A.L. Howard of the Connecticut National Guard had an interest in the company manufacturing the weapon and had provided one to the Canadian forces for use against the Métis.[4] Middleton had arranged for the HBC steamer, the *Northcote*, to meet with his forces at the village on Saturday, May 10. He expected that the steamer would come under attack at the river and divert the Métis, while his land forces attacked from the high ground on the east.

Dumont's scouts reported the movements of the government troops and he anticipated that the attack would come on Saturday morning. In the early hours of that morning, the Métis filed into the rifle pits that overlooked the church and Adolph Caron's farm to the south, and waited.

Unfortunately for Middleton, his plan foundered when the *Northcote* failed to do its part. Shortly after 8:00 a.m., smoke from the *Northcote* had alerted the Métis of its imminent arrival, and as the *Northcote* swung around a bend in the river and anchored, it immediately came under fire from the snipers on shore. The crew of the steamer, realizing that they had to move further downstream toward the ferry crossing between the village and the store to avoid the rifle fire, decided to lift anchor and proceed. However, when the steamer reached the ferry crossing, west of the town, the ferry cable slid over the ship, knocking off its smokestack and causing it to drift helplessly downstream in the current until it came to a stop on a sandbar, out of contention.

The Métis who had followed the steamer, intending to board it, abandoned their pursuit when they were alerted that Middleton's advance scouts were approaching the village. Middleton stationed his cannon at the edge of the clearing on high ground east of the river, overlooking the village, and began firing shells into the houses where the families of the Métis had gathered. Dumont's plan had been to wait until the soldiers had started down the steep slopes toward the flood plain and then to encircle them, while his snipers fired from the rifle pits hidden on the upper part of the slope. However, seeing the cannon shelling their homes, the Métis began to fire from the pits immediately, and Middleton pulled his cannon back from the edge of the cliff. As the cannon was being pulled back, the Métis, who had started their encircling movement, began to fire on the soldiers. Middleton, anticipating that strategy, ordered the Gatling gun into action. Startled by the noise and rapidity of the firing, the Métis retreated to the safety of their rifle pits. The soldiers, seeing the Métis retreat, began a frontal assault down the ravine, only to find themselves fired upon, not only by the defenders they knew about, but from both sides and even from behind. Unable to see their enemy, the soldiers fell back to safety on the higher ground.

Middleton ordered a second assault that afternoon. This time the soldiers moved more cautiously down the slope but still met stiff resistance from the rifle pits in front and on the sides. Unable to penetrate the Métis lines of resistance, the soldiers again fell back to the safety of the plateau while the Gatling gun covered their retreat. Scattered firing continued the rest of the afternoon while Middleton attempted unsuccessfully to find some weakness in the Métis position. In the end, he simply gave up, ordered his men to stop firing and set up camp at Caron's farm. Middleton had lost three soldiers and nine wounded while the Métis had not lost any men, and only a few were wounded.

The feeling by some of the Métis that they had won the battle and that Middleton's troops would go away was quickly dispelled by Gabriel Dumont, and Riel realized that there would be no negotiations with the Canadian government. It had finally answered his petitions, but not in the way he had wanted.

SUNDAY, MAY 10, 1885

The following morning, Dumont led his men into the rifle pits around the ravine and church, while the Indigenous Peoples took up a position near the cemetery and northeast of the church. In the meantime,

Middleton spent a good part of the day continuing to look for a weak spot in the Métis defences. He thought he had found it in the area behind the cemetery where Sioux warriors had been stationed and began to move some of his troops into this area. Dumont, realizing what was happening, brought up fresh Métis who were able to check the advance. Unable to press his advantage, Middleton withdrew his troops and marched them back to their camp at Caron's farm for the night.

MONDAY, MAY 11, 1885

The next morning, Middleton, wanting the Métis to believe that he intended to concentrate his attack again at the cemetery, decided to line up a squad of his troops near the church. However, his real intention was to launch a two-pronged attack from an area to the northeast known as La Belle Prairie. He then led a squad of soldiers to La Belle Prairie, telling his officers in command of soldiers in the area of the church and cemetery to launch their assault on the rifle pits when they heard a blast from his cannon. The cannon was set up and the troops got ready to launch their assault. Cannon shots were fired into the village to signal the attack but the troops near the church and cemetery did not advance. When they did not hear small-arms fire, they assumed that something had gone wrong. When Middleton discovered that there was no assault underway from his troops at the cemetery, the cannon was fired once more: but again no signal was received indicating that his troops around the church had started to move forward. In the end, the only casualties were a woman and a baby in the village, who had been killed by the cannon shot.

The rest of the day saw an exchange of rifle fire without any other casualties, other than a few wounded. Neither side had moved from its protected positions. Late in the afternoon, Middleton marched his men back to their encampment at Caron's farm for dinner. Some of his officers, unhappy with Middleton's leadership, quietly discussed launching another attack themselves through the cemetery, which they now knew was the weakest sector of the Métis defence. The medics had reported that many of the soldiers wounded that afternoon had been hit by nails and bolts. The Métis, the officers now realized, were running out of ammunition.

While there was excitement in the soldier's camp that evening, the atmosphere was entirely different in the Métis camp. With ammunition almost gone, the Métis and the Indigenous Peoples finally recognized that they had little chance of defeating the Canadian troops. Slowly, some who had run out of ammunition began to slip out of the village and vanish in the darkness. As morning approached, Dumont realized he had only eighty men that he could count on for the coming day, on which was expected to be the final assault. He also knew that the ammunition was almost exhausted, and they would have to use nails, even stones in their rifles, for ammunition.

TUESDAY, MAY 12, 1885

In the morning, Middleton's soldiers again started to probe the defensive positions around the church and cemetery. With little ammunition left, the defenders could only retreat from rifle pit to rifle pit, putting what little ammunition they had to good use. A flying squad under Dumont moved back and forth, trying to support the weaker sections, while Riel went from rifle pit to rifle pit, praying and comforting his men.

Around midmorning, a large troop of soldiers headed from their camp in the direction of La Belle Prairie, pulling a cannon and the Gatling gun. Middleton was going to attempt a repeat of the same two-pronged attack that he had attempted the day before. Fearful that Middleton was going to shell the village again, Riel quickly scribbled a note to him stating that the Métis would kill the Indian agent and a number of prisoners they were holding if their families were massacred. One of the prisoners, John Astley, was given the note and escorted through the lines to deliver it to Middleton. Middleton read the note and sent a reply: "Mr. Riel. I am anxious to avoid killing women and children and have done my best to avoid doing so. Put your women and children in one place, let us know where it is and no shot shall be fired on them. I trust to your honor not to put men with them." Riel immediately answered, agreeing to Middleton's suggestion.

During dinner, some of his officers started probing the area around the cemetery and the church for weak defences. With 250 men, Colonels William and Grasset started down the slope. Dumont, realizing what was happening, attempted to reinforce his men, but it was too late. At an arranged signal, the soldiers started to charge what they believed to be the last rifle pits. Hearing the noise, Middleton, who was having his dinner, realized what had happened and went to muster reinforcements. Although Dumont and his men fought bravely, moving back to another line of rifle pits that had been recently constructed behind them, it was too late. The reinforcements that Middleton sent were now split into two groups, one to clear out the rifle pits and the other to come in from behind Batoche.

Dumont's men decided to take their final stand in a semicircle of rifle pits around the village. Although they fought bravely, the odds of almost eight to one and the depletion of their ammunition made them realize that there was no hope for them. Slowly, they began to slip out of the rifle pits and vanish into the woods to the northeast of the village. By the time Middleton's troops were able to sweep around Batoche to the north, Riel, Dumont, and his men were gone.

WEDNESDAY, MAY 13, 1885

Major General Middleton had written a letter to Riel telling him that he would receive him and his council, offering them protection until the government decided what to do with them. Dumont and Riel met to discuss the letter. Dumont said that he would not surrender and would try to get to the United States with Michel Dumas, who had been one of the four men who had gone to Montana to persuade Riel to return to Canada. Riel told Dumont that he would stay, since he was not prepared to return to a life of exile in the United States. He knew that he was the person that the government wanted, and, if he gave himself up to Middleton, he would have a public trial and demand that the government give him and his people the justice they had never received.

On the evening of May 13, Riel crossed the river to leave his pregnant wife and their two small children with his friend Moise Ouellette.

Two days later, on May 15, he wrote a letter to Middleton saying that his council had dispersed and that he would surrender himself at Batoche. That afternoon, Riel arrived at Middleton's camp and surrendered to his soldiers. He was immediately taken to the general, who later recalled him as "a mild-spoken and mild looking man, with a short brown beard and an uneasy frightened look about his eyes which gradually disappeared as I talked to him." Middleton was said to have received Riel with courtesy and dignity. Later, stories of a dramatic capture of Riel were falsely spread by journalists.

Since there was some concern that Riel's presence in the camp would spark demonstrations, Middleton appointed Captain George H. Young of the Winnipeg Field Battery to escort Riel to Regina on the *Northcote*. They arrived in Regina with little fanfare. Ironically, no one recognized the man who had created so many problems for the government of Canada. Riel was turned over to the North-West Mounted Police and locked in a cell to await his trial. Although the Canadian government originally intended to have Riel tried in Winnipeg, frantic last-minute telegrams from Ottawa now ordered Riel to be kept in Regina.

CHAPTER 4

The Players

Prime Minister John A. Macdonald was undoubtedly elated that Riel, who had been a thorn in his side for fifteen years, had been defeated and captured. Now he could proceed with his dream to extend Canada west to the Pacific coast by railway without interruption. It was time to excise the thorn before it caused any further damage. As far as he was concerned, Riel had committed high treason and had to be prosecuted and hanged. The best lawyers in Ontario had to be engaged to ensure a successful prosecution. Two immediately came to mind — Christopher Robinson, Q.C., and Britton Bath Osler, Q.C. — and they were quickly retained. To ensure that they pursued the prosecution vigorously, Macdonald sent the deputy attorney general of Canada, George Wheelock Burbidge, to supervise their work.

If Macdonald was to have Riel removed permanently, then Riel had to be tried for high treason, a capital offence. Treason, the betrayal of one's superior, was considered the most heinous of crimes in British history. The common law recognized two kinds of treason: high treason, which was a breach of faith by a subject to his king; and petit treason, which was

The guard room at Regina barracks where Louis Riel was confined in 1885.

Louis Riel as a prisoner, standing beside a tent on a riverbank, with soldiers in the background.

committed when a subject killed his superior. Although the punishment for both treason (high and petit) and felony was death, a conviction for treason resulted in a forfeiture of the accused's lands and goods to the king, who could do whatever he wanted with them. A felony, on the other hand, resulted in a forfeiture of his land and goods to the accused's lord, not to the king. In early English history, the king wished to extend the law of treason at the expense of felony in order to fill his constantly depleting royal coffers. The lords, however, wanted to resist this intrusion on their rights to avoid losing their seigniorial dues. King Edward III finally settled the dispute in 1351 when he enacted the famous Statute of Treasons. This act confined high treason to three branches: actual attacks on the king's person; war actually levied against his authority; and adherence to his enemies. Although later British monarchs passed treason statutes broadening the definition of treason to prevent any form of dissent, those statutes were repealed and the act of 1351 remained essentially unaltered until 1848 when the Treason Felony Act was passed to quell disturbances in England arising out of revolutions that had been occurring in continental Europe.[1]

Although some of the offences defined under the 1848 act overlapped with some under the 1351 statute, such as intending to depose or levy war upon the king, an important distinction was the punishment. Punishment for treason under the 1351 statute was death by hanging. Punishment for felony treason under the 1848 statute was life imprisonment. For Riel, this meant that death or life imprisonment depended upon whether the government chose to proceed against him under the 1351 statute or the 1848 act. It was decided by the government that Riel should be tried with levying war against the Queen under the 1351 statute. If the decision was regarded as too harsh, the government could answer for it in the next election. The Protestant electorate of Ontario wanted Riel's neck for Scott's death. The Catholic electorate of Quebec wanted him saved from the hangman.

It had been originally intended to send Louis Riel to Winnipeg where he could be tried by a Superior Court Judge of the Manitoba Queen's

Bench with a jury of twelve members of the community, but the frantic telegrams at the last minute from Ottawa had given instructions that he be tried in Regina. In Manitoba, Riel would have the right to be tried by a mixed jury of twelve French- and English-speaking jurors and both French and English could be used in court. No such right existed if Riel were tried in Regina, which was in the North-West Territories. The North-West Territories Act of 1880, passed by the federal government, provided that an accused would be tried by six English-speaking jurors, not twelve, presided over by a magistrate, not a superior court judge, and only English could be used in court.[2] Prime Minister Macdonald was not going to give Riel an opportunity to escape the hangman by having French-speaking members on his jury.

Regina, a thriving western settlement, had been founded in 1882, three years before the Métis rebellion. Although it was initially assumed that the CPR, which began construction in 1881, would travel through the rich "Fertile Belt" of the North Saskatchewan River valley, this plan was discarded the next year in favour of a more southerly route across the arid Palliser's Triangle, a more direct route closer to the Canada-U.S. border, making it easier for the CPR to keep American railways from encroaching on the Canadian market. The southern route across the plains also allowed for easy construction and the CPR owned nearly half the land surrounding the proposed track. Since the proposed route was too far away from Battleford, the territorial capital, the CPR was instructed by the federal government to choose a new capital on the government's behalf. A location 245 miles to the southeast of Battleford was chosen, at the point where the railway crossed Wascana Creek, and Regina became the new territorial capital before the first train arrived on August 23, 1882.

By April 1883, less than a year after the first settlers arrived, Regina had approximately four hundred buildings — including fifteen stores, two banks, four feed stores, two carriage shops, four hotels, a church, and a post office — and a population of about a thousand. In the late 1870s, the headquarters of the North-West Mounted Police (NWMP) were located at Fort Walsh to deal with problems caused by whisky traders and by the presence of Sitting Bull in Cypress Hills. As settlers moved west with the railways, policing them became more important

North-West Mounted Police outside the Regina courthouse where Louis Riel was tried.

An illustration of the same Regina courthouse.

and the headquarters were transferred to Regina. Construction of the new North-West Mounted Police barracks began in 1882. In that year, the force was increased to five hundred to cope with the increased tasks being demanded of it, and the police began to use the railway to bring in recruits more easily from the eastern provinces.

Although Regina was on the planned route of the new transcontinental railway, the CPR had only reached Qu'Appelle (then called Troy), some eighteen miles to the east, at the time of the rebellion. Regina was originally called "Pile of Bones" because of the large piles of buffalo bones on the banks of Wascana Creek, a spring runoff channel rising a couple of kilometres to the east. The Cree people believed that the living buffaloes would not leave the bones of the dead buffalo; as long as there were bones in the area, there would always be buffalo to hunt. The pile of bones, which the Cree named "Okana ka-asateki," was at times six feet high and forty-two feet in diameter. However, the name "Pile of Bones" was not good enough for the capital of the North-West Territories. Although several names were suggested for this new town on the banks of Wascana Creek, it was decided to ask Princess Louise, the wife of Canada's governor general, to name it. She decided to name it "Regina," in honor of her mother, Queen Victoria. On December 1, 1883, Regina was declared a town and made the capital of the North-West Territories. By 1884, a public school and a newspaper (the *Leader*) had been established. In 1885, at the time of Riel's trial, there were two hotels: the Windsor, on Broad Street, and the Pacific, at the corner of Broad and South Railway Street, with hardly enough rooms to handle the press reporters, court officials, and the curious who had travelled from eastern Canada and the United States to witness the proceedings.

On July 20, 1885, only five days after two members of Louis Riel's defence team had arrived from Quebec City, Louis Riel was arraigned before Magistrate Hugh Richardson on six counts of high treason. Riel was asked to plead to the charge: "Are you guilty, or not guilty?" Just before he answered, Magistrate Richardson, as was the custom in court, inquired who appeared as counsel for the prosecution.

Christopher Robinson, Q.C., the sixty-two-year-old third son of John Beverly Robinson, Ontario's chief justice, rose to introduce himself as chief counsel for the Crown. Assisting him were Britton Bath Osler, Q.C.; George Wheelock Burbidge, Q.C.; David L. Scott; and Thomas Chase-Casgrain. Tall and austere, Christopher Robinson had built a reputation as one of the finest lawyers in Ontario. Born into Toronto's elite, he had been educated at Upper Canada College, had received a Bachelor of Arts degree from King's College, a Master of Arts from Trinity College, and had been called to the bar in 1850. Although his practice was mainly in commercial cases, he had been retained by the federal government as a prosecutor in a number of high-profile cases, developing a reputation as a successful prosecutor. In 1868, he had acted for the Crown in the unsuccessful appeal of Patrick James Whelan who had been convicted of the murder of Thomas D'Arcy McGee.

Britton Bath Osler was a member of a famous Toronto family that included his brother Sir William, Canada's best-known physician. He had received a law degree from the University of Toronto in 1862 at the age of twenty-three and had set up a law practice in Dundas, Ontario, eventually becoming Crown attorney for Wentworth in 1874. In 1882, he left his Crown attorney position and joined a leading law firm in Toronto where he was retained by the federal government to prosecute a series of murder trials, the most famous of which was the trial of Reginald Birchall, a notorious English swindler, for the murder of Frederick Benwell, the son of the biggest potential investor in one of his swindles.

However, the prosecutor who was to play the most influential role in the trial was thirty-eight-year-old George Wheelock Burbidge, Q.C. Burbidge, born in Nova Scotia, had been called to the bar of New Brunswick in 1872 where he had practised law until he was appointed deputy minister of justice in 1882. There he remained until 1887 when he was rewarded by Prime Minister Macdonald with the post of the first chief justice of the Exchequer Court of Canada. He and Robert Sedgewick were to co-author the first Canadian Criminal Code in 1892. Burbidge had been directed by Macdonald to assemble and lead the most effective prosecution team in the trial of Louis Riel. He was also the guiding hand behind the actual prosecution and was undoubtedly sent, as the trial transcript reveals, by Macdonald to ensure that the case against Riel was vigorously prosecuted.

The fourth member of the team, David Lynch Scott, who was almost forty at the time of the trial, had been elected mayor of Regina in 1884. Born in Brampton, Ontario, he had been called to the Ontario bar in 1870 and had practised law in Orangeville until 1882, serving as mayor from 1879 to 1880. In 1882 he had moved his law practice to Regina where he was elected mayor two years later; this time by acclamation. It was a well-known tactic to hire a local lawyer, particularly one who was an acclaimed mayor and popular with the citizens of his town, to sit at the counsel table. The Riel jury, drawn mainly from the local members of the Regina community, would know where the sympathies of their mayor lay. In 1894, nine years after Riel's trial, Scott was appointed to the newly created Superior Court of the North-West Territories. When the provinces of Saskatchewan and Alberta were created in 1907, Scott was appointed to the Supreme Court of Alberta.

The last member of the prosecution team, thirty-three-year-old Thomas Chase-Casgrain, who came from a family with an avid interest in politics, was a professor of law at Laval University, and was undoubtedly there to assist on points of law. He had been admitted to the Quebec bar in 1877, receiving the Governor General's medal, and was named professor of law two years later. Casgrain was the only French Canadian who had been invited to join the prosecution team. Pro-Riel sentiment in Quebec was so strong against Cagrain that he was burned in effigy during at least one demonstration. Nevertheless, his participation in the trial did not prevent his election to the Quebec Legislative Assembly a year after the trial and again in 1892. He was attorney general of Quebec from December 1891 to November 1892 and again from December 1892 to May 1896. In 1896, he was elected a Conservative member of parliament and served until his death in 1914. Burbidge, Scott, and Casgrain took active parts in questioning the witnesses for the Crown but left the difficult task of cross-examining the witnesses for the defence to experienced and skilled barristers like Osler and Robinson.

* * *

Although Louis Riel had no money to hire lawyers, Liberal supporters in Quebec had gathered funds to hire a defence team to represent him. After Robinson introduced the team of prosecutors, it was the turn of François-Xavier Lemieux, chief counsel for the defence, to rise and introduce the defence team: "I appear for the prisoner with Mr. Charles Fitzpatrick, J.N. Greenshields, and T.C. Johnstone."

Although Lemieux was only thirty-five years of age and had been called to the Quebec bar at the age of twenty-one, he had quickly built a solid reputation for himself in Quebec City as a brilliant and eloquent defence lawyer. He had been elected a member of the provincial legislature in 1883 for Lévis and for Bonaventure in 1894. Seven years after Riel's trial, he and Fitzpatrick successfully defended the premier of Quebec, Honoré Mercier, against a charge of having defrauded the public treasury. In 1896 and 1897, he was named *bâtonnier*, the president of the Quebec bar. He would eventually top off his career as a judge of the Quebec Superior Court and chief justice of Quebec in 1915 and receive a knighthood from the king of England.

François-Xavier Lemieux, member of the counsel for defence at the trial of Louis Riel.

Thomas Chase-Casgrain, representative of the Crown at the trial of
Louis Riel.

Britton Bath Osler, Crown attorney
at the trial of Louis Riel.

Charles Fitzpatrick, three years younger than Lemieux, was the son of a Quebec lumber merchant, and was a brilliant law student. He studied at Laval University, obtaining a Bachelor of Arts degree in 1873 and a law degree three years later. Called to the bar of Quebec in 1876, he established his practice in Quebec City and later founded the law firm of Fitzpatrick & Taschereau. He not only defended criminal cases but also prosecuted them as Crown attorney in the Quebec district. He was also the brother-in-law and law partner of Adolphe Caron, who was the minister of militia and defence in Macdonald's government. Five years after his defence of Riel, Fitzpatrick was appointed a professor of criminal law at Laval University and elected a member of the Quebec legislature. In 1896, he decided to run for a seat in the Parliament of Canada as a Liberal, was elected and immediately appointed solicitor general of Canada, at that time a position outside the cabinet. Six years later, he was promoted to minister of justice. Suddenly, on June 4, 1906, at the age of fifty-two, he left the cabinet and was appointed chief justice of the Supreme Court of Canada to fill a vacancy left by the retirement of Sir Henri Elzéar Taschereau. He was knighted in 1907. He served on the Supreme Court of Canada for twelve years, resigning on October 21, 1918, to accept the position of lieutenant governor of Quebec. He achieved his greatest reputation as a defence counsel, not only for Riel, but also, along with Lemieux, for his defence in 1892 of Honoré Mercier and Thomas McGreevy, a contractor, who had been implicated in the political corruption that had driven Mercier from office.

James Naismith Greenshields, a thirty-two-year-old member of the Montreal bar, made up the third member of the defence team. After graduating from McGill University Law school in March 1877 with the Gold Medal for the highest marks in his class, he was called to the bar of Quebec in January of the following year. His scholastic achievement had marked him as a counsel with a bright future. After the trial, he set up a law practice in Montreal with his younger brother Robert Alfred Ernest Greenshields, who was later appointed chief justice of Quebec and dean of McGill Law School.

Thomas Cooke Johnstone, the fourth member of the defence team, had moved from Toronto to Regina in 1882 to set up a practice of law.

Although known as one of the best authorities on criminal practice in the West, like Scott, his presence as a local Regina lawyer at the counsel table with the defence team would be of assistance when the witnesses for the Crown were being cross-examined by the defence counsel. He would also be appointed to the Supreme Court of the Northwest Territories in 1906 and would serve on that court until 1914, when ill health forced his retirement. Both he and Greenshields would play minor roles in the presentation and cross-examination of the witnesses.

Presiding over the trial was sixty-four-year-old Lieutenant Colonel Hugh Richardson. Richardson had been born in London, England, and had immigrated to Canada with his family as a child in 1831 when his father had been appointed manager of the Bank of Upper Canada in Toronto. He had been called to the bar of Osgoode Hall in Toronto in 1847 and practised law in Woodstock, Ontario, for twenty-five years, serving also as Crown attorney for Oxford County from 1856 to 1862. Richardson was active in the local militia and helped to organize the 22nd Battalion Volunteer Militia Rifles (Oxford Rifles) in 1862, becoming commander of the unit in April 1866. In 1866, he served as a militia colonel during the Fenian raids, and in 1872 was appointed by the Conservative government as chief clerk of the Department of Justice. There he remained until the federal government decided that it needed a magistrate to bring law and order to the North-West Territories. Section 61 of the North-West Territories Act of 1875 and Section 74 of the North-West Territories Act of 1880 (consolidating all previous acts), passed by the Parliament of Canada, had authorized the appointment of not more than three stipendiary (salaried) magistrates "who shall hold office during pleasure." In 1876, Richardson, having accepted one of the appointments, went with two other magistrates to Battleford, then the seat of the territorial government, to preside in the magistrate's criminal courts. In 1877 he had a large house built to accommodate his invalid wife and three daughters. When one of his underage daughters fell in love with a North-West Mounted Police officer who abducted and married her, Richardson had him charged and presided over his trial. Fortunately, the jury acquitted him.

After his wife died the following year, Richardson remarried and in 1883 moved to Regina with the territorial government. Besides conducting trials throughout the territories, Richardson served as legal adviser to the lieutenant governor, and also served as an ex officio member of the territorial council until that body was abolished in 1888. Besides presiding over the trial of Riel, Richardson also tried many of Riel's Métis followers, as well as prominent Chiefs Poundmaker, Big Bear, and One Arrow; and Riel's "secretary," William Henry Jackson.

Richardson returned to his normal routine of judicial work and legislative drafting after the Riel trial. When Parliament created a Supreme Court of the North-West Territories in 1887, Richardson was rewarded with an appointment as a judge of that court and made the senior judge. However, Richardson was passed over in February 1902 in favour of his junior colleague Thomas Horace McGuire when Parliament created the office of chief justice of the Supreme Court of the North-West Territories. In November of the following year, he retired and returned to spend his final years in Ottawa, a city that was also the home of one of his daughters.

Historically, a prosecution for treason had to be conducted before a judge of the superior court (in 1885 called a judge of the Queen's Bench), with a jury of twelve members of the community. Richardson, a stipendiary magistrate, the second-lowest judge in the judicial hierarchy, and only one level above a justice of the peace, was entitled to try only minor criminal cases. A stipendiary magistrate was a salaried judge who had all of the powers of a justice of the peace plus the power to hear any case that the common law or a statute required two justices of the peace to hear. Holding office "during pleasure" meant that he did not have security of tenure. He could be removed whenever the Canadian government felt that they didn't like his rulings.

Section 91(27) of the British North America (BNA) Act of 1867 had given the federal government jurisdiction over the procedure in criminal matters and section 96 gave it the authority to appoint judges of the superior, district, and county courts. Section 99(1) gave judges of the superior court security of tenure "during good behaviour," removable only upon a joint address of the Senate and the House of Commons. There was nothing in the BNA authorizing the federal government to appoint magistrates. The appointment of magistrates and justices of the peace had long preceded the act of 1867 and had been the bulwark of the British judicial system since 1361 when the Justices of the Peace Act had been put into statute by King Edward III. The system of justices of the peace had been imported into the judicial systems of the various provinces that had eventually joined Confederation. Even the Hudson's Bay Company had members of its staff appointed justices of the peace to deal with crimes during its tenure over Rupert's Land. Although the provinces were not specifically given authority to appoint judges under section 92 of the act, section 129 had preserved the existing office of magistrates and justices of the peace in the provinces of Ontario, Quebec, New Brunswick, and Nova Scotia.

Sketch #2 of trial: 1. Judge Richardson; 2. Magistrate Le Jeune; 3. Louis Riel; 4. Crown Attorney Osler; 5. Coroner Dr. Dodd; 6. Captain Deane (North-West Mounted Police); 7. Counsel Fitzpatrick; 8. Counsel Lemieux; 9. Counsel Greenshields; 10. Deputy Sheriff Gibson; 11. Crown Attorney Robinson; 12. Crown Attorney Chase-Casgrain; 13. Chief Stewart; 14. Nolin (witness); 15. Interpreter

Full rendering of sketch #2 on page 66.

In 1885, the federal government had not appointed judges of the superior court for the North-West Territories as it had done in all the other provinces. However, its North-West Territories Act of 1880 had authorized the lieutenant governor to appoint justices of the peace to administer justice throughout the territory. The 1880 act had also authorized the governor in council to appoint not more than three "fit and proper person or persons, barristers-at-law or advocates of five years' standing in any of the provinces to be a stipendiary magistrate within the North-West Territories." Section 76 had listed certain offences that were to be tried by a magistrate in a summary way and without a jury. Subsection 5 went on to authorize a magistrate to try, "with the intervention of a jury of six, … any charge against any person or persons for any crime."

The federal government could have sent the case to Manitoba, where there were superior court judges. But that would have meant that Riel would have been entitled to a jury of twelve, half of whom had to be French-speaking. Or it could have appointed a special commissioner (usually a barrister of ten years' standing) to sit as the judge. Either a superior court judge or a commissioner would be independent judges. As we shall see later, both Robinson and Osler were concerned that a magistrate was given authority to preside over a treason trial. A judge of the superior court, unlike a magistrate, would have security of tenure. He could not be removed from the bench if he failed to please the government like a magistrate could be. He could only be removed for cause, and then only by joint addresses of both houses of Parliament. "Cause" meant crimes, or physical or mental problems that affected his ability to judge impartially. It did not include rulings that annoyed the government. A superior court judge's independence ensured that his impartiality would remain intact in the face of any criticism by the government of his rulings, without fear of losing his job. Moreover, judges of the superior court were usually chosen from the most experienced trial counsel in the country and would be expected to be familiar with the criminal law, to ensure that the prosecution strictly adhered to the rules of evidence in presenting their case against an accused. In 1885, a magistrate was neither independent, as they are today (now called provincial judges), nor did he consider himself independent of the government that appointed him. A magistrate did not even have to have legal training. Appointed by the government "during pleasure" meant that his appointment could be withdrawn at the whim of the government whenever it was displeased with his performance. British kings had regularly fired superior courts who held their office "during pleasure," until the British Parliament had passed the Act of Settlement in 1700, which provided that judges should hold office during good behaviour, but subject to a power of removal upon an address from both houses of Parliament.

This, and the fact that a magistrate usually operated out of an office in the police station, was the reason why they were called "police magistrates." A magistrate was appointed and removed by the attorney general of the province or, in the case of a federal appointment, by the minister of justice upon the recommendation of his deputy. This meant that George Wheelock Burbidge, Q.C., the deputy minister of justice, was appearing for the prosecution before the very magistrate over whom he had the power to recommend removal if the magistrate did not perform satisfactorily.

Richardson even regarded himself as an employee of the federal government, not an independent judge. In March 1885 he had taken part in a meeting with Lawrence Clarke, chief factor of Fort Carlton, the Hudson's Bay Company's trading centre in the Saskatchewan valley area; A.G. Irvine, the commissioner of the North-West Mounted Police; and Indian Commissioner Hayter Reed, at which it had been decided to send a hundred mounted policemen to put down the Métis unrest.

Sitting with Magistrate Richardson was justice of the peace Mr. Henry Le Jeune, whom Richardson introduced as the "associate justice for the approaching trial." Section 76.5 of the North-West Territories Act of 1880 required a justice of the peace to preside with a stipendiary magistrate in all cases that were to be tried by a jury. After introducing Le Jeune, Richardson then introduced the court clerk and the court reporters.

After Lemieux introduced the defence team, he announced to Richardson that the defence would be attacking the jurisdiction of the court. It was customary in a criminal trial, as it has been for the last five hundred years, for an accused to raise all preliminary matters dealing with the jurisdiction of the court before being asked to plead to the charge. If the court had no jurisdiction to try Riel, then there was nothing to plead to and he would be entitled to go free. Riel's lawyers were objecting strongly to the jurisdiction of the court to try him.

> Mr. Lemieux: I hold in my hand a plea to the jurisdiction of the court, supported by the usual affidavits, and we have agreed that Mr. Fitzpatrick shall argue that part of the case.

As was the custom where a formal attack on the jurisdiction of the court to try the case was entered, Riel was required to swear to an affidavit supporting the plea. The "plea to the jurisdiction of the court" was then read and the case adjourned until one o'clock.

When court resumed at one o'clock, Fitzpatrick began his long attack on the jurisdiction of the court to try Riel. The first argument was on the validity of the North-West Territories Act of 1880 passed by the Parliament of Canada, which the prosecution relied upon to give the court jurisdiction to try Riel. The second was whether the language of that act overrode the provisions of Magna Carta, which guaranteed every British subject accused of high treason the right to be tried by a superior court judge with a jury of twelve of his peers.

Fitzpatrick began by pointing out that the North-West Territories became part of the British Dominions either as having been part of the territory covered by the Hudson's Bay Charter of 1670, or as part of Canada ceded to the English by the French in 1763. If it were the former, then the provisions of Magna Carta guaranteed trial by jury of twelve men, impartially selected, who had to unanimously concur in the guilt of the accused Riel before he could be legally convicted. If it were the latter, then the common law rule was that the criminal law of the conquering power — England — became the criminal law of the North-West Territories. In either case — whether 1670 or 1763 — British subjects were entitled to trial by jury, particularly if they were subject to the death penalty if convicted. Here, only six, not twelve, citizens had been selected as the members of the jury who were to hear the case against Riel. This was not only contrary to British law, Fitzpatrick argued, "it is also contrary to the laws in the other provinces of Canada." Moreover, the panel of jurors (from whom six eventually would be selected to hear the case against Riel) had been hand-picked by Judge Richardson from the citizens of Regina. This was not the impartial selection guaranteed by Magna Carta and was contrary to the usual British custom where the sheriff of the county or district returned a panel of prospective jurors from a list of voters in the community. Allowing the judge to select the prospective jurors could hardly be considered as providing an impartial jury of Riel's peers.

Section 146 of the British North America (BNA) Act, under which the North-Western Territory was admitted into Canada, he argued, guaranteed a constitution similar in spirit to that of the United Kingdom. The BNA Act was a treaty scheme between all of the provinces, and to which all were parties. Even Prime Minister Macdonald had said this at the time of Confederation. When the territory entered into this treaty, it acquired the same rights as the other provinces and Parliament had no power to alter any of the provisions guaranteed at the time. Would Parliament have dared to deprive Quebec or Ontario of the right of trial by jury, he asked Richardson?

In an impassioned speech, Fitzpatrick argued that trial by jury was the birthright of every British subject. Trial by jury, he said, "is generally understood to mean ... a trial by a jury of twelve men, impartially selected, who must unanimously concur in the guilt of the accused before a legal conviction can be made. Any law therefore dispensing with any of these requisites may be considered unconstitutional."

The law under which Riel was being tried, the North-West Territories Act of 1880, enacted by the Parliament of Canada, was in conflict with Magna Carta, he argued, and therefore was unconstitutional. The charge was treason, the most serious crime known to the common law, and could only be tried by a judge of the superior court. Magistrate Richardson was a mere magistrate, not a judge of the superior court. Moreover, as Fitzpatrick delicately put it, magistrates and justices of the peace were appointed at the pleasure of the government and could be easily removed if they did not do the bidding of the government. Judges of the superior court, on the other hand, had security of tenure and could not be removed except for cause, and then only by joint addresses of both houses of Parliament.

Finally, he pointed out, the selection of a jury was particularly important where the charge was one of treason, which involved an attack on the Crown. The Crown was a party to the suit and it had long been the law that selection of the panel of jurors had to be taken out of the hands of the Crown; otherwise an accused could not be said to have had a fair trial. To ensure impartiality, the responsibility for selecting a pool of prospective jurors fell upon the sheriff of the county or district where the trial was to take place. Here, the very judge who was to try the case, not the sheriff, had selected the panel of prospective jurors.

When Fitzpatrick had finished his argument, he turned to his colleague James Greenshields, who was to raise another reason why the court did not have jurisdiction to try Louis Riel. Greenshields's argument was that all of the laws affecting Canada that had been passed by the Parliament of Great Britain prior to Confederation in 1867 had never been repealed by the Parliament of Great Britain. If the laws had never been repealed, he said, they were still in force and superseded the North-West Territories Act of 1880. Those British laws said that where a person was charged with an offence punishable by death (and treason was automatically punishable by death), the case had to be sent to be tried by a judge of the superior court with a twelve-man jury, in either Upper Canada or British Columbia. Since Riel was being tried in Regina in the North-West Territories by a magistrate, not a judge of the superior court, particularly one who had hand-picked the panel of jurors from which six, not twelve, jurors were selected as was required by Magna Carta, the court had no jurisdiction to try the case.

After Greenshields completed his argument, it was the Crown's turn to reply, and Christopher Robinson answered the submissions, with contempt. As far as he was concerned, the issue was not whether the laws passed by Parliament were reasonable or unreasonable. The only issue was whether Parliament had the authority to pass them. Parliament, he said, was supreme over all of the ancient customs that British subjects had fought and died for, such as the right of trial by a jury of twelve independently chosen British subjects. The Parliament of Canada, under the British North America Act of 1867, had the power to pass any laws that it was specifically empowered to do under that act, even if the effect was to sweep away individual rights acquired over many centuries of struggle against the British Crown. The supremacy of Parliament was a theme that was to be hammered home to Richardson by Robinson over and over again. The British Parliament had the right to do anything but "to make a man a woman and a woman a man." The Canadian Parliament had the right to do the same within those specific areas granted to it by the act of 1867. Section 91(27) gave the Canadian Parliament absolute jurisdiction over criminal law, including "the procedure in criminal matters." If Parliament decided that treason trials in the North-West Territories should be conducted before a magistrate with a jury of six instead of a superior court judge with a jury of twelve, it could do so and no court could override it.

If Robinson's submissions were correct, it meant that Parliament could decree that a treason trial could be conducted before a magistrate (or even a justice of the peace) without a jury. It did not matter that the right to be tried by a superior court judge with a jury of twelve had become an integral part of the British judicial fabric for five hundred years. Nor did it matter that although the British Parliament had the same power as the Canadian Parliament — indeed probably more, since its powers were not limited by section 91(27) — it would have never dared to abolish the right to be tried by a superior court judge with a twelve-man jury. The British public would simply not stand for it.

Could the Parliament of Canada sweep aside five hundred years of fundamental rights that had stood as a strong oak against governmental abuses by a simple act of Parliament? It was an argument that was to engage legal scholars in Canada until the middle of the 20th century, when a movement to create a Bill of Rights modelled after the American Bill of Rights was initiated by Prime Minister John Diefenbaker. It would continue until the Charter of Rights and Freedoms in April 1982 would enshrine in Canadian law the right to trial by a jury.[3] However, this was 1885. What made it worse was that the North-West Territories had no representatives in Parliament to fight for its rights.

Charles Fitzpatrick was given the usual right of reply to Christopher Robinson's argument. He pointed out that if Robinson's argument was correct then Parliament could deny the inhabitants of one part of Canada the rights given those in another part.

> Where people assemble together and give to their representatives whom they elect to the Legislature certain

powers, they say that this power must be exercised subject to the principles of the common law, and subject to
certain restrictions. Now why should those powers delegated and transferred to the Federal Parliament be exercised with any greater freedom and without the same
restrictions? Why should the powers delegated by the
Imperial to the Federal Parliament be exercised in such
a way that you can interpret them as meaning one thing
with reference to one province, and a different thing
with reference to another?

The argument that the Parliament of Canada had no right to pass laws
that did not treat all of the citizens of Canada equally fell on deaf ears.
Richardson (as he would demonstrate throughout the trial) had no difficulty agreeing with Robinson, here in sustaining the Crown's right to try
Louis Riel with a jury of six rather than twelve. After lengthy and learned
argument by all counsel on the jurisdiction of the court, one would have
expected the judge to adjourn to consider the submissions and give some
reasons for his decision. Richardson treated the defence's arguments with
the same contempt as had Robinson. They were perfunctorily dismissed
without reasons. Better to say nothing than to give reasons that might be
faulty and jeopardize the expected verdict of guilty on appeal.

"Well, as I cannot hold that," the magistrate said, "I must sustain the
demurrer. I must now call upon Louis Riel to plead."

However, the legal skirmishes were not over. The defence now launched an
attack, not on the court, but on the indictment — the document that had
set out the charges against Riel. The Crown had alleged six acts of treason
by Riel in the indictment. The first three each said that Riel had led a rebellion against Her Majesty the Queen: one at Duck Lake, one at Fish Creek,
and one at Batoche *while a subject of Her Majesty*. The second three said
that he had led the same rebellions against Her Majesty at Duck Lake, at
Fish Creek, and at Batoche *while under the protection of Her Majesty*.

T.C. Johnstone objected to the wording of the charges against Riel because the second set of charges were simply a restatement of the first. The indictment, he pointed out, "contains these charges twice over in the same words, the same identical words, the same overt acts." There was no difference between committing treason *while a subject of Her Majesty* and committing treason *while under the protection of Her Majesty.* The second set of charges should have stated that Riel was the citizen of a foreign state — the United States — that was at peace with Her Majesty. How was Riel to properly defend himself when he had been charged with two sets of charges that were identical? To do so infringed a fundamental rule of pleading in criminal cases that prevented the Crown from charging a person with the same crime more than once.

However, the Crown had not alleged two separate offences in the same count of the indictment. What the Crown was saying was that Riel had committed an act of treason, for example at Duck Lake, as a British subject in one count and, alternatively, if he was not a British subject (there was some concern that he had become an American citizen), as an alien who owed allegiance because he was in Canada under the protection of the Canadian government. The Crown had filed alternative charges to ensure that Riel could not claim he was not subject to Canadian law.

George Burbidge was not going to let Richardson be persuaded by any such technical argument raised by the defence. He quickly got on his feet to reply to Johnstone's argument.

> In three counts we have charged him as a British subject and having violated his natural allegiance, and in three counts we have charged him with having acted contrary to his local allegiance. It is quite sufficient that a man may live in a country to be guilty of treason. With reference to the two sets of counts, I do not need more than to refer to the School's case. In that case, counsel for the prisoner were called upon to say whether their prisoner would be tried as an alien or a British subject, before the Crown would be called upon to amend or to make any election. I need not pursue this question further I think.

Judge Richardson, again without reasons, agreed with the Crown and dismissed Johnstone's argument. "Were there any further objections?" he asked the defence. There were none.

Now that all of the preliminary motions had been dismissed, the clerk of the court asked Riel to formally plead to the charges.

> Clerk: "Louis Riel, are you guilty or not guilty?"
> Prisoner: "I have the honor to answer the court I am not guilty."
> Clerk: "Are you ready for your trial?"

At this point, Fitzpatrick rose to ask the court to adjourn until the following morning to enable the defence to prepare some affidavits to show why they were not in a position to proceed with the trial at that time. The defence needed time to arrange for the appearance of witnesses, some of whom were in Montana, and a one-month adjournment was suggested. Although Fitzpatrick did not indicate what witnesses the defence intended to call, it was obvious that one of the witnesses would be Gabriel Dumont, who was now living in Montana. However, Canadian jurisdiction does not extend beyond its boundaries and a subpoena issued by a Canadian judge to a Montana resident would probably be ignored by Dumont. Judge Richardson knew this and reminded the lawyers that he had no way of compelling the appearance of witnesses residing in Montana. Moreover, Dumont and the other witnesses would hardly be prepared to appear willingly, unless the Crown gave them immunity from prosecution, and this was unlikely. Furthermore, there was little that Dumont or the others involved in the rebellion could say that would assist Riel in his defence, unless they intended to say that he and the council had led armed rebellion over Riel's objections. Justification for the rebellion, that Riel wanted to advance as his defence to the charges, was no defence in law and his lawyers knew it. Robinson indicated that the Crown was not prepared to consent to an adjournment for a month and would oppose the request. But it was up to the judge to decide if and how long an adjournment would be granted, not the Crown. Richardson agreed to adjourn until the following morning.

Was the request for an adjournment for a month an unreasonable one in the circumstances? Lemieux, Fitzpatrick, and Greenshields, once retained to defend Riel, had only had a few days to pack their bags and to set out for Regina in order to arrive before July 20, the date fixed for Riel's arraignment on the charges. On the way, they stopped at Saint Boniface, just long enough to visit the Riel family and receive a rosary and some water from the shrine at Lourdes from Riel's sister Henrietta to take to him. Continuing their journey, they arrived in Regina at three o'clock in the morning of July 15, five days before Riel's arraignment, to find that there were no rooms at the local hotels.

After interviewing Riel, his lawyers realized that their task would not be an easy one. Before leaving Quebec, they had been given a long rambling letter written by Riel to J.B.R. Fiset, one of Riel's oldest friends and classmates, who had been the prime mover in gathering funds for his defence. The letter had indicated that he wanted to be tried, not by a judge and jury in Regina, but before the Supreme Court of Canada in Ottawa. There was, of course, no legal precedent for such a trial. The Supreme Court of Canada was an appeal court, not a trial court. Riel had to be first tried and convicted before the Supreme Court could eventually hear an appeal. Moreover, he wanted his defence to be based on the merits of his actions, and there was no legal justification for his actions. Armed rebellion, even one that might be justified on moral grounds, was no defence in law. Since there was ample evidence that he had been involved in the rebellion, the only defence left was that he was of unsound mind at the time. The problem was to convince Riel that he should allow his counsel to present the defence that he was insane. If he did allow them to present that defence, it would take time to arrange for the necessary witnesses on his behalf.

The following morning, three affidavits requesting an adjournment were presented to Judge Richardson by James Greenshields, who read them to the court. They pointed out that the charge was the most serious one that could be preferred against a British subject and that it was usual for the court to grant the defence an adjournment to enable counsel to prepare their case. Furthermore, the defence had no funds and needed money to pay for the subpoenas to the witnesses. Richardson interrupted Greenshields to point out that the court also had no funds. Greenshields replied that it was customary for the federal government to provide funds for the defence where the accused was indigent, suggesting that Richardson ask the government for funding. Richardson did not respond, remaining silent to the request.

The affidavits filed set out two reasons why the adjournment should be granted. The first was to obtain the presence of Gabriel Dumont, Michel Dumas, and Napoleon Nault, who were in Montana, to show that Riel came to the North-West Territories "with pure and good motives" to redress the grievances which they "unquestionably had." They wanted the Crown to assure the witnesses that they could enter Canada to give evidence without being arrested. The defence also needed all of the documents, petitions, writings, and representations sent to and ignored by the federal government. The evidence of Dumont, Dumas, and Nault

> will prove facts that are of the highest importance to the defence; they will prove that Mr. Riel if he had been listened to, not one drop of blood would have been shed … that the alleged rebellion was commenced and conducted under the direction of a council of fourteen persons, of which council the prisoner was not a member; that he did not participate in any engagement or permit or countenance any overt act of treason.

The second reason was that an adjournment was needed to obtain the appearance of the medical witnesses to give evidence of Riel's mental condition at the time of the battles.

However, the Crown opposed any adjournment of the trial. Robinson argued that "we have no power whatever to give any of those persons who have fled justice anything approaching protection or safe conduct, if they choose to enter this province." He was wrong. The Crown always had the power to grant Dumont, Dumas, and Nault immunity from prosecution if they came to give evidence. Burbidge, as deputy minister of justice, was the second-highest-ranking justice official in Canada and had authority to grant Dumont, Dumas, and Nault immunity from prosecution. But the Crown was not prepared to do this, with anti-Riel feeling running high in Protestant Ontario. As to the production of the documents or petitions requested, Robinson argued that they were inadmissible "under any circumstances" by the defence. His reason, he said, was that any correspondence seized from Riel was regarded by the Crown as state documents, since many implicated others, and the Crown was entitled to suppress the production of anything that could be considered in the nature of treasonable correspondence, or which could implicate others in any matter. Again, Robinson was wrong. All the defence wanted were the documents sent to the government by Riel and other Métis requesting that their grievances be resolved, and the answers received. They were hardly state secrets.

However, Robinson was correct when he said that evidence of the government's refusal to redress the grievances of the Métis was not a legal defence to treason. What the Crown was trying to prevent was evidence that Riel had always wanted to use peaceful means, not rebellion, to obtain redress and that it was the council, not Riel, who was not a member of the council, who had decided on armed rebellion. Evidence that Riel was encouraged out of compassion, not greed, to come to the aid of the Métis would remove the prejudice that had already been built up in the press about Riel's motives, knowing that the Crown would stress over and over again to the jury that Riel's reasons for representing the Métis were not altruistic at all, but designed to extract money from the government for himself, after which he would quickly abandon their cause.

Although the Crown was ready to proceed and Crown witnesses ready to testify, Robinson finally indicated that the Crown would agree to a postponement for a week and would pay the expenses of the defence witnesses. It is the judge who must decide whether it is in the interest of justice to grant an adjournment, not the Crown prosecutors. Richardson did not seem to understand his responsibility as trial judge. As in other rulings during the trial, he simply went along with the position taken by the Crown and denied the defence the one-month adjournment. As far as he was concerned, a week was a reasonable time and "the means of communication are very quick now compared with what they were, and a witness can be brought from Quebec."

Even by standards of the day, the request by the defence for a month's adjournment to prepare its case was certainly reasonable, considering the distance that the witnesses (including medical witnesses who could address Riel's mental state) were expected to travel by train. The defence also needed time to brief the witnesses. Today, such a request, even in a less serious case, would be routinely granted for a much longer period, even with rapid air travel. However, criminal trials during the 19th century in Canada were usually conducted with dispatch, especially if for treason. Would a month adjournment, as requested by the defence, have assisted them? Unfortunately, defence counsel themselves never publicly commented on how the refusal of a longer adjournment created prejudice against them.

CHAPTER 5

The Evidence of Treason

After all the attacks on the jurisdiction of the court had been quickly dismissed, it was now the turn of the Crown to prove its case against Riel. The common law system does not require an accused to prove his innocence, or to even declare his defence in advance. An accused is entitled to remain silent and to say to the Crown, in effect, "prove your case before I am called upon to explain mine."[1]

This meant that the Crown had to prove beyond a reasonable doubt that Riel had committed treason contrary to the 1351 Statute of Treasons. The specific allegation was that Riel had attempted and endeavoured "by force and arms to subvert and destroy the Constitution and Government of this Realm as by law established, and deprive and depose our said Lady the Queen." In other words, that he levied war against Her Majesty in her realm in the territories.

There was no evidence that Riel had been personally involved in any of the skirmishes with the soldiers or volunteers under the command of Superintendent Crozier or General Middleton. It was not necessary to prove that he had been. If the Crown could establish that Riel was the leader of the Métis and the Indigenous Peoples, and had led or incited them into rebellion, this would be sufficient proof of treason under the

1351 statute. Then Riel's lawyers would have to decide whether to answer the Crown's case by calling evidence to refute that evidence, or to present nothing of their own and simply argue that the Crown had not proven his guilt beyond a reasonable doubt.

Remaining silent, presenting nothing of their own, was not an option. The Crown was planning to call many witnesses to show Riel's involvement as the leader of the rebellion and his lawyers realized that it was unlikely that they could successfully shake that evidence. They were entitled, of course, to cross-examine those witnesses in an effort to attack the reliability or to test the honesty of their evidence. They might be able to poke holes in their testimony, but it was unlikely they could persuade the jury to reject all of the evidence. There was no doubt that many of the witnesses would be hostile to Riel; cross-examination could expose their bias against him. The defence lawyers might also be able to bring out evidence of Riel's devotion to the Métis cause. Although that might cause some jurors to feel sympathy for Riel, they had taken an oath to "render a true verdict according to the evidence" and would have to find him guilty if the evidence established treason.

Riel's lawyers realized from the beginning that the evidence of Riel's treason was overwhelming. They decided that if they were going to save his life they would have to show that he was legally insane at the time of the rebellion. Evidence of his insanity would have to come from the medical experts who knew Riel's mental state and would give evidence in support of that defence. The problem was that Riel did not want to be found not guilty by reason of insanity. As far as he was concerned, he was not insane then or now. A verdict that he was insane would destroy all he had worked for and struggled to achieve. Riel felt that he was legally justified in fomenting rebellion. The Métis and the Indigenous Peoples had been abandoned and treated abominably by the federal government and they were only asserting their rights. After all, the Indigenous Peoples were the First Nations of Canada and, together with the Métis, had developed the west. If, Riel felt, he could only be given the chance to explain his motives in leading the rebellion, the people of the West would understand, and he would be exonerated. They would even call him a hero for standing up to the federal government. They had done it before. Had they not cheered him when he had stood up to the federal government in the Red River Settlement a decade earlier and helped create the province of Manitoba?

High treason is the crime of disloyalty to the Crown. Before 1351, there was no clear common-law definition of treason. It was for the king and his judges to decide what constituted treason. However, this open-ended determination of what was treason was open to abuse, and decisions were often arbitrary. English kings had directed the courts to expand its scope in order to stifle dissent. Discontent by the nobility forced Edward III in 1351 to enact the Statute of Treasons to clarify precisely what it was. The act distinguished two varieties of treason: high treason and petty treason (or petit treason), the first being disloyalty to the Sovereign, and the second being disloyalty to a subject. At the time, the practical distinction was the consequence of being convicted: for a high treason, the penalty was death by hanging, drawing, and quartering (for a man) or drawing and burning (for a woman), and the escheat (loss to the Crown) of all the traitor's property; in the case of petty treason, the penalty was drawing and hanging without quartering, or burning without drawing; and property escheated only to the traitor's immediate lord. By the 18th century, the punishment for high treason was simply hanging without all of the other indignities to the accused's body.

In 1795, another Treason Act was passed after King George III was subjected to stoning on his way to open Parliament. It did not abrogate the 1351 act, but this act made it high treason to, "within the realm or without compass, imagine, invent, devise or intend death or destruction, or any bodily harm tending to death or destruction, maim or wounding, imprisonment or restraint, of the person of ... the King." This was derived from the Sedition Act 1661, which had expired. The 1795 act was originally a temporary act, which was to expire when George III died, but it was made permanent by the Treason Act 1817.

By the 19th century, it was realized that juries were often reluctant to convict people of capital crimes. It was thought that the conviction rate might increase if the sentence was reduced to exile to the penal colonies in Australia, or, later, to life imprisonment. As a result, in 1848 three categories of treason were reduced by the Treason Felony Act 1848, from treasons to felonies. During the period in Britain, the death penalty was being abolished for a great many offences. It was now treason felony to "compass, imagine, invent, devise, or intend": (1) to deprive the Queen of her crown, (2) to levy war against the Queen, or (3) to "move or stir" any foreigner to invade the United Kingdom or any other country belonging to the Queen. Transportation to a penal colony was abolished in 1868, leaving life imprisonment as the only penalty.

The 1848 act did not prevent prosecutors from charging somebody with treason instead of treason felony if the same conduct amounted to either offence. They could charge Riel with high treason under the 1351 act with "levying war against the Queen," in which case he would be executed if found guilty, or with treason felony under the 1848 act with "levying war against the Queen," in which case he would be imprisoned for life if found guilty. Christopher Robinson and B.B. Osler decided to charge Louis Riel with high treason under the 1351 act. They had been instructed by Burbidge that Riel was to be given no quarter. A sentence of life imprisonment would rally the Métis and the Indigenous Peoples to interrupt and possibly obstruct Macdonald's plan to build a railway to British Columbia within ten years, as he had promised the province if it would join Canada. He wanted no further obstructions. More seriously, Canada faced the prospect of a rising by the Indigenous Peoples, who were desperately resisting the development of more settlements. They had soon discovered that the deal they had made with the Crown, their lands in exchange for confined reserve life, was not a fair one. A sentence of death for Riel would solve both of Macdonald's problems.

The common law system of justice, the adversary system, assumes that if two champions of relatively equal ability are pitted against one another in a courtroom, truth will emerge. The champions are, of course, the lawyers. The champion for each side is given the opportunity to prove their case by calling witnesses to tell what they know about the matter; the opposing champion is then allowed to test the reliability and honesty of each witness by cross-examination. The role of the judge is different. The judge is required to ensure that the battle is conducted fairly and according to the rules of evidence, intervening only when a rule is breached by the champions. This does not mean that the judge must sit silently like a sphinx until one side objects to the breach of the rules by the other. The judge has the duty to intervene as soon as a breach occurs. The judge is the helmsman of a ship ensuring that it follows its course, deviating neither to the port nor the starboard. It is the judge who must ensure that each side adheres to the rules of evidence and procedure without waiting for the lawyers to intervene.

Witnesses are required to restrict their evidence to first-hand knowledge of the events — observations made with their eyes, ears, nose, etc. They are not allowed to say what they were told by others that may be relevant. Called the rule against hearsay or second-hand evidence, it is based upon common sense. The reliability and the honesty of second-hand evidence cannot be tested by cross-examination. All the witness can say is that he heard it from another. The person who said it must be called so that his honesty and reliability can be tested. Another rule requires the judge to ask the jury to leave the courtroom where the admissibility of certain evidence is contested, while he rules in their absence. It would be ludicrous for a judge to rule that certain evidence that the jury has just heard is inadmissible and then instruct them to ignore it.

Witnesses are also required to give their evidence spontaneously to questions asked by the lawyer who has called them. The examiner is not allowed to suggest to the witness the answer. Where this occurs, the trial judge must intervene immediately and rule the question to be improper, and not wait for the other side to object. In Canada, tradition has always prevented lawyers, particularly Crown counsel, from asking a question that they know to be improper. Crown lawyers are expected to be fair and impartial, particularly when an accused is on trial for his life. Cross-examination is different. The cross-examiner is allowed to suggest the answer to the witness and will often try to get the witness to agree with the suggestions put to him, or to bring out testimony that is favourable to his side. Once cross-examination is completed, a witness may be re-examined to clarify his answers, particularly where he may have been confused by the cross-examiner. Again, since this round is not cross-examination, the rule that answers must not be suggested to the witness applies. And new matters may not be raised: the side that calls a witness gets only one kick at the can.

Throughout the trial, these basic rules were regularly broken by the Crown prosecutors, particularly George Burbidge. Burbidge was allowed to put into a witness's mouth whatever he wanted the witness to say. When the witness did not give him the answer he wanted, Burbidge repeated the question, prompting the witness about the answer he wanted. Judge Richardson never intervened when he should have, giving the prosecutors a free hand to improperly put testimony in the mouths of their witness. But probably the worst offenders were Riel's lawyers, who allowed the prosecutors to get away time after time with breaches of the rules. They never objected. The only time they ever objected to hearsay was near the end of the case, when the evidence was not even harmful to Riel's defence.

The process of screening the evidence heard by the jury may seem to the layman an obstacle to the discovery of the truth. Why not let the jury hear all of the evidence, first-hand, second-hand, or third-hand, and let them separate the wheat from the chaff? Unless the jury hears all of the evidence, there is a risk that the guilty may escape punishment. There is a great deal of truth in that argument. However, long ago, it was decided that strict adherence to the procedural rules is the only way that juries will not be influenced by extraneous matters. The adversary system attempts to ensure that everyone, good or evil, will enjoy freedom from state interference unless the state has reliable and trustworthy evidence of misconduct. Although some guilty persons occasionally escape justice under the adversary system, it is considered a small price to pay to ensure that our democratic ideals of justice and fair play are maintained.

The common law assumes that truth will emerge if the witnesses called for the Crown are effectively cross-examined to determine whether their evidence is reliable and honest. It also assumes that if an accused has an experienced and competent lawyer to defend him, the weakness in the testimony of a Crown witness will be exposed by his lawyer. Of course, it should be noted that it was not until late in the 18th century that an accused in a serious case was allowed to hire a lawyer, if he could afford one, to defend him and to cross-examine the witnesses against him. Before that, the courts had rationalized that an innocent person could always effectively defend himself against an accusation. Ironically, it was not until feuding British nobles, who used accusations of treason against each other, decided that they needed the assistance of lawyers at their trials, that Parliament was prepared to pass legislation to allow defence counsel in court at all. It took another century for the courts to recognize that an accused should be allowed the assistance of a lawyer, to level the playing field.

The Crown could only prove treason by Riel through witnesses who could give direct or circumstantial evidence of Riel's participation in the rebellion. A witness who could say that he saw Riel shoot at the Canadian soldiers would be giving direct evidence. A witness who could say that he saw Riel encourage the Métis to order his men to fire on the Canadian soldiers would be giving direct evidence. A witness who could say that he saw Riel behind enemy lines speaking to the Métis sharpshooters firing on the Canadian soldiers would be giving circumstantial evidence, from which it could be inferred that he was inciting rebellion.

The success of a cross-examination will often depend upon knowing in advance what a witness is going to say. In 1885, the Crown was not required to disclose to the defence what its witnesses were going to say, although the law does require the Crown to do so now, even if the evidence is favourable to the accused. No provision had been made under the North-West Territories Act of 1880 for a preliminary inquiry, as in the other provinces, permitting the defence to question Crown witnesses to determine whether there was sufficient evidence to put Riel on trial at all. Nor was there provision under the 1880 act for an indictment to be presented to a grand jury to decide whether Riel should be sent for trial. All the Crown had to do was present an indictment to a judge authorized to conduct a treason trial. Because Riel's defence team was not entitled to know what the Crown witnesses were going to say, they were hampered from effectively preparing questions for cross-examination.

It has been the custom of Crown counsel for many years to open its case with a speech to the jury explaining how it intended to prove the guilt of the accused. The opening statement is not evidence; its purpose is to explain what witnesses will be called and what they are expected to say. Crown counsel must be careful not to overstate its case, otherwise it will leave an opening for the defence to point out to the jury that the "Crown said that they would prove this or that and they have not done so." They must also be careful not tell the jury that certain evidence will be called if the judge must first rule on its admissibility. An admission of guilt, for example, because the judge would first have to decide whether the admission was voluntary. If the admission turned out to be involuntary, the jury would have heard that the accused admitted his guilt and a mistrial might be declared.

B.B. Osler opened the Canadian government's case against Riel by giving the jury the usual warning to put aside any preconceived notions of the guilt of Riel.

> The prisoner stands before you charged with the highest crime known to the law, and you are charged with passing upon his life or death. It is for you to remove from your minds any impression you may have had, or possessed from the knowledge of public facts, as to his guilt or innocence. You must endeavor to bring upon the evidence, and upon the evidence alone, your reasoning; and upon the evidence, not upon your knowledge of that which is public property, you must pass upon his guilt or innocence. He is to be presumed, as everybody

is in the criminal dock, innocent until the evidence brings home, to your satisfaction, guilt.

The indictment filed against Riel had charged him with six counts of treason by levying war against Queen Victoria. The first three described him as a subject of the Queen and alleged that he had levied war in three locations: Duck Lake, Fish Creek, and Batoche. The last three charged him with levying war against the Queen, not as a subject of the Queen but under her protection, at the three locations. Osler went on to explain why Riel was charged with six counts, "the three last being in fact a repetition," because if they found that Riel was not a subject of the Queen, then he owed allegiance as every other resident of Canada.

If any juror wondered why there were only six jurors trying Riel instead of the usual twelve jurors, Osler explained that Parliament had decided that the sparseness of the population made it impossible to have more jurors until the North-West Territories were more settled.

What had Riel done that amounted to treason against Her Majesty? he asked rhetorically.

> We first find him acting in concert with prominent men of both the English and French half-breeds and holding meetings. At those meetings apparently for some time nothing more than ordinary constitutional agitation for the redress of grievances, supposed or real, took place. The first overt act which we find against the prisoner is his calling his immediate friends — the French half-breeds — to bring their arms at the last of this series of public meetings; that meeting was held, I think, on the evening of the 3rd of March. At that meeting arms were brought. That is the first act that we find indicating that the prisoner intended to resort to violence. Now we find matters getting worse and worse, and on the 17th of March, we will give evidence of a statement made by the prisoner to the effect that he intended effecting a change in the government of

the country, probably referring to that particular section of the country known as the Saskatchewan district; he said that he intended to become the ruler of that country or perish in the attempt. We find him progressing from that until the 18th of March, when we find him sending out armed bodies of men, who took prisoners the Government Indian agent, Mr. Lash and some store-keepers. We find them looting or taking possession of the contents of stores at and near Batoche; we find armed men stopping freighters and taking their freight from them. Matters had become very serious, and the authorities much alarmed. On the 21st of March the French half-breeds, speaking generally, may be said to have been in arms under the guidance of the prisoner, and they were joined by Indians, Indians incited to rise, as I think the evidence will satisfy you, by the prisoner.

Many regarded Louis Riel a folk hero who had fought a government a thousand miles away and indifferent to the plight of the western settlers. Any sympathy for Riel had to be quickly swept away by painting him, not as a selfless hero, but as a scoundrel whose true motives were not to help his people but to sell them out for a government bribe.

The prisoner was not there for the purpose so much of aiding the half-breeds, as he was there for the purpose of utilising the half-breeds for his own selfish ends. You will find throughout the evidence in this case that it was not so much the rights of the half-breeds he was seeking as the power and benefit of Louis Riel, and the money that Louis Riel wanted to extract from the Government. It will appear that this so-called patriot, leader of an oppressed people, was willing to leave the country and go wherever the Government wanted him if he got a sum of money from the Government.

* * *

The Crown called nineteen witnesses — eight on Tuesday, July 28, and eleven more on Wednesday, July 29, to prove its case. The first, Dr. John Willoughby, a doctor from Saskatoon, said that on March 16, 1885, he and Norbert Walsh, who wanted to see Riel, left Saskatoon for Batoche, fifty miles away. Arriving two days later, they went to "the house of a half-breed named Rocheleau" located six or seven miles south of Batoche, where Riel was staying. Riel told him that "the time had come for the half-breeds to assert their rights" and that "he and his people intended to strike a blow to gain their rights ... No one knew better than he did as to the grievances of the settlers — my people have time and time again petitioned the Government to redress our grievances, and ... the only answer we received each time has been an increase of police." While he was there, sixty or seventy armed "half-breeds" arrived and Riel pointed to the men standing at the door and said, "Now I have my police; in one week that little Government police will be wiped out of existence."

Witnesses at the trial who had been held by Riel at the time of the battle of Batoche.

Riel said that the time had come when he was to rule the country or perish in the attempt. His plans were to have a new government in the North-West "composed of God-fearing men, they would have no such Parliament as the House at Ottawa." He intended to divide the country into seven portions and distribute the portions among the Bavarians, Poles, Italians, Germans, Irish, etc. "There was to be a New Ireland in the North-West." This rebellion was to be of a far greater extent than the former — and "they would have no Orangeism in the North-West."

Riel told him of a telegram that had been sent last fall by the residents of Saskatoon to the residents of Battleford offering to kill off "the half-breeds and the Indians." The same offer had been made again eleven days earlier. The people of Saskatoon had no right to ask for his protection.

Riel's lawyers decided to raise the question of his legal sanity with Dr. Willoughby, the first witness. Fitzpatrick, who cross-examined Willoughby, asked whether he thought Riel's proposal to apportioning various parts of the North-West to various nationalities was not peculiar:

Q. In regard to the plan he submitted to you, did you ever hear of such a plan before?
A. No, I never did.
Q. Did it strike you as being at all peculiar?
A. Rather; a little.

And moments later:

Q. Of course the plan he unfolded to you about the conquest of the North-West did not strike you as anything extraordinary for a man in his position to assert?
A. It did, certainly.
Q. It appeared to you a very rational proposition?
A. No, it did not.

The next eight witnesses called by the Crown were men who had been arrested by the Métis and held until the hostilities were over. Their evidence was to give the jury a first-hand description of Riel's direct involvement in the rebellion. It was not enough for the Crown to show that Riel talked of rebellion. It had to show that he actively participated by leading the rebels or by inciting them to rebel.

Thomas McKay from Prince Albert was called to describe the battle at Fish Creek. He was allowed, without objection by Riel's lawyers, to give hearsay evidence that he had *heard* that Riel was inciting the Métis to take up arms and that Riel had sent a letter (which he had not seen) regarding the surrender of Fort Carlton, which was being held by a force of mounted police under Superintendent Crozier. On March 21, he and Hillyard Mitchell went to Batoche to point out to the Métis the danger they were getting into by taking up arms.

At Duck Lake, they met two or three Métis and tried to persuade them to end the movement. They met with Riel who told him that the Métis had waited fifteen years to have their grievances redressed and blamed him for having neglected his people. McKay said that while speaking with Riel, he suddenly became agitated and said, "You don't know what we are after — *it is blood, blood, we want blood; it is a war of extermination, everybody that is against us is to be driven out of the country.* There were two curses in the country — the Government and the Hudson's Bay Company."

Riel wanted to put McKay on trial as a traitor to his people and called various Métis present to testify against him. McKay told the Métis that "Riel is threatening to take my life. If you think by taking my life you will benefit your cause, you are welcome to do so." Emmanuel Champagne assured him that they did not wish anything of the kind and "wanted to redress their grievances in a constitutional way." Riel later apologized, saying that it was not McKay personally but his cause that he was against and invited him to join them. Riel said that unless Crozier surrendered Fort Carlton, they would attack the fort that night at twelve o'clock. McKay and Mitchell returned to fort Carlton and reported what had happened to Crozier.

On the morning of March 26, McKay accompanied Sergeant Stewart and mounted policemen to get provisions and flour from Mitchell's store at Duck Lake. Three or four miles from Duck Lake, they noticed a group of Indigenous people lying in the snow watching the trail. About a mile and a half from Duck Lake, they saw some mounted policemen riding at full gallop, followed by a number of mounted men. A short distance later,

Gabriel Dumont and about thirty or forty men rode up and blamed him for the trouble, saying it was his fault that the people were not assisting the Métis. After some excited discussion and accusations, McKay and Stewart were allowed to return to Fort Carlton where they met a hundred men led by Crozier on their way to Duck Lake. They decided to go along.

About four miles from Duck Lake, their advance guard warned that there were Indigenous people waiting in a house. When an advance guard of Métis and Indigenous arrived, Crozier told his men to make a barricade and take the horses to the rear. Suddenly a white blanket appeared and Crozier, with an interpreter, went out to meet two men coming toward them. He then noticed the Métis and Indigenous people starting to surround them from the rear. Suddenly shots rang out from the other side and, for the next thirty or forty minutes, shots were exchanged. They then retreated to Fort Carlton. Nine of their men were killed and one wounded.

Although Greenshields, in cross-examination, suggested to McKay that Riel's comment about wanting blood referred to eating blood as part of their meal, McKay quickly dismissed the suggestion.

John W. Astley, a civil engineer and land surveyor from Prince Albert, was examined by George Burbidge, the federal deputy minister of justice. Astley had been employed by Superintendent Crozier as a scout in March and had posted proclamations from Crozier telling those who had been forced into rebellion that if they gave themselves into the charge of the police, they would be protected. On the morning of March 23, he and Harold Ross, a deputy sheriff at Prince Albert, had gone over to see if the French Métis were trying to intercept Crozier and were themselves captured by Gabriel Dumont and a party of Métis and Indigenous people. They were taken to Duck Lake and put in the telegraph office with a number of other prisoners. Around noon, Riel arrived; he seemed to be in command of about 550 men, 150 of whom were Indigenous.

Astley said that he heard the sound of a cannon, and an hour or so later, a prisoner, Newett, was brought in with a leg wound, which he dressed. Riel spoke to him and told him that Crozier's men had fired first.

Astley told Riel that from what he knew of Crozier, a gun might have gone off by accident. He said that he was kept a prisoner with a number of others until all the hostilities were finally over.

Astley said that after the Fish Creek and Duck Creek battles, he was concerned that he and the other prisoners would be harmed by their captors, and spoke to Riel to see if he could persuade him to agree to a ceasefire. Riel refused, saying that they had won two battles (Fish Creek and Duck Lake) and if they won another, they could get better terms.

On May 12, during the battle at Batoche, Astley testified, he was involved in running notes back and forth between Riel and General Middleton. Riel was concerned that the women and children were coming under fire from the Canadian soldiers. Middleton told him to tell Riel that if he would get the Métis to stop firing, he would stop his advance. Riel replied, "You know the men I have; I cannot go among these men and tell them to stop firing. You know that." Astley went back and told Middleton that Riel was willing to surrender but Middleton refused to accept a surrender from Riel until his men stopped firing. Middleton gave him a note to Riel indicating that if he should surrender, he would be kept safe until he had a fair trial.

Burbidge wanted to get Astley to say that Riel was acting only in his own self-interest and to refute any suggestion that he was concerned about the Métis, and improperly asked him,

Q. Did he speak to you of his personal safety?
A. He had very little to say about the half-breeds, *as far as regards himself seemed the principal object.**

Surprisingly, Riel's lawyers did not object to the leading question and Burbidge continued to press Astley about Riel's concern for his personal safety.

Q. What did he ask you in regard to himself?
A. If I would explain what risk he ran personally himself. He said to me that we knew that he never carried a rifle, of course, at the

---

* Here and elsewhere, italics added.

same time that we had seen him carry a rifle on one occasion. I told him he ran no danger as I could look at it. He suggested that I should broach the subject of the Church to the General and it would give him a chance to broach the subject when he came to be interviewed by the general. He would say that he was not to blame, that the council was to blame.

Although Astley had never said that Riel was in command, Burbidge again improperly suggested to Astley that he tell the jury about Riel's role as commander.

Q. During the time you saw the prisoner there *did you see him in command?*

A. He ordered the men into the pits on that occasion when some of them were leaving them. He took one half-breed and made him go back, saying that he would be able to do some fighting with the troops at all events.

Again Burbidge improperly suggested without objection that Riel must have been armed asking Astley when had he seen him armed, even though there was no evidence that Riel was ever armed.

Q. *When did you see him armed?*

A. Sometime before the Fish Creek fight, it must have been a week before I was talking to Riel before the council chamber one day, when a French half-breed came up with a report that the troops were coming. Shortly after, myself and the rest of the prisoners saw him passing the front of the house quickly with the half-breeds going towards the river, *armed.*

Burbidge had been allowed to put in Astley's mouth the evidence he wanted him to give; conduct improper and shameful on the part of a prosecutor, especially one who was the deputy attorney general of Canada.

T.C. Johnstone, who cross-examined Astley, wanted to show that Riel was excited, obviously to raise the issue of his legal sanity. However, his method of cross-examination was clearly ineffective and produced damaging answers.

> Q. You say you were speaking to him for a considerable time, did he at this time strike you as being excited or excitable, *or was he calm?*
> A. *He was cool enough, a little elated at his victory.*

Another attempt was even more ineffective and damaging:

> Q. What did he say at Batoche about his church?
> A. He said that he wanted me to mention to the General that he was to be recognized as the founder of the new church and that if the subject was mentioned to the General he could continue the subject when he met him.
> Q. What did you understand by founding a new church?
> A. *I understood it as a sharp trick to get the upper hand of the unfortunate half-breeds.*
> Q. When did you think it was to get advantage of the half-breeds?
> A. I considered that he was using them for his own ends.
> Q. Did you consider his actions eccentric?
> A. He seemed intelligent and in many respects a clever man.

A few more questions attempting to show Astley was biased against Riel and personally involved in the prosecution of Riel were quickly dismissed by Astley. Finally, Johnstone mercifully completed his cross-examination. A witness as important and as damaging as Astley should have been cross-examined by a more skillful advocate than T.C. Johnstone.

Harold Ross testified that he had gone up to Duck Lake with Astley on March 23 to see if the "half-breeds" would intercept Colonel Irvine, who was on route from Regina. They had been taken prisoner by Gabriel Dumont and about a hundred men and put into the telegraph station at Duck Lake.

After the Duck Lake battle on March 26, Riel came and told him not to be afraid. He related a conversation he heard between Astley and Riel:

A. Mr. Riel said that the troops fired first, and Mr. Astley suggested that perhaps the shot went off by accident and Mr. Riel said — well he did not agree with him for some time afterwards, he said perhaps that was the way.

Q. Did he say anything else?

A. And he said, *when I heard the shot I called on my men in the name of God to fire, and he seemed quite proud of it.*

Q. Did he say so?

A. No, judging from his actions, that is all.

Ross said that on March 31 Riel ordered all seven prisoners to be taken by sleighs under guard to Fort Carlton where they were kept until April 3 and then taken to Batoche. He saw Riel periodically thereafter and had a conversation with him after the Fish Creek battle.

> After the Fish Creek battle, I remember Riel one time — I can't tell you the day or date — saying that they had gained two victories, and they wanted to gain a third, and they could make better terms with the government.

He said that on May 12 during the battle at Batoche, Riel opened the hatch in the cellar where the prisoners were being kept and said to Astley, "Mr. Astley ... come up and stop the troops advancing, for if they hurt any of our families, we will massacre all the prisoners in the cellar."

Fitzpatrick cross-examined Ross to show that Riel had not even been at the Duck Lake fight and Ross reluctantly agreed.

Q. You say you saw the troops leave for the Duck Lake fight also?

A. *His troops yes, the rebels.*

Q. Did you see Riel with them?

A. No, not going away I did not see him.

Q. If he had been there, of course, you would have seen him?

A. I saw him outside.

Q. When they were going away did you see Mr. Riel with them, going away to Duck Lake?

A. I did not.

So far, so good. He had established that Ross did not know if Riel had been at the Battle of Duck Lake. He then committed a fundamental mistake all good cross-examiners avoid. Instead of moving on to another topic, Fitzpatrick continued to hammer home that Riel was not with the rebels at the Duck Lake battle. "Had he been with them you would have seen them, would you not?" Ross, realizing that he might have helped the defence by saying Riel was not with the rebels, turned on Fitzpatrick.

A. I might not. *There was a big crowd going away.*

Fitzpatrick then got Ross to admit that it was Dumont, not Riel, who had taken him prisoner and put him in the cellar with the other prisoners. But Ross's admission was turned against Riel when Scott was permitted, during re-examination of Ross, to improperly suggest that even though it was Dumont who had made them prisoners Riel was part of that company.

Q. Did you see any others of the party who took you prisoner afterwards?

A. One Indian is all I can remember.

Q. *Then Gabriel Dumont formed part of the same party that you saw Riel in company with afterwards?*

A. *Certainly.*

Again, there was no objection to this improper leading of the witness.

* * *

Peter Tompkins was the next witness. He, who lived at Duck Lake, and McKean, the miller, were repairing telegraph lines when about thirty Métis under the charge of Joseph Delorme and Jean Baptiste Paranteau arrested them and took them to the Walters and Baker store in Batoche. There they were kept with the others as prisoners. The next morning, they were taken across the river, to the church that was being used as barracks, council room, prison, and restaurant. Riel addressed a crowd of men in the church. Although Riel spoke in French (Tompkins did not understand French), he did understand Riel to say, "what was Carlton, or what was Prince Albert? They're nothing. *March on my brave army.*" The following evening, Tompkins testified, he and McKean were taken to Duck Lake and kept under guard in Mitchell's house with Astley and Ross. While they were there, a council was elected.

Although Tompkins testified about an election of the council, he had never said that Riel had anything to do with it. Casgrain suddenly slipped in the suggestion that it was Riel's council, and Riel's lawyers and the judge said nothing.

> Q. Well where did you go from that church? How long were you kept there.
> A. We were kept there till nine o'clock the next evening, and then we were sent down to Garnot's place
> Q. Philippe Garnot's place?
> A. Yes.
> Q. What capacity was he acting in, do you know?
> A. He was acting as secretary to the council.
> Q. *To Riel's council.*
> A. *Yes. We were told that ...*

Tompkins said he heard a cannon go off a couple of times and saw Riel ride up on a horse waving his hat, cheering his men, and thanking Sainte-Marie, Saint Jean-Baptiste, and Saint Joseph for his victories. Riel then came into the house and said that the police or volunteers had fired first and that he had ordered his men to fire "in the name of the Father Almighty who created us." Riel seemed to be running the whole thing, he said, and that whenever they wanted something, they had to ask Riel. On the day Batoche was finally taken by Middleton's troops, he heard Riel tell Astley, "If they massacre our women and children, we will massacre you prisoners."

Tompkins admitted in cross-examination that Riel took no part in the election of the council except that he spoke in favour of some person that another councilman had objected to. He also admitted that Riel took no part in his own arrest and was not present when he was put in the cellar at Batoche.

Tompkins's cousin William was employed by the Indian Department in the territories as a farm instructor and interpreter for the Indigenous people. On March 18, he had gone with John Lash, the Indian agent for the Canadian government at Fort Carlton, to Duck Lake, where they were taken prisoner by Riel, Gabriel Dumont, and other Métis, and taken to the church where a council was being elected. Riel, he said, took no part in the election. The next day they were taken to Batoche, then, on March 26, they were all taken back to Duck Lake and put in Hillyard Mitchell's house. After the Duck Lake battle, Tompkins heard Riel say to Astley that the police had fired first, and he gave the word to his men "in the name of God, to fire." He said that at Batoche, Riel appeared to be in charge, and he saw him armed with a Winchester rifle. On April 12, he said, Riel took Astley out of the cellar and told him that if the army did not stop shelling the houses, he would massacre the prisoners. Although Greenshields, in cross-examination, tried to get Tompkins to admit that he might have been mistaken about what Riel had said because Riel spoke French and Tompkins did not understand French; Tompkins said he understood Cree and an interpreter translated for him in Cree.

John Lash, the government's Indian agent at Fort Carlton, followed William Tompkins on the stand, and gave devastating evidence against Riel. On March 18, he said, he and Tompkins had been returning from the One Arrow reserve when they came upon a crowd of armed men near Batoche. Gabriel Dumont approached Lash and said that Riel wanted to see him. Riel arrived and told him that he was going to detain him because "the rebellion had commenced and that they intended fighting until the whole of the Saskatchewan Valley was in their hands."

Q. Who seemed to be in authority when Riel came up.
A. He seemed to command the whole thing. It was by his orders that the mules I was driving were unhitched, and he took possession of them and the trap.

He and Tompkins were taken to Batoche and put in the Walters and Baker store with the other prisoners and taken to the church the following day. He saw Riel at the church addressing the crowd and had several conversations with Riel who told him:

> He had three enemies ... the Government, the Hudson Bay Company and the police.
> He would give the police every opportunity to surrender, and if they did not do so, there would be bloodshed.
> He had heard that the Lieutenant Governor was on his way up and that he had sent an armed body to capture him.
> As soon as they had the country, it would be divided up, and so forth. He was going to give a seventh to the Indians, a seventh to the half-breeds, and I don't know what was to become of the balance.
> He had been waiting fifteen years, and at last his opportunity had come.

Asked if he ever saw Riel armed, he replied that he had.

Q. With what?
A. It was a rifle of some kind.
Q. When?

A. Prior to the Fish Creek fight, I cannot give you the date.
Q. Did Riel say anything about the Fish Creek fight?
A. Yes, he claimed the victory there.

Fitzpatrick wisely chose not to cross-examine him.

George Ness, a farmer and justice of the peace who lived near Batoche, said that in July or August of 1884 he had spoken to Riel, who had been trying to assist the people to have their grievances righted. From the beginning of his examination, Burbidge put the answers he wanted into the mouth of the witness. He tried to get Ness to say that Riel was fomenting trouble from the very beginning. Surprisingly, neither Riel's lawyers nor the judge objected to his improper tactics.

Q. *Speaking of getting up an agitation?*

Ness obviously did not understand what Burbidge meant by "agitation" and repeated the word but explained what Riel really intended.

A. Yes, an agitation or a bill of rights.

Burbidge unsuccessfully tried again, without objection by Riel's lawyers.

Q. *Did he at that time make any suggestion of using force?*
A. *No.*

Ness said he *heard* that Gabriel Dumont was inciting the Indigenous people on the One Arrow reserve and felt it was his duty to report this to Major Crozier at Carlton. On March 18, he was returning home to Batoche when he saw a big crowd opposite Kerr Brothers' store. Dumont stopped him and said that he had to keep him prisoner until Riel arrived. When Riel arrived, he told him to go down to the church. Burbidge again improperly suggested the answer he wanted:

Q. *Did every one appear to obey him?*
A. Yes.
Q. Dumont and all the rest?
A. Yes.
Q. Tell us about their taking you to the church?
A. When we got to the church they were in front of the church. Mr. Riel commenced saying that he was a prophet, that he could foresee events.

Ness and the other prisoners were taken across the river to the Walters and Baker store and returned the next day to the church. Burbidge again suggested the answers he wanted, without intervention by the judge or objection by Riel's lawyers.

Q. *Was the prisoner giving orders?*
A. Yes, he appeared to be at the head of affairs: he was giving orders.
Q. What was the chief event of that day as far as you can remember?
A. He was giving orders to go and take William Boyer and Charles Nolin prisoners.
Q. Did you hear them say why they were to be taken prisoners?
A. Because they would not take up arms.
Q. *Did he say anything about, because they had been movers up to that time?*
A. *Because they had been movers, and had left it at the time of taking up arms.*

Ness said that he was then taken before the council and charged with communicating with the police and insulting Gabriel Dumont. As a penalty, his horse and cutter were confiscated and he, for his liberty, was forced to promise to do nothing against them. He told the court he agreed because he had no alternative. When he arrived home, he said, his wife was in a great state of excitement because "Sioux Indians" had told her he was to be shot. At this point, James Greenshields finally rose to object: "There should be a limit to this hearsay evidence."

Why he chose to object to this evidence as hearsay is difficult to understand. It was irrelevant to the case. The issue was whether Riel had led or incited rebellion, not whether the Sioux had told Ness's wife that Ness was to be shot. Hearsay evidence had been led by the Crown frequently on issues critical to Riel's defence without objection, yet, when Burbidge improperly suggested the answer in critical questions that followed, neither the defence objected nor the judge intervened.

Q. Did you have any of the rebels quartered on you during that time?
A. Yes, they told me my property was public, every body's property was public.
Q. *The prisoner and others with him took whatever they saw fit?*
A. Yes.

By now the defence must have realized that the evidence of Riel's involvement in the rebellion was overwhelming. They had allowed Burbidge to put the answers he wanted into the mouths of the witnesses. If the jurors were going to acquit Riel, they would have to sympathize with his motives, even if those motives did not constitute a defence in law to rebellion. Fitzpatrick began his cross-examination by going to the heart of the reason for the rebellion. Ness confirmed that Riel had been sent for by the Métis because of some agitation in the country.

Q. The agitation was to obtain by *constitutional* means to redress certain grievances that the half-breeds pretended to exist?
A. Yes.
Q. That agitation had been going on for some years?
A. Yes.
Q. Riel told you when you first saw him that he had come for the purpose of taking part in that agitation at the request of the persons interested?
A. Well, I could not say he exactly said that, but I understood that he came for that purpose.
Q. You saw him frequently from July last up to the month of March?
A. Yes.

Q. *Did you, during all that time, hear of anything either for himself or any person else which would lead you to believe anything in the shape of rebellion was pretended by him?*

A. No sir, not till the 17th of March.

Fitzpatrick had now established that Riel's purpose was to obtain redress of Métis grievances by peaceful and constitutional means, not rebellion. Ness confirmed that different petitions had been in circulation in the country and had been forwarded to Ottawa, and that the last petition had been prepared under Riel's direction, had been approved by Ness (as the federal Indian agent), and then forwarded to Ottawa. He also confirmed that no answer had been given to any petitions that had been sent in. Instead, *the police force had been increased.*

Q. *That was generally considered among the people there as being the answer to their petition?*

A. I could not say.

Fitzpatrick now turned to the issue of Riel's sanity, and obtained from Ness the acknowledgement that Riel had acted differently with respect to the priests and religion between July or August, 1884, when he first met him, and March 17, 1885, when Riel had proclaimed that "the Spirit of God was in him and that Rome had tumbled, and he could tell future events." During July, August, September, and October, immediately after his return to Canada, Riel had attended church as a Roman Catholic and acted very devoutly, but by March 17 he was arguing with a priest, Father Moulin, and said Rome had fallen: "*Rome est tombée.*"

Q. *The first time you heard of the rebellion, heard it talked of, was at this time of the 17th March, and it is on that day he gave expression to this extraordinary language you have just told us about?*

A. Yes; on the 18th of March.

Fitzpatrick had carefully implanted in the jury's mind that Riel had shown signs of insanity on March 17 that had not manifested prior to that time. It was now Burbidge's opportunity to re-examine the witness to clarify any answers that Ness had given during cross-examination. Burbidge once more, improperly, put damaging answers in Ness's mouth. Riel's lawyers and Richardson remained inexplicably silent.

Q. When you told Mr. Fitzpatrick you understood the Government had refused Mr. Riel, *I understood you to be referring to Mr. Riel's own personal claims, is that what you mean?*

A. No, I said the Government had declined to accede to Riel's terms.

Q. *You were referring to Riel's own claims?*

A. *Yes; from what I understood, it was his personal claims.*

The suggestion that the claims were Riel's personal ones would haunt the defence throughout the trial. To remove any sympathy for Riel, the Crown had decided that it had to hammer home to the jury that Riel was concerned, not with the plight of the Métis, but with what he could get from the federal government. One has to ask why the judge remained silent during Burbidge's improper questioning? It was his duty to stop him, whether or not Riel's lawyers objected. Ness was the last witness called on this day, Tuesday, July 28, 1885.

The Crown led off the next morning with George Kerr, who had a store in Batoche. Examined by Casgrain, he said that on March 17, Gabriel Dumont and Riel had called a meeting to be held in Batoche. The next day, Riel and about fifty of his followers came to the store and asked for his guns and ammunition. Kerr told them to take the guns. When the Métis jumped over the counter to take them, Riel told them that they had no right behind the counter. Riel told Kerr to give his men what they wanted and charge it. Kerr said that he then left the store to get his cattle, about three miles away and returned to discover that "half-breed women and Indians" had stripped his store of everything. The next day, he was arrested by two Métis and taken to the home of Ludger Gareau, where there were about fifty or sixty men. A council was being held and Gabriel Dumont was in charge. Kerr said that he and his brother were charged with attempting to inform the authorities of their activities, but the charges were dismissed after Riel spoke to the council on his behalf.

It was obvious that he felt no animosity toward Riel and Fitzpatrick found him to be helpful on cross-examination. He said that he had attended a meeting back in January when money, gathered by the people, was presented to Riel.

Q. Were any speeches made at the table?
A. *Yes, Riel proposed the health of our Sovereign Queen Victoria.*

Riel had not approved of the Métis and Indigenous people breaking into his house and had sent him a letter protesting their conduct. Riel also took his part before the council.

Q. *Was there any treason talked?*
A. *No, not one word.*
Q. *They were all pleasant together as loyal subjects?*
A. *Yes.*

Fitzpatrick knew that Charles Nolin, Riel's cousin, was to be called by the Crown to say that he was not in favour of rebellion. He now used the opportunity to bring out from Kerr evidence that Nolin was active in the Métis meetings that were taking place so that he could discredit Nolin's later evidence.

Q. You knew that there were meetings being held alternatively in the vicinity of Batoche?
A. Yes.
Q. By all the people?
A. Yes.
Q. You knew that Nolin took an active part in these meetings?
A. Yes.

* * *

The next witness, Henry Walters, was co-owner of the Walters and Baker store in Batoche. He was obviously hostile toward Riel. On March 18, at about six o'clock in the evening, he had an intimation that the rebellion had broken out when he looked out the window and saw a party of armed men driving toward the door of his store. When they came into his store, Riel, whom he did not know before, said to him, "Well, Mr. Walters, it has commenced." Riel asked him for his arms and ammunition. When he told him that he could not have them, Riel asked him again to give them up quietly and peaceably. Riel, he said, told him "if they succeeded in the movement, they would pay me, and if they did not the Dominion Government would pay for them."

He asked Riel about the movement and was told that if successful, they were going to divide the land: "One seventh to the pioneer whites, and one seventh to the Indians, one seventh to the French half-breeds, and one seventh to the church and schools and the balance was Crown lands — I suppose Government lands." Riel also said that "if the whites struck a blow, a thunderbolt from Heaven would strike them; that God was with their people." Riel, he said, supervised removal of the goods from his store.

In the face of this damaging evidence, Greenshields decided to cross-examine him on Riel's motives for leading the rebellion.

Q. You heard that he had been sent for by the half-breeds?
A. Yes
Q. Did you know for what purpose?
A. No, I heard that the half-breeds had grievances.
Q. *And they wanted Riel to assist them?*
A. *Yes.*

* * *

Hillyard Mitchell, who owned the store in Duck Lake and was a trader and a justice of the peace, was the next witness. He had been coming back from Sandy Lake when he was told by a priest to get back to

Duck Lake because the Métis were up in arms and intended to take his store. On March 19, he went into the Métis council room and had a long conversation with Riel. Riel explained that the Métis had petitioned the government several times to have their grievances redressed and the reply they were now getting from the government was "five hundred policemen to shoot them." Although he told Riel the rumour was false, Riel said that it did not matter whether it was true or not; the Métis intended to show the government that they were not afraid to fight five hundred government soldiers. Riel spoke about the Métis' grievances, that he had suffered himself and had been kicked out of the House of Commons and out of the country fifteen years ago. Riel said that "he intended to bring Sir John to his feet and talked a great deal of bosh." Mitchell told him he had done a foolish thing and should repair the telegraph wires, which the Métis had cut. Riel said that he would consider it. When Mitchell returned the next day to get Riel's answer, he was told by Charles Nolin, *who was speaking for the Métis council*, that they wanted the unconditional surrender of Fort Carlton and if the police did not surrender, they would be attacked "with eight hundred strong."

Mitchell said he went to Fort Carlton and spoke to Superintendent Crozier, who told him he was willing to meet with Riel "man to man, with or without an escort, and at any place suited," but refused to put it in writing. He returned to Batoche and told Riel what Crozier had said. Riel became very excited and said that he would not take Crozier's word of honour. Riel asked Mitchell to put in writing what Crozier had said and Mitchell did. Riel, however, refused to meet Crozier personally and, instead, named two people to meet with him. Mitchell carried the message back to Crozier. After he arranged the meeting, he said that he told Nolin to tell Riel and the people that he would have nothing more to do with them and had done what he could to quiet them down.

Thomas E. Jackson, called next, was a druggist from Prince Albert who sympathized with the Métis movement. His brother, William Henry

Jackson, was Riel's secretary. He said that on Sunday, March 29, he went to Duck Lake to see his brother and, while there, spoke with Riel who told him that they had taken up arms in self-defence. Speaking about the Duck Lake fight, Riel said that he had gone there in person and, after Crozier had fired the first volley, urged his men to fire, "first in the name of the God the Father; secondly, in the name of God the Son; and thirdly, in the name of God the Holy Ghost; and repeated the commands in that manner throughout the battle."

Riel told him that his quarrel was not with the people but with the government, the police, and the Hudson's Bay Company. Riel had given him a letter to the people of Prince Albert indicating that if they remained neutral he would not bring in the Indigenous Peoples. If they did not, he would attack Prince Albert with them. If the settlers did not stay home, but stayed in town with the police, he would attack all of them. Riel, Jackson said, was in charge and only Riel was giving orders. Jackson was worried about his brother, Riel's secretary, and went to Batoche to see if he could get his brother away. Riel, he said, told him that his brother was sick, that his mind was affected, and that it was a judgment on him for opposing Riel himself. Although Jackson tried to get his brother away from there, Riel refused, saying that he was "getting along very nicely there and that he would recover."

Riel, he said, wanted him to write some letters to the newspapers and "to place a favourable construction on his action in taking up arms." He wanted him to write that he had applied to the government for indemnity of his losses through his being outlawed and his property being confiscated, and he claimed $100,000.

Q. *Do you know from him anything as to his personal motives in taking up arms?*

A. Yes. He disclosed his personal motives to me on this occasion. He became very much excited and angry, and attacked the English and the English constitution, and exhibited the greatest hatred for the English, and *he showed his motive was one of revenge more than anything else.*

Although Jackson was entitled to repeat what Riel had said to show his hatred for the English, he should not have been allowed to go on and say that this showed that his motive *was one of revenge more than anything else.* Again, Riel's lawyers did not object and Richardson continued to remain silent. Jackson was again allowed to comment on his opinion of Riel's motives, although the evidence should not have been admissible. The comments were prejudicial and no attempt was made to stop him.

Q. Revenge for what?
A. For his *supposed* ill-treatment, his property being confiscated and he being outlawed.
Q. Did you hear anything about the half-breed struggle?
A. Yes, he spoke of their grievances.
Q. In his communications with you whose grievances were the most prominent?
A. *I think his own particular troubles were the most prominent.* Of course, he spoke of the half-breeds' troubles.

Fitzpatrick started his cross-examination by asking Jackson to explain the nature of the agitation going on in the Saskatchewan district during the previous autumn. Jackson said that the agitation was for provincial rights principally, for "half-breed" claims, and against duties that they felt were onerous.

Q. *You were in sympathy with the agitation?*
A. Yes.
Q. You were aware Riel was brought into the country for the purpose of taking part in the agitation?
A. He was brought to this country on account of his supposed knowledge of the Manitoba Treaty.
Q. The people of the Saskatchewan district were of the opinion Riel could be useful to them in connection with the agitation?
A. Well, he was brought in principally by the half-breeds. The Canadians knew nothing about it till he was very nearly here.

Q. *Almost the whole of the people in that district had joined together for the purpose of this agitation?*
A. *They had.*
Q. *That agitation had been going on for a considerable length of time?*
A. *For some time.*
Q. Can you say for about how long?
A. *Five or six years, or longer.*

Fitzpatrick got Jackson to agree that Riel's intention was that the movement was to be entirely peaceful and constitutional. If they could not get what they had agitated for in five years, they would agitate for another five years: "constitutional agitation would get what they wanted."

Q. *Did you at any time hear that he wished to resort to any means other than constitutional up to March?*
A. *Nothing.*

So far so good. Fitzpatrick wanted to show that it must have been after March that Riel began to believe that he had a mission from God and therefore the onset of Riel's insanity. Jackson testified that Riel had told him his brother William had become insane because he had opposed Riel, and that was punishment from God for his opposition to Riel. Riel told Jackson that after he chased the Canadians out of the territory, he intended to divide up the territory into seven parts and give various nationalities a part. Riel had told him that he would put the word "Exovede" after his signature on official documents, to convey that he was simply one of the flock.

Q. *That he had no independent authority but simply acted as one of the others?*
A. *Yes, it was simply an affectation of humility.*
Q. You are aware that all the documents signed by him, as far as you know, bore the word "exovede"?
A. The most of them.

Riel had explained to him that his new religion was a "new liberal religion." The pope had no rights in this country and "I think very likely he intended himself to take the position, that the Pope was in his way." Fitzpatrick then put the question that was the basis for his insanity defence.

Q. *The first time you heard of this new religion and these new theories of religious questions was after the rebellion had begun?*
A. *Yes.*

* * *

Finally, the Crown called the conquering hero of Batoche, General Frederick Middleton. A British officer noted for his service throughout the British Empire, he had been appointed General Officer Commanding the Militia of Canada in the summer of 1884. On March 23, 1885, Joseph-Adolphe Caron, the minister of militia, sent for him to quell the disturbances in the Saskatchewan district. Two hours later, he boarded a train for Winnipeg, where he found his troops ready to go. It was two days after the battle at Duck Lake. That evening, he and his troops took the train to Qu'Appelle, where they disembarked and started their march to Fort Qu'Appelle and then to Fish Lake. He had between 420 and 450 soldiers.

Middleton's first skirmish was at Fish Creek on April 24, where nine or ten of his men were killed and forty wounded. On May 8, he started for Batoche, arriving the following day. An engagement began immediately upon his arrival and Batoche was eventually taken on May 12. He said that during the battle at Batoche, Astley came galloping from the direction of the enemy, with a flag and carrying a letter from Riel indicating that "if you massacre our families we are going to massacre the Indian agent and other prisoners." Middleton said that he took the letter and wrote on the back that he was anxious to avoid killing women and children, who should be put in one place, and, if he was told where, "no shot shall be fired on them. I trust to your honor not to put men with them." He said that by a series of rushes, they forced their way and the enemy was dispersed. Six of his men were killed and twelve or thirteen wounded.

On May 15, two scouts brought Riel to his tent, and Riel spoke freely with him. However, the only thing he remembered was the following:

> General, I have been thinking whether, if the Lord had granted me as decided a victory as he has you, whether, I should have been able to put it to a good use.

Middleton said that he was eventually directed to send Riel to Regina, which he did under the charge of Captain Young with twelve men and a sergeant. Greenshields, who cross-examined the general, asked him whether he had had any conversation with Riel about his religious views, and what he might have said.

A. I could hardly tell you. It was a disconnected thing. He told me that Rome was all wrong and the priests were narrow-minded people. There was nothing particularly, except the ideas of an enthusiast on some religious point.

Q. Did he say to you he was a prophet?

A. No.

Q. And endowed with the spirit of God?

A. No, nothing of that sort.

* * *

Captain George Holmes Young followed, and was examined by Burbidge. He was with the forces that arrived at Batoche and was present during the fighting that took place from May 9 to May 12. He was also with the charge of soldiers that went over the pits in the last charge and one of the first that entered the house that was known as the council chamber of the rebels. There he found a number of papers, which he gathered and gave to an artillery sergeant to give to Colonel Jarvis. General Middleton sent for him to identify Riel, whom he had known from the rebellion of 1869 and 1870, and Riel was then put in his charge. Burbidge knew that

Riel had made some damaging admissions to Young and wanted him to tell the court what Riel had said.

For two hundred years or more, the common law has recognized that statements made by an accused to a person in authority are not admissible unless freely given. The rule was born out of the excesses of the British government in the 18th century in suppressing any form of criticism of state action. Torture and trickery were frequently used by the authorities to extract confessions from people suspected of subversion. The judicial decision in the Warickshall case in 1783, however, clearly stated that "confessions ought to be voluntary and without compulsion."

This meant, and still means, that no statement of an accused given to a person in authority may be introduced at his trial until the judge first decides whether it was given freely and voluntarily. The obligation is upon the Crown to establish that the statements are voluntary, not upon the accused. Today, the Crown has the obligation to ask the judge to make his ruling on any such point in the absence of the jury. The reason is obvious: a jury present in court would have difficulty ignoring an incriminating statement made by the accused subsequently ruled to be inadmissible. The Crown is then required to call all of the witnesses present during the making of the statement to relate the circumstances under which it was made. It is not enough or relevant to ask the witnesses whether the statement was voluntary, since the question of voluntariness is one for the judge to decide, not the witnesses. It is only where the judge is satisfied beyond a reasonable doubt that the statement was made freely and voluntarily that the jury will be allowed to hear it.

Young, as custodian of Riel, was certainly a person in authority and Burbidge, the senior minister of the department of justice had to be well aware of this fundamental rule. It was his sworn duty to ensure that it was applied, especially where the prisoner was on trial for his life. But he was driven to obtain a conviction at any cost and pressed on, ignoring that sworn duty. Though Richardson and Riel's lawyers said nothing, Burbidge began by asking Young in the presence of the jury whether he had frequent conversations with Riel and whether Riel spoke "freely and voluntarily." It was not up to Young to make that assessment. It was not until Burbidge asked Young whether Riel spoke to him about the Indigenous people he expected to act with him that Fitzpatrick finally got to his feet and objected to the question.

Richardson, who did not seem to know that he, not Burbidge, had to rule on whether the statements were voluntary, inquired, "What is your objection?"

Fitzpatrick replied, "A statement made by a prisoner when in custody to the person in charge of him is not admissible."

Richardson ignored the objection and said nothing. Burbidge took his silence as a cue to press on and improperly put the answers that he wanted into Young's mouth in the presence of the jury.

Q. *Did you hold out any inducement to him to make a statement to you?*
A. *No.*
Q. *His statements were voluntary entirely?*
A. *Yes.*
Q. *Did you offer any inducements or make any promises of any kind?*
A. *No.*

Although the jury had heard the evidence, Fitzpatrick objected again that the evidence was not admissible and once again, Richardson ignored him. Burbidge, now in control of the courtroom, pressed on as if the objection had never been made.

Q. What did he say about the Indians?
A. On the Saturday the general wished to know as to the movements of some bands who intended to join the rebel forces, and the prisoner spoke about a messenger, Chi-ci-cum, whom he had sent towards Prince Albert and Battleford to bring men with him to Batoche. He gave this information to the general as it might be possible to divert the Indians from their intention.

Q. Did he say anything about sending runners out to the bands?

A. Yes, in the North-West, and also towards Cypress Hills.

Q. Did he speak to you of any other aid he expected to receive?

A. I was instructed to speak about possible aid from Irish sympathizers in the United States.

Fitzpatrick again objected, this time not about the fact that Burbidge had not proved that the statement was voluntary but whether Young "was instructed to speak to him about" aid from possible Irish sympathizers in the United States. Burbidge knew that he had gone too far. But he had been successful in getting the jury to hear this prejudicial evidence. The harm was done. They would not forget it although it was improper. Then, condescendingly, as if he was trying to show the jury that he was really fair, he withdrew the question: "We will not say anything about that." However, he continued to ask Young about other conversations that he had with Riel. Again no objection or ruling by Richardson. Young was allowed to relate to the jury everything that Riel had told him about his involvement in the battle at Duck Lake, even though the judge had never ruled whether that evidence was admissible. It was a confession of his involvement in the rebellion that effectively sealed his fate.

To make matters worse, Fitzpatrick in cross-examination conceded that Riel's admissions were free and voluntary by asking Young whether Riel was co-operative with Middleton.

Q. He gave information for the purpose of enabling the general to take such measures as were necessary to prevent any difficulty with the Indians?

A. He did.

Q. *He gave that freely and voluntarily, without pressure?*

A. *Yes; entirely of his own accord.*

The last questions put an end to any possible argument on appeal that the judge had admitted the conversations without ruling on whether they were given voluntarily. Fitzpatrick had done Burbidge's work for him.

* * *

The indictment against Riel had charged him with leading a rebellion on three occasions: at Duck Lake on Thursday, March 26, 1885; at Fish Creek on April 24, 1885; and at Batoche on May 9–13, 1885. The Crown lawyers decided to call Superintendent Crozier to give his version of the events that led to the incident at Duck Lake. The government lawyers wanted the jury to hear that it was the Métis who had started the fight, not Crozier's men. The Métis wanted the jury to know that it was Crozier's men who had fired first and they had only returned fire defending themselves from being killed by Crozier's men. Who had started the fight was an important issue for the jury to decide.

Crozier said that on March 26, he had left Fort Carlton with his force of police officers and Prince Albert volunteers for the purpose of getting some provisions from a store at Duck Lake, when they were met by a large party of rebels. Osler wanted to ensure that Crozier got the story right, so he decided to put into his mouth the Crown's version. Again, Riel's lawyers did not object and Richardson allowed Osler to breach the rules and lead the witness.

Q. *The result was a contest?*
A. *Yes.*
Q. *Your force was fired upon?*
A. *Yes.*
Q. *And several killed and wounded?*
A. Yes.
Q. *Did you get the provisions?*
A. *We did not.*
Q. *Why?*
A. *We could not proceed; we were prevented by an armed force of rebels.*

It had now been improperly suggested to the jury that the government forces had been suddenly ambushed by the Métis and the Indigenous people on their way to Duck Lake.

The Métis' position, on the other hand, was that the battle had started when Crozier's interpreter, Joe McKay, shot Assiyiwan and the Métis had responded *in self-defence*. Now was the opportunity for Riel's lawyers to show that if McKay had not shot Assiyiwan, a confrontation might never have occured and the Duck Lake incident would never have happened. However, Fitzpatrick's opening questions indicated that he had not fully grasped this.

Q. When you reached the place where the fight took place you advanced yourself, did you not?

A. Yes, I did.

Q. A short distance in advance of your troops?

A. Yes.

Q. You were met by one from the opposite side?

A. Yes.

Q. Who was that?

A. I do not know — he appeared to be an Indian.

Q. What became of that man?

A. *That man I heard was killed.*

Q. *Did you see him drop?*

A. *I cannot say that I saw him drop.*

Crozier may have been telling the truth when he said that he did not *actually* see Assiyiwan drop, but he knew a great deal more about the incident than he was prepared to admit. He was being evasive to a possible suggestion that the Métis were only defending themselves. The confrontation between McKay and Assiyiwan happened right in front of him. Surely, he knew who had fired the first shot. Fitzpatrick asked him a few more questions about who was the first man killed and whether he saw any men killed, to which he replied that he did not know because he was too busy giving directions to his men. The opportunity to obtain evidence that might have demonstrated that the Métis were only defending themselves was soon lost and Fitzpatrick sat down.

Charles Nolin, Riel's cousin, was called next. Riel and his family had lived with him for four months after he came back from Montana. Nolin had been a member of the original group of Métis, along with Gabriel Dumont, in favour of an all-out war against the whites, and had been named to the council. However, he changed his mind when he was convinced by the clergy that he should oppose the movement and try to split the Métis. On March 19, he was arrested by Dumont's men and put on trial for treason. To save his life, he agreed to join the movement. When he was arrested after the Battle of Duck Lake, he agreed to become a witness for the prosecution and turn against his cousin in exchange for immunity from prosecution. His evidence against was the most damaging of all the witnesses.

Nolin testified that it was about December 1, 1884, that Riel said he had a divine mission to fulfill and showed him a plan to destroy England and Canada and then Rome and the pope. Riel told him, at first, that the Canadian government owed him about $100,000 and he wanted $10,000 or $15,000. Father André told Riel he would use his influence with the government to obtain $35,000 for him. He said Riel agreed, saying that he would settle with the government himself for the balance of $100,000 he was owed. Riel told him that if he got the money he wanted from the government, he would go wherever the government wished to send him. Riel also told him that if he got the money, he would go to the United States and start a paper and raise the other nationalities in the States: "Before the grass is that high in this country, you will see foreign armies in this country." Riel said "he would commence by destroying Manitoba, and then destroy the North-West and take possession of the North-West."

In January 1885, the government had asked for tenders to construct a telegraph line between Edmonton and Duck Lake. Nolin had tendered and had been awarded the contract. He said that on January 27, Riel and Dumont tried to persuade him to withdraw his tender in favour of Riel because the government had not given Riel any answer to his claim of $35,000. It would show the government that the Métis were not satisfied because they had not given Riel what he asked for. Nolin said that he had refused but proposed to Riel that if he abandoned his plan to return to the United States and raise up an army to come to Canada, and would renounce his American citizenship, he could accept a seat in Parliament when the North-West was divided up into counties. Riel, he said, agreed.

Nolin said that the next day he received a telegram from David Macdowall, the district's representative on the Territorial council, indicating that the government was going to grant the "half-breeds" their rights, but nothing was said about Riel's claim for compensation. He showed the telegram to Riel the following Sunday. Nolin said that at a meeting of the Métis that was scheduled for February 24, Riel wanted him to participate in a scheme whereby Riel would tell the French and English Métis that he was going back to Montana and five or six members would say, "No, no," and then Riel would be asked to stay and be their leader. On March 2, Nolin said, Riel met with Father André and asked for permission to declare a provisional government before midnight but Father André refused.

The following day, about sixty armed men arrived with Riel and had a meeting. Riel wanted to take up arms but Nolin suggested that they have public prayers for nine days. A vote was taken and Nolin's suggestion was adopted. When nine days of prayers ended, Nolin was taken prisoner and brought before the council for trial, with Riel making accusations against him. He said he told the council that Riel was making use of the movement to get his $100,000 from the government, and he was acquitted. But Riel protested against the decision, and the council condemned Nolin to death. To save his life, he said, he had to agree to join the movement.

Q. Do you remember the 26th of March, the day of the battle at Duck Lake?

A. Yes.

Q. Was the prisoner there?

A. Yes, after the news came that the police were coming, the prisoner started one of the first for Duck Lake on horseback.

Q. What did he carry?

A. *He had a cross.*

With the exception of this last answer, Nolin's evidence that Riel's true intention in leading the rebellion was to obtain an indemnity of $100,000 from the government and not help the Métis to gain their rights was devastating to the defence. If Riel's lawyers were to convince the jury that Riel's motives were entirely altruistic and that he had returned from Montana to help the Métis cause, then Nolin had to be shown to be a liar who had agreed to testify falsely against Riel to save himself from prosecution. The problem was that Riel's lawyers had not been told ahead of time what Nolin was going to say. In 1885, the law did not require the prosecution to reveal what a witness was going to say. The North-West Territories Act had not established the right of an accused to a preliminary inquiry as there was in other provinces. If there had been that right, Nolin could have been questioned about the evidence he planned to give. Although it must have been apparent to Riel's lawyers that, since Nolin had not been charged with any involvement in the rebellion, his evidence was going to be helpful to the Crown, and harmful to Riel. If it could be established that he had agreed to testify against Riel to purchase prosecutorial immunity, it could be argued to the jury that he should not be believed.

Lemieux, who was to cross-examine him, had a formidable task. He started off by showing that Nolin himself had been active in political movements in the West.

Q. You took a very active part in the political movements in this country since [18]69?

A. Yes....

Q. You thought the presence of the prisoner would be good for the half-breeds, for the claims they were demanding from the Government?

A. Yes.

After a few more questions and answers:

Q. A constitutional movement took place in the Saskatchewan to redress the grievances?

A. Yes.

Q. The half-breeds of all religions took part?

A. Yes

Q. The whites?

A. Not directly, they sympathised very much with us. The whites did not take direct action in the movement, but sympathised greatly with the half-breeds.

Unfortunately, the transcript of the trial at this stage suddenly becomes a narrative of Nolin's evidence rather that an exact record of the questions and answers. Nolin was questioned about his breakup with Riel and replied that he broke with Riel about March 18. When Lemieux pressed Nolin to admit that he continued to deceive the "half-breeds" about Riel's declared intention to return to Montana, he said that he only did it because Captain Gagnon, representing the federal government, was there and he hoped it would bring about a satisfactory result for Riel. However, he was never questioned about the fact that he had not been prosecuted and must have sold out his cousin to save himself.

Lemieux then turned to the issue of Riel's sanity and asked if Riel had ever considered himself a prophet. Nolin said that he had and related an unusual incident that had occurred at his home when Riel and his family were living with him. One evening after dinner, Riel's bowels were making noise. Riel asked if he heard the noise and, when Nolin said he did, Riel told him that the noise was his liver and that *he had inspirations that worked through every part of his body.* Asked about Riel's intention regarding Canada, Riel, he said, showed him a book written with buffalo blood indicating that when he had taken over Canada, Canada would be divided up and Quebec would be given to the Prussians, Ontario to the Irish, and the North-West Territories would be divided up into various parts between European nations including the Jews, the Bavarians, and the Hungarians.

Suddenly, Riel's lawyers were faced with a serious problem: Riel wanted to take over the questioning of Nolin. Richardson did not seem to know how to deal with this unusual situation. The first thing that Richardson should have done was to send the jury to their room while the problem was being discussed. An experienced judge would have known that Riel was about to say something that would prejudice his right to a fair trial.

RIEL: Your Honor, would you permit me a little while —
RICHARDSON: In the proper time, I will tell you when you can speak to me, and give you every opportunity — not just now though.
RIEL: If there was a way, by legal procedure, that I should be allowed to say a word, I wish you would allow me before this prisoner (witness) leaves the box.
RICHARDSON: I think you should suggest any question you have to your own counsel —

After further discussion between the judge and Riel, Charles Fitzpatrick finally addressed the court:

I think the time has now arrived when it is necessary to state to the court that we require that the prisoner in the box should thoroughly understand that anything that is done in this case, must be done through us, and if he wishes anything to be done, he must give us instructions. He should be given to understand that he should give any instructions to us, and he must not be allowed to interfere. He is now endeavoring to withhold instructions.

Richardson was at a loss what to do. Should Riel be allowed to question the witness when he was represented by lawyers, he inquired of Fitzpatrick?

FITZPATRICK: I think the statute provides that he may make statements to the jury.
RICHARDSON: The prisoner may defend himself under the statute, personally or by counsel.
FITZPATRICK: Once he has counsel, he has no right to interfere.
ROBINSON: He has the right to address the jury. I am not aware of any right until then.

But Riel would not be silenced. He wanted the opportunity to question Nolin personally.

> RIEL: If you will allow me, your Honor, this case comes to be extraordinary, and while the Crown, with the great talents they have at its service, are trying to show I am guilty — of course it is their duty, my counsellors are trying — my good friends and lawyers, who have been sent here by friends whom I respect — *are trying to show that I am insane —*
>
> RICHARDSON: Now you must stop.
>
> RIEL: Now I will stop and obey your court.
>
> RICHARDSON: I will tell you once more, if you have any questions which you think ought to be put to this witness, and which your advisers have not put, just tell them quietly and they will put it, if they think that it is proper to do so.
>
> FITZPATRICK: I don't think he ought to be allowed to say anything more.

All of these matters should have been raised in the absence of the jury as a precaution against Riel, or even his lawyers or Crown counsel, saying anything that might prejudice his case. The problem was not unusual and could arise anytime there was an issue about the sanity of the accused, a potential nightmare that every defence counsel representing a client who may be legally insane fears. How will the accused react when he discovers that his lawyers are trying to prove that he is insane when he does not think he is? If the accused has some understanding of the proceedings that are going on, he may not wish to be found not guilty by reason of insanity.

Once Riel agreed to have lawyers represent him, they were entitled to exercise complete control over the conduct of his defence. It was their responsibility to ask whatever questions they believed were in his best interests. Although Riel was entitled to ask his lawyers to put certain questions to a witness or to adopt a certain defence, they had the right and duty to ignore him if they believed that it was not in his best interests. If Riel had persisted, his lawyers could have advised Richardson that Riel would not take their advice and ask to be allowed to withdraw from the case. Riel also had the right to discharge his lawyers and defend himself. The difficult issue for Richardson was whether to allow Riel to fire his lawyers when there was some concern that he was possibly insane and could not properly defend himself.

Riel's lawyers were also in a difficult position. Riel did not want to discharge them, but he did not want them to ask questions of Nolin that would suggest that he was insane at the time of the rebellion. What he wanted them to do was to show that his rebellion was justified because the petitions of the Métis had been ignored. But his lawyers knew that justification was not recognized as a defence to treason. If they were going to save his life, the only defence available was that he was insane at the time of the rebellion.

The discussion between the judge and defence counsel continued — unfortunately, in the presence of the jury. Richardson finally understood that he had to do something that he should have done earlier.

> RICHARDSON: Prisoner, are you defended by counsel? Are you defended by counsel? Are you defended by counsel? Answer my question, please, are you defended by counsel? Is your case in the hands of counsel?
> RIEL: Partly, my cause is partly in their hands.
> RICHARDSON: Now, stop; are you defended by counsel or not? Have you advisers?
> RIEL: I don't wish to leave them aside. I want them, I want their services, but I want my cause to be, your Honor, to be defended to the best which circumstances allow.
> RICHARDSON: Then you must leave it in their hands.

Richardson should have adjourned the proceedings to allow Riel to reflect upon his situation and possibly consult with his lawyers. Riel's life now depended upon the choice that the judge was forcing him to make, and he was expected to make it immediately. Richardson was not prepared to give him time to make a considered decision. He was bound and determined to speed up the process of the trial and rush to judgment.

Riel tried to explain his position to the judge. It was simply that his lawyers came from Quebec, a faraway province, and were not familiar with the witnesses as he was. "Athough I am willing to give them all the information that I can, they cannot follow the thread of all questions that could be put to the witnesses. They lose more than three-quarters of the good opportunities of making good answers ..."

Riel was correct in some respects but not in others. It was true that his lawyers had come a long way and were not as familiar as he was with the witnesses. More time to prepare would have enabled them to become more familiar with the evidence that the Crown witnesses would be expected to give and be more effective in their cross-examination. But Richardson was not prepared to give Riel's lawyers adequate time to prepare for such an important trial and had been instructed to get the trial over with as quickly as possible. Riel, on the other hand, would not have helped his defence if he had been allowed to question the witnesses. He wanted to justify his rebellion and any attempt to justify his conduct would have been harmful to his defence.

After some further discussion between Riel, the judge, and the lawyers, Richardson decided to do what he should have done in the first place and grant Riel's lawyers an adjournment to discuss whether he wanted them to continue to defend him. But it was only a five-minute adjournment, and Riel was instructed to go with his lawyers. Unfortunately, the adjournment did not resolve the problem. When the court resumed, François Lemieux advised the court that Riel wanted them to continue to represent him, but he personally still wanted to put some two hundred questions to Nolin. Christopher Robinson rose and facetiously advised Richardson that the Crown had no objection to Riel questioning the witness. Of course the Crown would not object, as it would have demonstrated that Riel was probably sane. Again, the consent of the Crown was irrelevant, since it was a matter between Riel and his lawyers, not the Crown. Richardson expressed the opinion that if "this man" insisted on putting a question, he could not refuse. He was wrong. Defence counsel could not conduct the defence in a manner that they felt was in Riel's best interest if he were allowed to ask questions that they were not prepared to ask, and which might counteract their efforts on his behalf. Richardson finally and correctly explained to Riel what might happen if he decided to ask questions:

> Listen to me for one moment. I say that I shall not stop you from putting a question. I could not stop you from putting a question, but if you do it, you do it with the knowledge that those gentlemen will abandon you at once. I think that is the position you gentlemen put it in, and you will have to take the responsibility of that.

Riel would not accept his ruling. He wanted to be able ask the questions himself and to have his lawyers "there to give him advice necessary to stop me when I go out of the procedure." Richardson again explained to him that this was a matter between him and his counsel. After further discussion back and forth between Riel and the lawyers, Richardson ruled:

> I think that I will have to tell you, too, that you are in your counsel's hands, and if you and they cannot agree, then will come another question, whether the court will not further interfere, and say counsel must go.

When Riel continued to inquire why he could not ask questions, Richardson simply ignored him and asked the lawyers whether they had any further questions to ask the witness. The cross-examination continued and Nolin was asked about Riel's influence on the Métis. He said that Riel gained influence by working against the clergy and by making himself out as a priest, the "half-breeds" were ignorant, and they were taken advantage of because of their ignorance and simplicity.

Nolin's answers understandably angered Riel. He repeated that he wanted the right to ask questions and at the same time be defended by his lawyers. Richardson told him again that he could not have both, noting that Riel's counsel "say that they cannot accept the responsibility of conducting his case if he insists upon it." Richardson then made an astonishing admission that accurately summed up his incompetence to conduct the trial:

> If it were an ordinary criminal case, I should not hesi-
> tate, but this is beyond the ordinary run of cases that I
> have had to do within my whole career.

Riel was not silenced by the ruling. This time he wanted to know if his counsel could insist upon being his counsel "if I thank them for their services." What he meant was not clear. Richardson again warned him that if his lawyers decided not to continue their services, then he could assign counsel to defend him and Riel would be bound by his ruling. Richardson was wrong. He had no right to foist on an accused a lawyer that he did not want. Riel responded that "it is not against their dignity. I cannot see it in that light." Again what he meant was not clear. Richardson ignored the remark and directed the Crown to call their next witness.

Thomas Sanderson, a farmer living at the Carrot River Settlement, was the eighteenth witness for the Crown. On March 20, he was at Hoodoo, which was fifty miles away from his home, between Batoche and Humboldt, when some rebels rode up and took him and Edward Woodcock, who was in charge of the Hoodoo station, to Batoche as prisoners. There he had some conversation with Riel.

Q. Did he tell you anything else about the [Duck Lake] battle?
A. I asked him who fired first and he said the police, and he said afterwards he then gave orders for his men to fire, three distinct orders.
Q. Did he say how he gave the orders?

A. "In the name of the Father Almighty, I command you to fire," was the first time; I think those are as near the words as I can repeat them. I think he said the second time, "in the name of our Saviour who redeemed us, I command you to fire," and the third time, "in the name of the Father, Son and Holy Ghost, I command you to fire."

Riel wanted to send a message to Crozier to pick up his dead but none of his men wanted to volunteer for fear of being taken prisoner. Sanderson agreed to go and left the following day with a letter for Crozier. Although Sanderson promised to return, he was detained by Crozier after delivering the letter and assisted Crozier to recover the dead policemen.

The defence again saw an opportunity to question Sanderson about Riel's unusual plans to divide up the territory once a government was formed.

Q. Now, at the time you spoke to him regarding the formation of a government, did he give you any idea of what kind of a government he proposed forming?

A. Yes; he was going to divide the country up into seven parts. One part was to be for the Canadians, or white settlers, one-seventh, another seventh for the Indians, another seventh for the half-breeds, and he named over what he was going to do with the rest, I don't recollect the names of the people.

Q. Did he tell you he was going to give other sevenths to other nationalities, the Poles, the Hungarians and Bavarians and Jews?

A. He did not.

Q. Did you hear him say anything about giving a portion of it to the Germans?

A. No; not to my knowledge. He named over, I think it was three-sevenths of it was to remain to support the Government.

Q. That was for himself, I suppose?

A. Yes, I suppose, for the government he was about to establish.

[...]

Q. Did he talk to you anything about religion?

A. Yes.

Q. What did he tell you about that?

A. He told me that he had cut himself loose from Rome altogether, and he would have nothing more to do with the Pope, that they were not going to pay taxes to Rome. He said if they still kept on with Rome they could not agree with the Canadian and white people who came there to live, because their government would have to keep all Protestants out of the country, if they kept on with Rome.

Q. That is, if the Riel government kept on with Rome they would have to keep all Protestants out of the country?

A. Yes.

Q. And abandoning Rome, they would be able to allow Protestants to come into the country?

A. Yes, that is what I understood from him.

* * *

Robert Jefferson, the nineteenth and last witness, was called to identify a letter that Riel had sent to Poundmaker, one of the chiefs of the Cree, urging him to join him in the rebellion. Jefferson had been in Poundmaker's camp when he saw the letter from Riel and eight members of the council urging the "half-breeds and Indians" of Battleford to rise up, take Battleford, and destroy it. The letter also requested the Indigenous Peoples to send a detachment of forty to fifty men. Jefferson testified that he heard the letter read to Poundmaker in French and then translated for him into Cree. The Crown had now demonstrated that Riel had also incited the Indigenous Peoples to rebellion.

It was now almost six o'clock in the afternoon. The Crown had completed its evidence and Robinson asked the judge to adjourn the proceedings until the next day at 10:00 a.m. The Crown had presented an overwhelming case of treason against Riel with nineteen witnesses in only two days of evidence. Riel's lawyers now realized that if they expected to save his life, they would have to convince the jury that he was legally insane at the time of the rebellion. The next day, Thursday, July 30, was the defence's turn to call their witnesses.

CHAPTER 6

The Defence of Insanity

Before the prisoner can be convicted *you must be satis-fied* that he was implicated in the acts charged against him. If you are satisfied that he was implicated in the acts in which he is said to have been implicated, *he must as completely satisfy you* that he is not answerable by reason of unsoundness of mind. (italics added)

— Judge Richardson, Charge to the Jury

When the attacks on the jurisdiction of the court to try Riel failed, the only defence left to save Riel's life was to show that he was insane. The Crown had presented overwhelming evidence that Riel had led or incited an armed rebellion of his Métis followers against the Canadian government. There had also been very damaging evidence from Riel's cousin Charles Nolin that Riel had been prepared to abandon the Métis and Indigenous Peoples' cause and go back to Montana for a payment of $10,000 to $15,000 from the federal government. Any sympathy that the jury might have for Riel, who claimed to be fighting government indifference and abandonment, would be quickly dashed by this revelation unless it was shown to be a lie. A prophet does not abandon his people for forty pieces of silver. If Riel's lawyers expected that they could persuade the jury that he was truly insane then they would have to show that Nolin's evidence was false. Had Nolin not bought prosecutorial immunity in exchange for that evidence? Had Nolin not been one of the original rebels? Was he not now giving evidence against his cousin to save his own skin? Ordinary jurors would have difficulty believing a person like Nolin, who had turned on his own kinsman.

The trouble was that Lemieux had failed during his cross-examination of Nolin to show that his evidence was self-serving. Instead of concentrating on attacking Nolin's credibility, Lemieux's questions were directed toward getting Nolin to agree that Riel considered himself to be a prophet, ordained by God to help his Métis people and the Indigenous Peoples achieve their rights. However, Nolin's evidence that Riel said he would go back to Montanan for $10,000 would come back to haunt him during the Crown's summation, Richardson's charge to the jury, and the Manitoba Court of Appeal. There could be no sympathy for a leader who was prepared to bargain his people's cause away for a paltry $10,000.

Armed rebellion was treason and the only punishment for treason was death by hanging. To save him from the gallows, his lawyers would have to convince the jury that at the time he led the rebellion, he was insane as defined by the law, notwithstanding Nolin's evidence.

Canadian law in 1885 and now provides that a person is not guilty of a crime if at the time that the crime was committed the person was legally insane. A finding of insanity, however, does not allow him to go free. He will be committed to an institution for the criminally insane, usually for the rest of his life. If Riel were found not guilty by reason of insanity, he would not be free. However, he would at least still have his life.

Although English law, even in its harshest days, recognized insanity as a possible defence against execution, mere existence of insanity did not exempt the insane from criminal responsibility. Proof of madness did not entitle a man to be acquitted, but to a special verdict that he committed the offence when mad. This gave him a right to a possible pardon. Before the 18th century, few early legal writers were prepared to put pen to paper to discuss what was meant by madness or what Blackstone called lunacy. Trial judges were left individually to define what they understood to be madness in their instructions to the juries. As late as 1724, Mr. Justice Tracey, the judge in the *Arnold* case, instructed the jury that no mentally affected person should be allowed to escape punishment (the gallows) unless it should appear that he is "totally deprived of his understanding and memory, and doth not know what he is doing, no more than an infant, than a brute, or a wild beast." It was not until the *Hadfield* case in 1800 that the attitude of the courts began to change, after the great advocate, and later Lord Chancellor, Thomas Erskine was able to convince the trial judge, Lord Kenyon, to accept the test of insane delusion and direct the jury to find Hadfield, who had attempted to kill King George III, not guilty by reason of insanity.

The British Parliament had never defined what constituted legal insanity. Unlike treason, Parliament had left the law of insanity to be developed by judges. Yet it was not until 1843 that any definitive statement finally emerged from English courts. It occurred in the curious case of Daniel M'Naghten.[1] M'Naghten had delusions of persecution. He believed that a number of persons were conspiring against him and used to send people into his room at night to worry him. One of the people he thought had conspired against him was Sir Robert Peel, the prime minister of the day. M'Naghten, a Scotsman, had decided to come to London with a pistol and get rid of Peel, whom he believed was "in the conspiracy to make my life impossible." Arriving in London, he went to 10 Downing Street, the official residence of the prime minister, and shot the first person that emerged from the residence. That person was not Sir Robert Peel, but his secretary, Edward Drummond. In law, it made no difference that M'Naghten had shot the wrong man. He was still guilty of murder unless the defence could show that he was legally insane.

The case was tried by Chief Justice Tindal of the English Court of Queen's Bench. At the conclusion of the evidence, he directed the jury that the question they had to consider was whether M'Naghten "had competent use of his understanding so that he *knew* that he was doing a wicked and wrong thing. If he was not sensible that it was a violation of the law of God or man, undoubtedly he was not responsible for the act or liable to any punishment whatsoever." The jury found M'Naghten not guilty on account of insanity. The verdict raised such a clamour throughout England that the matter was debated in the House of Lords. The Lords didn't know what to do, so it was decided to ask all fifteen judges of the day to give their opinion on the law of insanity as a defence to the commission of a crime. What were the proper directions to be put to a jury where the defence of insanity is raised, they asked? The answer given was this:

> The jury ought to be told in all cases that every man is presumed to be sane, and to possess a sufficient degree of reason to be responsible for his crimes, *until the contrary is proved to their satisfaction.* That, to establish a defence on the ground of insanity, it must be clearly proved that at the time of committing the act the accused was labouring under such a defect of reason from disease of the mind *as not to know the nature and quality of the act he was doing, or if he did know it that he did not know he was doing what was wrong.* (italics added)

This answer was not entirely satisfactory to everyone. What did "know" mean in law? Did "wrong" mean contrary to the "law of the land," or contrary to the "law of God"? The judges were concerned that if the definition of wrong was restricted to the law of the land, it might "confound the jury by inducing them to believe that an actual knowledge of the law of the land was essential to lead to a conviction; whereas the law is administered on the principle that everyone must be taken conclusively to know it without proof that he does know it." The judges decided that the best way to avoid any confusion was to simply leave the question for the jury without further explanation and let the jury make up their own minds.

In 1885, the criminal law of Canada was the same as English common law. Seven years later, in 1892, Parliament passed the first Criminal Code and made an important change to the law of insanity. It changed the word "know" to "appreciate" in the first branch of the test. To be found insane, the accused had to be suffering from a disease of the mind that rendered him incapable of "*appreciating* the nature and quality" of his acts. Mere knowledge of his actions was not enough. He was not guilty if he did not have the capacity to *appreciate the consequences of his conduct*, a wider definition. In 1885, however, the existing law only required the offender to *know* the nature and quality of his acts. The law presumed, as it still does today, that a person accused of a crime is sane unless he proves otherwise. Once the Crown proved that Riel had committed treason, the onus shifted to the defence to prove that Riel was insane at the time — that *he did not know he was doing what was wrong.*

Although the sanity or insanity of a person is essentially a medical question, whether an accused has a disease of the mind that renders him incapable of "knowing the nature and quality of his actions" or "knowing that his actions are wrong" is a legal question, not a medical one. Lawyers and judges are not experts on the workings of the mind and have to turn to medical experts — psychiatrists and psychologists — for assistance. However, psychiatrists and psychologists do not diagnose mental illness by the legal standard of insanity and often disagree with their colleagues on whether an accused is or is not legally insane. As a result, it is neither unusual nor difficult for each side of a case to line up one or more psychiatrists and psychologists to give opposing opinions on the very issue that the jury must decide, and leave it up to the jury to decide which opinion to accept. The task of Riel's lawyers was to engage medical experts who would testify that Louis Riel *did not know the nature and quality of his actions when he led the Rebellion, or if he did know, that he did not know that what he was doing was wrong.*

The common law rule that an accused is presumed sane until he proves the contrary is simply a rule of common sense. Since an accused is entitled to remain silent and say nothing to his accusers, without the presumption of sanity the state would be unable to have its medical experts question the (silent) accused to determine his sanity, and that would make it virtually impossible for the Crown to obtain a conviction. The defence could simply say the accused was insane, and that would be that. But with the presumption of sanity, there is no obligation upon the Crown to lead evidence as to the sanity of the accused at the time he committed the offence. It is up to the accused to raise his insanity as a defence after the Crown has proved its case against him. The Crown is then entitled to call evidence to refute the claim of insanity after the defence has completed its case.

Tradition, at least since the 19th century, has always imposed a duty upon the Crown to be impartial in the prosecution of a person accused of having committed a crime. Impartiality excludes any notion of winning or losing. In 1935, the English Court of Appeal in the *Sugarman* case eloquently stated that tradition:

> It cannot be too often made plain that the business of counsel for the Crown is fairly and impartially to exhibit all the facts to the jury. *The Crown has no interest in procuring a conviction.* Its only interest is that the right person should be convicted, that the truth should be known, and that justice be done.[2] (italics added)

"That justice be done!" Words that strike a resounding chord for British justice. Justice is not done when a person who is insane — or not mentally fit to stand trial — is prosecuted by the state. Even before Riel was put on trial, the Crown had the duty to have him examined by a psychiatrist to determine whether he was fit to stand trial. For some reason no effort was made to do this, even though there had been clear indications to everyone that Riel's mental condition was unstable.

This is curious when one considers how Riel's secretary, William Henry Jackson, was treated by the Crown. Jackson was not a Métis. He was born into an anglophone Methodist family in Toronto on May 13, 1861. Several years later, the family moved to Wingham, Ontario, 150 miles northwest of Toronto where his father opened a general store. After completing high school, he attended the University of Toronto where he studied classics for three years. Unfortunately, his father went bankrupt before he was able to finish his degree and the family decided to move to Prince Albert, Saskatchewan. There his father started a farm implement business. Soon after, Jackson was elected as the secretary of the Settlers' Union, which had been organized by a group of farmers and townspeople to fight for the Prince Albert District's rights. At meetings held throughout the district, Jackson attacked the federal government's harsh land regulations and its misadministration of the North-West Territories. He also called for a union with the Métis at Batoche, who were already concerned about their land claims.

Jackson met Riel, soon began to admire him, and became sympathetic to the Métis cause. He became Riel's secretary and supported him to the end. He wrote at the time that "the oppression of the aboriginals has been the crying sin of the white race in America and they have at last found a voice." On May 12, 1885, he was arrested for his involvement in the rebellion and sent for trial in Regina.

Jackson's trial took place before Judge Richardson just four days before Riel's trial was scheduled to begin. He was charged with treason felony, not high treason, as was Riel. When he was arraigned, the charges read to him and asked how he pleaded, his defence counsel J.B. McArthur, Q.C., answered, "not guilty on the ground of insanity." Instead of proceeding with the prosecution, B.B. Osler, the same person who was to lead the prosecution against Riel four days later, advised the court that

> evidence that has come to the knowledge of counsel for the Crown during the course of preparation for other trials is conclusive that at the time he committed the acts he was not responsible for them.

Dr. Augustus Jukes, senior surgeon for the North-West Mounted Police, who was later to give evidence for the Crown against Riel, was then called by the defence to give evidence on behalf of Jackson. It was his opinion that Jackson was unquestionably of unsound mind and had become much worse as preparations for his trial progressed. As far as he was concerned, Jackson was "labouring under a mild form of insanity" and "would be incapable of conducting his trial or doing justice to himself in any manner," because "he holds peculiar ideas on religious matters in connection with this trouble, and in connection with the new religion of which he thinks Riel is the founder."

Jukes was satisfied that if Jackson had committed any acts of treason while in his present mental condition, he was probably insane. Based on Jukes's testimony, Osler felt satisfied that the jury should return a verdict of not guilty by reason of insanity and, on behalf of the Crown, recommended to Richardson that they be so instructed. Richardson did and the jury promptly found Jackson not guilty by reason of insanity.

Richardson then ordered Jackson to be in strict custody until the pleasure of the lieutenant governor was known, which meant "until he was considered no longer insane." Jackson, who was sporting a full beard and a Métis headband, was committed to the lunatic asylum at Lower Fort Garry, north of Winnipeg, to await the lieutenant governor's pleasure. However, he did not remain there very long. On November 2, that same year, he escaped and walked to the American border. When Riel was executed two weeks later on November 16, he decided to renounce his race. Reaching Chicago, he identified himself as a Métis and changed his name to the French-sounding Honoré Jaxon. In Chicago, he became a union organizer for the carpenters' fight for an eight-hour day. Until his death in New York on December 12, 1951, his lifelong mission was the establishment of a library for the Indigenous Peoples of Saskatchewan.

Although Riel held the same peculiar ideas on religious matters as did Jackson, the Crown did not feel that he should also be found not guilty by reason of insanity and kept in strict custody awaiting the lieutenant governor's pleasure. Prime Minister Macdonald had plans for the northwest and Riel was in the way, though Jackson was not. Osler was instructed to prosecute Riel even though his mental fitness was in doubt.

* * *

A delusion is frequently defined as a false belief having no foundation in fact, and which will not yield to reason or argument. The difficulty with this definition is that it is not very different from a stubborn or unreasonable mistaken belief in some fact. The role of the medical expert is to determine how intense the delusion really is and how it dominates and controls the mental processes of the person suffering from it. Riel had such stubborn delusions. The task of his lawyers was to show that at the time of rebellion his beliefs had passed from being stubborn or unreasonable to delusional, impervious to reason or argument, and therefore he had been insane within the legal definition.

After the Crown had presented its case against Riel, it was the turn of the defence. His lawyers planned to call two medical men to give expert evidence on Riel's behalf. But before they did that, it was necessary to lay the groundwork by calling persons familiar with Riel who could testify as to statements made and conduct exhibited by him consistent with his alleged insanity. The three witnesses that the defence proposed to call were Father Alexis André, the superior of the Oblates in the District of Carlton, who had lived in Saskatchewan since 1865 and knew Riel intimately; the second was Phillippe Garnot, a former resident of Batoche, who had been involved in the rebellion; and the last was Father Vital Fourmond, an Oblate priest at Saint Laurent, who had arrived ten years earlier. After they gave evidence, two medical experts would be called: Dr. François Roy, who had treated Riel years before but had not seen him in many years; and Dr. Daniel Clark, who had only had a short interview with him before the trial.

Surely, the defence must have realized the danger in calling Father André. He had opposed Riel's attempts to encourage the Métis to civil disobedience and had wanted to get him out of the country at any cost. Riel had berated him for not showing enough enthusiasm and support for the Métis cause. More importantly, Charles Nolin had said that Riel had told Father André that he was prepared to abandon the Métis for the sum of $35,000. If Father

André were not called, it could be easily argued that Nolin was not credible because he had agreed to testify against Riel in exchange for immunity from prosecution. But if it were true that Riel was prepared to abandon the Métis for the sum of $35,000, and André confirmed it, Riel would be branded as a Judas to the Métis cause, and any sympathy the jury might have had for the way Riel had been treated by the federal government would quickly vanish. If the defence lawyers had interviewed Father André, as they should have and probably did, they would have discovered that Nolin's story was true. There had been a great deal of evidence by witnesses for the Crown of Riel's peculiar religious views. The evidence of Phillippe Garnot and Father Fourmond would have been icing on the cake. Riel's lawyers probably thought that if they limited their questions to Riel's irrational conduct and peculiar religious views, the lawyers for the Crown would restrict their cross-examination to those issues and not get into whether Nolin had told the truth. If they honestly believed that, they would be soon disappointed.

When examined by chief defence counsel François Lemieux, Father André testified that he was aware of the unrest of the English and French Métis who were having difficulty getting the federal government to settle their claims and to answer their petitions. He was also aware that they had gone to Montana to get Riel to help them. Before Riel arrived, the Métis had demanded patents for their land, frontage on the river, abolition of taxes on the woods, and the rights of those who did not have scrip in Manitoba.[3] Resolutions and petitions were sent to the government but only one evasive response was received. The silence of the government, he said, "produced great dissatisfaction in the minds of the people." The people had confidence in Riel and he had returned to Canada to try to help them get what they wanted from the government.

Lemieux then turned to the key issue that he wanted the jury to consider — Riel's unusual behaviour. Father André said that he did not like to speak of religion and politics with Riel. Although upon matters such as literature and science, Riel was in an ordinary state of mind,

> upon politics and religion *he was no longer the same man*. It would seem as if there were two men in him, he lost all control of himself upon these questions.

So far so good. Father André said that Riel had accomplished some good since his arrival. Although it did not justify rebellion, many of the claims of the Métis had been settled after the rebellion. Whether his beliefs were so delusional that they would not yield to reason or argument would depend upon the experts. However, other witnesses had also testified about Riel's peculiar ideas of dividing up the North-West Territories among various races and religions and how he was going to replace the pope with a new one. Father André had not really added anything to what the other witnesses had said.

No sooner had Father André finished than the danger Riel's lawyers should have anticipated happened. Thomas Casgrain immediately went to the heart of the issue and asked him whether it was true that Riel had agreed to abandon the Métis if given money. If Father André confirmed this then the Crown could argue that Riel was an opportunist, ready to abandon the Métis for a bribe.

Q. I believe in the month of December '84, you had an interview with Riel and Nolin with regard to a certain sum of money which the prisoner claimed from the Federal Government?

A. Not with Nolin. *Nolin was not present at the interview.*

This meant that Nolin's evidence on this important issue had been hearsay. It should never have been admitted in the first place. But the jury had heard it.

Q. The prisoner was there?

A. Yes.

Q. Will you please state what the prisoner asked of the Federal Government?

A. I had two interviews with the prisoner on that subject.

Q. The prisoner claimed a certain indemnity from the Federal Government, didn't he?

A. When the prisoner made his claim I was there with another gentleman, and he asked from the Government $100,000. We thought this was exorbitant, and the prisoner said: "Wait a little, I will take at once $35,000 cash."

Q. And on that condition the prisoner was to leave the country if the Government gave him the $35,000?

A. Yes, that was the condition he put.

Q. When was this?

A. This was on the 23rd December '84.

[...]

Q. Is it not true that the prisoner told you that he himself was the half-breed question?

A. He did not say so in express terms, *but he conveyed that idea*. He said, if I am satisfied, the half-breeds will be. I must explain this — this objection was made to him, that even if the Government granted him $35,000, the half-breed question would remain the same, and he said, in answer to that, *if I am satisfied the half-breeds will be*.

Q. Is it not a fact he told you he would even accept a less sum than the $35,000?

A. Yes. He said, "use all the influence you can, you may not get all that but get all you can, and if you get less, we will see."

Father André's evidence had sealed Riel's fate. It was no longer possible for Riel's lawyers to argue that Nolin was not a credible witness or that Riel was acting selflessly in the interests of the Métis. It had now been firmly established that Riel was prepared to abandon the Métis cause as early as December 23, 1884, if the government would pay him some money. How could his lawyers argue that he was delusional and legally insane if he was rational enough to make a deal to abandon the Métis for money. This point would be hammered over and over again by Crown counsel in their address to the jury and by the judge in his charge, and later by the Manitoba Court of Appeal.

The defence decided to call two more witnesses to testify as to Riel's peculiarities. Phillippe Garnot said that Riel had slept at his home on occasion. Riel said he wanted to change the pope, that the spirit of Elias was in him, and he wanted the people to acknowledge him as a prophet. During the nights that he spent with him, Riel prayed loud all night, prayers that Garnot had never heard before. He also spoke of Riel's desire to divide up the territory into seven separate provinces for seven different nationalities. Riel had no doubt that he would succeed, as he had a divine mission from God. He thought that Riel was crazy because "he acted very foolish." But, under cross-examination, Garnot also damaged Riel's defence. He said that he followed Riel against his will and, because Riel had an armed force, "I had to go." He thought that Riel had lots of influence among the "half-breeds," who relied upon his judgment and advice.

Father Vital Fourmond, the last witness called before the medical experts, was also asked whether Riel was sane about religious and political matters.

> Before the rebellion it appeared as if there were two men in the prisoner. In private conversation he was affable, polite, pleasant and a charitable man to me. I noticed that even when he was quietly talked to about the affairs of politics and government and he was not contradicted, he was quite rational; but as soon as he was contradicted on these subjects, then he became a different man and he would be carried away with his feelings. He would go so far as to use violent expressions to those who were even his friends. As soon as the rebellion commenced, then he became excited and he was carried away and he lost all control of himself and of his temper.... he often threatened to destroy all the churches. He says: There is danger for you, but thanks for the friendship I have for you I will protect you from any harm.... He has extraordinary ideas on the subject of the Trinity. The only God was God the Father, and that God the Son was not God; the Holy Ghost was not God either; the second person of the Trinity was not God, and as a consequence of this the Virgin Mary was not the mother of God but the mother of the Son of

God. That is the reason why he changed the formula of the prayer which is commonly known as "Hail Mary." Instead of saying "Hail Mary, mother of God," he said "Hail Mary, mother of the Son of God." He did not admit the doctrines of the Church of the divine presence; according to his idea it was not God who was present in the host, but an ordinary man six feet high. As to his political ideas, he wanted first to go to Winnipeg and Lower Canada and the United States and even to France. He said we will take your country even, and then he was to go to Italy and overthrow the Pope, and then he would choose another Pope of his own making.

Fourmond said that as the agitation was progressing, he noticed that Riel was a great deal more excitable. At the time of the rebellion, he formed the opinion that Riel was insane.

Once he was asked by the people to explain his views on religion, on religious matters, so they could see through them. When he found out the clergy were against him, that he was contradicted, he turned against the clergy, particularly against me, and opposed the clergy, and kept following me into the tents wherever I would go. He compelled me to leave the place, go down to the river and cross to the other side. There were several women there who came to shake hands with me. The prisoner had a very extraordinary expression upon his face, he was excited by the opinion he gave upon religion. The prisoner spoke to the women and said: "Woe unto you if you go to the priests, because you will be killed by the priests." All of a sudden, when I came to the boat, which was not very easy to get into, the prisoner, with great politeness, came up and said: "Look out father, I will help you to get on the boat."

Casgrain attempted to show that his opinion of Riel's insanity was coloured because "you had a great deal of friendship for him."

Fourmond answered him gracefully, "Yes, *as I would have for you.*"

The first medical expert for Riel was Dr. François Roy, who was the medical superintendent and one of the proprietors of "the lunatic asylum at Beauport" in Quebec. He was eminently suited to give evidence of Riel's insanity. He had been a psychiatrist for over fifteen years and it had been his duty, in his words, "to go to the principal asylums in the United States and see how the patients were treated there." He had also been the superintendent of Beauport in 1875 and 1876 when Riel was a patient there for about nineteen months. During that period, he had seen Riel often and had reached an opinion as to Riel's mental condition.

Questioned by Fitzpatrick, Dr. Roy told the court that Riel was suffering from the condition known as "megalomania":

> They sometimes give you reasons which would be reasonable if they were not starting from a false idea. They are very clever on those discussions, and they have a tendency to irritability when you question or doubt their mental condition, because they are under a strong impression that they are right and they consider it to be an insult when you try to bring them to reason again. On ordinary questions they may be reasonable and sometimes may be very clever, in fact without careful watching they would lead one to think that they were well.

One of the problems facing the defence was that, except for Riel's peculiar views on religion and his belief in his prophecies, Riel acted like a normal person and generally gave the impression that he was of sound mind. If the jury were expected to find that Riel was insane, Dr.

Roy would have to explain in layman's terms why an insane person could appear normal to people around him.

Q. Did you hear the witnesses describe the actions of the prisoner as to his peculiar views on religion, in reference to his power, to his hoping to succeed the Pope, and as to his prophecies, yesterday and today?

A. Yes

Q. From what you heard from those witnesses and from the symptoms they prove to have been exhibited by the prisoner, are you now in a position to say whether or not at the time he was a man of sound mind?

A. I am perfectly certain that when the prisoner was under [our] care, he was not of sound mind, *but he became cured before he left, more or less.* But from what I heard here today I am ready to say that I believe on these occasions his mind was unsound, and that he was laboring under the disease so well described by Dagoust.

Being of unsound mind was not sufficient to establish that Riel was insane within the meaning of the M'Naghten rules. The defence had to prove that Riel was insane in a legal sense — "that he did not know the nature and quality of his actions, or if he did know, he did not know he was doing what was wrong." Fitzpatrick would have to get Dr. Roy to say that Riel's insanity existed at the time that the offence was committed, not when he was confined in Beauport in 1875 and 1876, eight or nine years earlier.

Unfortunately, in describing Riel as he remembered him at Beauport, Dr. Roy had said that Riel had been cured "before he left, more or less," obviously attempting to justify why he had released Riel in 1876. His opinion was compromised by the fact that he had not had the opportunity to examine Riel now, before he testified at his trial. The evidence he was now giving was based on "what I heard here to-day"; that is, on what others were saying about Riel at the trial. Such testimony was dangerous and could be easily destroyed under cross-examination.

Fitzpatrick now had to press for an answer that would fit Riel within the M'Naghten rules. Riel was legally insane if he fell under either test. It was an either-or test. He put the first test to Dr. Roy:

Q. Do you believe that under the state of mind as described by the witnesses and to which you referred that he was capable or incapable of knowing the nature of the acts which he did?

A. No, I do not believe that he was in a condition to be the master of his acts, and I positively swear it, and I have people of the same character under my supervision.

Having received an answer to the first insanity test, Fitzpatrick decided to put the second test to Dr. Roy:

Q. That the man did not know what he was doing or whether it was contrary to law in reference to the particular delusion?

A. No, and for another reason, the same character of the disease is shown in the last period, the same as when he was with us, there is no difference. If there was any difference in the symptoms I would have doubts, but it was of the same character so well described by Dagoust, who is taken as an authority and has been adopted in France as well as in America and England.

Q. The opinion you have formed as to the soundness of his mind is based upon the fact that the symptoms disclosed by the witnesses here yesterday and to-day are to a large extent identical with the symptoms of his malady as disclosed while he was at your asylum?

A. Yes.

He had got the best answers he could expect from Dr. Roy. It was time to sit down.

In cross-examination, B.B. Osler's first attack was on the fact that Dr. Roy was one of two owners of a private for-profit asylum. If he could show that Roy ran an asylum for profit, then it might be suggested to the jury that a financial motive coloured his testimony, a well-known, frequently used tactic of cross-examiners against experts, who are often paid handsomely for their services.

Q. It is a private asylum under Government supervision?

A. It has the character of a private asylum as to the condition of the board of the patients, but it is a public institution in the sense of the word. We receive patients by order of the Government.

Q. But it is a private asylum as far as the financial basis is concerned?

A. No, because it is ruled by the Government.

Q. It is owned by the Government or by the proprietors?

A. By the proprietors.

Q. It is only subject to inspection by the Government?

A. To inspecting and visiting besides.

Q. Is the profit or loss of the establishment borne by the proprietors?

A. Yes, by the proprietors.

Q. What is the extent of your accommodation? How many patients?

A. *I do not know whether you have a right to ask these questions.*

Why Dr. Roy suddenly became defensive to what was a very simple question seems odd, unless he was anticipating an attack on his professional integrity. Osler, the consummate cross-examiner, was not to be deflected from his task. He ignored his response and asked the question again.

Q. How many patients have you got?

Osler repeated his question aggressively and got his answer. Dr. Roy knew that any further objection, or even hesitation, could cause the jury to believe that he had something to hide. Neither the judge nor Riel's lawyers had supported his objection to the question.

A. Sometimes the number increases and sometimes it diminishes, according to discharges. I think that there would be an average of from 800 to 900.

Q. Is it from the profit of keeping these patients that the proprietors make money?

A. And to pay expenses and the interest upon a large capital put in.

Q. You are paid by the Government and paid by private patients?

A. When we have them. [He had just said that there would be an average of from 800 to 900.]

Q. And the proprietors manage it as a place to cure, and where they board these thousand people?

A. We have a place to cure and take care of these poor people who cannot take care of themselves.

After a few more questions about the operation of Beauport, Osler asked about Riel.

Q. Will you tell me whether you ever prescribed or looked personally after the prisoner?

A. I did.

Q. Under what name was the prisoner in the asylum?

A. Under the name of La Rochelle.

Q. Under what name does he appear in your books?

A. That is it.

Q. Did you know his right name?

A. No, I was not present when he entered the first day.

Did Riel enter Beauport under the name La Rochelle because he wanted anonymity or was it a symptom of his illness? Osler did not pursue the question. What he did, however, was criticize Dr. Roy for failing to bring his records with him. Dr. Roy had only brought along a few notes that he had made of his actual records. Based on his own estimate of an average eight hundred to nine hundred patients, Dr. Roy must have seen thousands of patients between 1877 when Riel was a patient at Beauport and July 1885. How could he recall details of Riel's insanity almost eight years earlier without the actual records?

Q. You have no book or copy of the book here?

A. No.

Q. You have brought us nothing?

A. Except what I am able to tell you from memory.

Q. You knew a long time before that you were going to be examined as a witness in this case, you had been spoken to about it shortly after the capture of the prisoner?

A. No, I was asked by telegraph.

Q. You were seen by the friends of the prisoner shortly after he was arrested?

A. No.

Q. When were you spoken to about giving evidence at the trial?

A. Some days before the trial came on.

Q. Did it not strike you that it would be important to have a written history of the case, the cause of his commitment; did it not strike you that that would be a matter of importance in considering a case of this kind?

A. No, I thought they would ask me my opinion of the case.

Q. That is what you thought would be satisfactory?

A. I never thought of coming at all, at first.

[…]

Q. How many patients had you under your immediate treatment in the year '77?

A. I am not able to tell you.

Q. One hundred cases?

A. No, we have not 100 cases of acute mania under our hands, fortunately.

Q. How many did you have under your personal treatment?

A. The cases of which I made a special study are acute mania.

Q. How many of such cases would you have in a year.

A. Not many, fortunately.

Q. How many in a year?

A. Twenty-five or thirty would be about the average of acute cases.

Q. We will speak of '77; can you give me the names of those men whom you treated in '77?

A. I will give you some of the names. I cannot tell you all. If you mention the names, I would know about them.

Q. The treatment of those persons is gone from your mind?

A. More or less.

Q. *You see the value of written testimony here?*

Osler had established that Dr. Roy was relying entirely on his memory of Riel, whom he had treated eight years earlier. He had not examined or spoken to Riel since. Memory is notoriously unreliable. Osler had nailed down the first weakness in Roy's expert testimony and it was now time to test the weakness in his opinion of Riel's insanity.

Q. You say the main feature of this disease is what? What is the leading feature of this disease do you say? Do you say that it is a fixed idea incapable of change?

A. That one thing I may say.

Q. Will you answer the question? Do you say that the leading feature of the disease is a fixed idea incapable of change by reasoning?

A. I did not succeed in changing —

Q. I ask you is that the leading feature of the disease?

A. It is one of them, it is one of the characteristic features.

Q. Is it the leading feature?

A. *It is one of them — it is one of the characteristic features.*

Q. A fixed idea with a special ambition, incapable of change by reasoning?

A. Yes, we did not succeed in changing the idea of the patient.

Q. Well, that fixed idea is beyond his control?

A. I would not be prepared to say entirely.

Q. If it is beyond his control, he is an insane man?

A. Yes.

Q. If within his control, it is an indication of sanity?

A. That he was trying to get better, he may have had intermissions in which he understood his condition.

Osler was attempting to pin down Dr. Roy to an all-or-nothing definition of Riel's condition. Either Riel believed that he had a divine mission to lead the West and the Métis people out of Canada and to form a new country, and that belief could not be changed by reason, in which case he was insane within Roy's definition; or he did not, in which case he was sane. Osler's purpose was to demonstrate that the premise upon which Roy based his opinion was faulty and not borne out by the true facts. He would in time suggest to Roy that Riel's "insane" belief could easily be diverted by the payment of money, but Roy would not be drawn in. Riel's insanity was not an all-or-nothing proposition. There could be, as he said, "intermissions when he can control himself because then the insanity disappears." As Osler continued to prod Dr. Roy, trying to pin him down to the answer he wanted, demanding that he "answer the question," Fitzpatrick finally rose to object.

> FITZPATRICK: This witness has been speaking in English for some time past. If the witness does not understand the questions properly he should answer the questions in French.
> OSLER: *If the man wants to hide himself under the French, he can do so.*
> OSLER TO ROY: You understand what I mean?
> ROY: *Parlez-moi en français.*
> OSLER: *It will be for the jury to say whether he is making the change at his own suggestion or at that of counsel on the other side.*

Osler's anti-French bias was not worthy of a lawyer of his stature. His attitude toward Roy was offensive and designed to inflame the members of the jury, none of whom were francophones, against Riel. An impartial judge would have immediately chastised him for his comments, but Richardson was not impartial and was obviously in awe of a famous lawyer like Osler.

Dr. Roy now chose to give his answers in French, which were more responsive to Osler's questions. Riel's illness, he said, was that he had a fixed idea, namely, that he was on a mission directed by God and that this fixed idea could not be changed by reason. If Osler could get Roy to concede that Riel could be dissuaded from his mission by reason, then his opinion would fall apart. Osler needed to ask Roy a few more questions to set him up to destroy that opinion.

Q. Having given a rule to test this insanity, what fact is there disclosed in the evidence which leads you to say that the prisoner comes within the rule?

A. That part of the evidence given by the clergy to-day shows in a positive manner that the prisoner has manifested symptoms that we meet in megalomania.

Q. That is not an answer to my question. I want the fact on which you bring the prisoner within the rule that you have laid down?

A. I want to take the fact proved by the evidence.

Q. Tell me the fact upon which you rely?

A. The prisoner gets his theory from the idea that he has a mission.

Q. Do you understand that to be a fixed idea not controllable by reason?

A. I believe so, because *reason has never so far succeeded in changing that idea that he has.*

Q. Is that the only reason you have for saying that the prisoner is insane?

A. It is, and I believe it to be sufficient.

Osler finally had the answer that he wanted from Dr. Roy. Now was the time to drive home to the jury that Riel had been prepared to abandon the cause of the Métis for the payment of $35,000.

Q. Is it consistent that a man laboring under an idea not controllable by reason, that he would abandon that idea for $35,000?

Throughout the cross-examination, Riel's lawyers must have sat uncomfortably as Osler slowly and methodically led Dr. Roy into his trap. As Osler sprung the trap on the unsuspecting Roy, they realized that Roy needed time to formulate a response to the question that he had been asked. Time to allow Roy to think could be obtained if the tempo of cross-examination could be interrupted, and Fitzpatrick was quickly on his feet, arguing, "I object to that. That has not been proved."

But it had been proved — by the defence, in fact, when Riel's lawyers had called Father André to testify for Riel.

Judge Richardson was obviously not paying attention, because he wanted to know, "What is the question?" Osler repeated the question and even agreed to let it be a hypothetical question. Fitzpatrick again objected and Richardson ruled that Osler could put a hypothetical question, although this was not really one. Osler became angry with Fitzpatrick's objection and accused him of deliberately interfering with his cross-examination to give Roy "a cue."

Fitzpatrick denied it. "I did not have any such intention. We have the right to object, and we intend to exercise that right."

Osler would not back down. "You should not exercise it in such a way as to give the witness a cue. That is the second cue you have given the witness. You have given him a cue in regard to speaking in French."

It was the duty of Richardson to stop the two lawyers attacking each other in front of the jury, especially with Osler's disparaging remarks about Dr. Roy's use of French. But Richardson had abdicated control of the courtroom to the Crown's lawyers from the beginning of the trial. Osler repeated his earlier question, and insisted that it be answered. Roy was prepared to concede only that it was "possible that the prisoner might want to obtain the money to obtain the object he has in view."

What followed was a series of devastating questions put to Dr. Roy, which he tried to answer, with Osler repeatedly insulting him with suggestions that he was not answering the question or that he "did not have the capacity to understand it."

Q. Do you agree with this proposition: "An insane delusion is never the result of reasoning and reflection"?

A. I don't understand what you want to get at.

Q. I want you to give an answer. Do you agree with that proposition, that "An insane delusion is never the result of reasoning and reflection"?

A. I believe that he makes false reasoning from a false principle.

Q. Is delusion produced by reasoning and deduction?

A. It has been by hallucination and —

Q. That is not an answer to my question. I want to know whether a delusion — an insane delusion — may be the result of reasoning and deduction, or is it always the production of the disease?

A. Sometimes, not always. Sometimes by false inspiration.

Q. Sometimes by sane inspiration?

A. Yes.

Q. You won't answer my question? [He had, but he had not given the answer Osler wanted.]

A. I have done my best.

Q. *Have you not the capacity to understand it?*

A. That may be your opinion.

Q. Take an insane delusion in a man's head, can it be brought about by reasoning and deduction, or is it the outcome of the disease?

A. It is the consequence of his disease.

Q. And, therefore it has nothing to do with reason and deduction?

A. I believe that when the patient is under the influence of hallucination he is quite beyond control.

Q. You say it is the first principle of irresponsibility, whether it is the result of disease or whether it is the result of reason (distorted reason if you will), it is only by disease that the insane delusion is produced?

A. Yes, by the disturbance of the brain which there is in every case.

Q. And it is by reason of its being a product of the disease that it is not controllable?

A. It is a consequence of it.

Q. Why do you say this prisoner during this time had no knowledge of right from wrong?

A. I say that the prisoner was under the influence of his delusion that he had a special mission to fulfill.

Q. From what facts in evidence do you say that the prisoner could not distinguish between right and wrong?

A. They never could prove to him that that mission never existed.

Q. I want you to state the facts that the witnesses spoke of from which you came to your conclusion?

A. The facts are that he believed that he had a mission to fulfill in the North-West.

Osler decided it was time to level the suggestion that Riel's insanity was also consistent with fraud on his part.

Q. Do you say that any man claiming to be inspired is insane so as not to distinguish between right and wrong?

A. It is possible.

[...]

Q. *Might it not be evidence of fraud on the part of the man making it?*

A. Not when the same idea has been sustained, at different times, without reason.

Q. When the idea is sustained from time to time, it is only sustained with insanity, is that the answer?

A. Yes, particularly with that kind of delirium.

[...]

Q. Does not the whole evidence sustain the theory that it was a skilful fraud?

A. I don't think so. I saw the prisoner at my place. He always retained the impression that he had a mission when he could have none and had nothing to gain by it.

Q. I am asking the general question whether the evidence, upon which you have formed your opinion, is not consistent with a skilful fraud?

A. It might be possible, there might be such an understanding, but it is not my opinion.

Q. It may be that it is consistent with a skilful fraud?

A. There is no evidence in this case that can prove there was fraud.

Q. Do you say that the evidence is inconsistent with a skilful fraud?

A. When I had the prisoner under my care —

Q. I am asking about the fact in evidence upon which you found your opinion?

A. In the mental condition of the prisoner, I think he is not —

Q. That is not an answer at all. Can you give me an answer?

A. Put another question in another way.

Unable to get Dr. Roy to say what he wanted him to say, Osler resorted to sarcasm. That he would simply dismiss Dr. Roy, the most important witness for the defence, and probably the only one who had any real insight into Riel's mental capacity, was unpardonable for an officer of the Crown, and especially so since there was no impartial judge to stop him. Osler delivered his final sarcastic blow:

> If you cannot answer it in English or in French, I may as well let you go. You can go.

The defence decided not to re-examine Dr. Roy to clarify any confusion that may have been caused by Osler's cross-examination, and called their next medical expert, Dr. Daniel Clark.

Prior to Dr. Clark giving his evidence, one must assume that Riel's lawyers interviewed him to find out whether he would be able to give a medical opinion that Riel fell within one or both of the M'Naghten tests of insanity and were satisfied that he could. Experienced and competent counsel do not call a witness, especially an expert, to give an opinion unless he or she can be of assistance to them. It was not enough for Dr. Clark to say that Riel was *medically* insane. What he had to be able to say was that Riel was *legally* insane — that he did not *know* at the time of the rebellion the nature or quality of his actions or, if he did, did not *know* that they were wrong.

Dr. Clark was also eminently suited to give evidence about Riel's mental condition at the time of the rebellion and at trial. He was the superintendent of the Toronto Asylum for the Insane and had been treating the insane for ten years. He had also been called to testify in court as an expert on lunacy, as he said, "very often." If he did, then he must have known the difference between medical insanity and legal insanity as defined by the M'Naghten case. Although he had only recently arrived in Regina, he had since examined Riel three times. He also had been in court and had listened to the evidence of all the witnesses.

Fitzpatrick began by asking whether, based on his examination of Riel and the testimony of the other witnesses, Dr. Clark was able to form an opinion as to the soundness or unsoundness of Riel's mind.

A. Well, assuming the fact that the witnesses told the truth, I have to assume that — assuming also that the prisoner at the bar is not a malingerer — that is English, I believe — then of course there is no other conclusion that any reasonable man could come to, from my standpoint, of course, than that man who held these views and did these things must certainly be of insane mind.

What did he mean by "must certainly be of insane mind"? Did he mean medical insanity or legal insanity? To bring Riel within the M'Naghten test, Fitzpatrick had to put to Dr. Clark the first test and ask whether Riel was capable of knowing the nature and quality of his actions. Dr. Clark's response must have caused Riel's lawyers to wonder whether they should have called him at all. He continued with his opinion:

A. Why, the insane understand, many of them, the nature of the acts which they do, except in dementia cases, and melancholia, and cases of mania even; they often know what they do, and can tell me what they did, tell all about it afterwards. It is all nonsense to talk about a man not knowing what he is doing, simply because he is insane.

What he was saying was that except for certain "cases of mania," the insane know the nature of the acts they are doing. If Fitzpatrick was concerned about his answer, he made no attempt to clarify it. However, he may have been concerned because he immediately put the second test to Clark.

Q. Do you think that man was, in the circumstances detailed by different witnesses, in a position to be able to say or be able to judge of what he was doing as either wrong or contrary to law?
A. Well, that is one of the legal metaphysical distinctions in regard to right and wrong, and it is a dangerous one, simply because it covers only part of the truth. I could convince any lawyer if they will come to Toronto Asylum, in half an hour, that dozens

in that institution know right and wrong, both in abstract and in concrete, and yet are undoubtedly insane; the distinction of right and wrong covers part of the truth; it covers the largest part of the truth, but the large minority of insane do know right from wrong. It is one of those metaphysical subtilties [*sic*] that practical men in asylums know to be false.

The last thing that the defence needed to persuade this Western jury of six anglophones that Riel was legally insane was an academic discussion about the legal metaphysical distinction in regard to right or wrong. A simple answer was all he wanted, preferably one in favour of Riel, but Clark was one of those experts who find it difficult to speak in ordinary language to ordinary people. Having given evidence as an expert before, he must have known that an answer in accordance with the M'Naghten test was what was expected of him. If he was not prepared to testify that Riel was legally insane, why had he not told Riel's lawyers? Had Riel's lawyers really interviewed him before calling him or had they simply assumed that he would give the opinion they expected?

Fitzpatrick decided to put the second test to him again and ask whether Riel knew right from wrong. Surely, Clark would give them the answer they wanted this time. His answer must have shaken the defence.

Q. Do you consider from the knowledge which you have of this individual that at the time of the events detailed by the witnesses here took place, that is to say, in March, April and May last, that he was labouring under such a defect of reason from disease of the mind, that he did not know that what he was doing was wrong?

A. *I think he did know; I think he was quite capable of distinguishing right from wrong.*

Fitzpatrick realized that he had to approach it another way if he expected to get the answer he wanted.

Q. Was he in a position to be able to say at that time, and to act at that time as an ordinary sane man would have done?

A. Assuming the evidence given by the witnesses, he did not act as a sane man would have done, for this reason, that no sane man would have imagined that he could come into the Saskatchewan, and that he could gather around him such a force as would enable him to become monarch of this country, that it could be divided up into seven divisions, giving each to a different nationality. He was not an ignorant man. He was not like an Indian who never read a newspaper, and knew nothing of the country around him. He had travelled, he had been in Ottawa, he had been in the United States, and he knew all about the power of Britain and the Dominion, and for him to imagine that he could come here and raise a few half-breeds in the Saskatchewan and keep up a successful warfare, and divide the country into seven divisions and with different nationalities, was certainly not a thing that a man with an ordinary understanding would ever think he could succeed in.

What Clark was saying was that any intelligent person who commits an irrational act should be considered insane; a view that might appeal to psychiatrists, but not to ordinary persons on the street, like a Regina jury. Surely, Clark knew this. He was not speaking to a room of psychiatrists. He was speaking to a jury of laymen in a court of law. B.B. Osler was to ridicule this answer in his cross-examination.

Clark ended his testimony trying to assure the court that he was trying to be as impartial as he could.

A. I might say, if the court will allow me, that when I come to cases of this kind, I am not subpoenaed for one side more than another. I am here only subpoenaed to give a sort of medical judicial opinion, and, therefore, I stand in that capacity.

What did he mean, that he was "not subpoenaed for one side or another," and that he was "only subpoenaed to give a sort of medical judicial opinion"? Surely, Riel's lawyers did not subpoena him to give an independent "medical judicial opinion." They had subpoenaed him to give evidence that Riel was legally insane. The Crown had enough medical evidence that Riel was legally sane and didn't need Clark's assistance. If he could not give evidence on Riel's behalf, he should have told Riel's lawyers so. Why did he hold back this opinion? He said he had been subpoenaed — but a subpoena from the North-West Territories could not compel a witness from another province to come to court. Was he anxious to get involved in the most important treason case in the country and to make a name for himself? Had Riel's lawyers even interviewed him before they called him to the witness box? If they had, and he had not told them what he was going to say, then his conduct was unpardonable. If he had been interviewed and had told them what he would say, then calling him was an act of incompetence by Riel's lawyers. If they had not interviewed him before he gave evidence, that also would be an act of incompetence. Clark's evidence had put the last nail into Riel's coffin.

Osler rose to begin his devastating cross-examination.

Q. Then, doctor, he would know the nature and quality of the act that he was committing?

A. He would know the nature and quality of the act that he was committing, subject to his delusions, assuming them to be such.

Q. He would know the nature and quality of the act he was committing and *he would know if it was wrong*?

A. If it was wrong, based upon his delusion; yes.

Q. And all the facts are quite compatible with a skilful shamming by malingering?

A. Yes, I think so. I think that no one — at least I say for myself, of course — that in a cursory examination of a man of this kind who has a good deal of cunning, who is educated, that it is impossible for any man to state on three examinations whether he is a deceiver or not. I require to have that man under my supervision for months, to watch him day by day, before I could say whether he is a sham or not.

Osler had now established that, in Dr. Clark's opinion, Riel was not legally insane within either test under the M'Naghten rule, although

Clark regarded him as medically insane. After a few more questions, Osler then put to Clark that Riel's conduct was "consistent with fraud."

A. Consistent with fraud? Yes, anything is consistent with fraud that is not discovered.
Q. You cannot say that it is not fraud?
A. No, I cannot.
Q. And there is nothing here to show you in the state of his intellect that he was not able to distinguish between right and wrong, and know the quality of the act which he was committing?
A. No, I say that I think that he knows what right is from wrong, subject to his delusions; but mind you, I want to add to that, *that many of the insane know right from wrong.*

Osler did not stop there but attempted to get Clark to admit that there were doctors who believed that all who suffered from a mental disease should be acquitted of crime. Clark disagreed and said that not all doctors felt that way.

Q. It is so that a large number then, I should say, of insane persons, ought to be responsible to the law?
A. There are some that are.

* * *

There was the danger that if Clark were re-examined, he might add to the damaging answers he had already given to Osler's questions. Fitzpatrick decided to risk it anyway since the damage was already done. Clark might say something that could be used in his address to the jury. He decided to go over again Riel's knowledge of right from wrong. A "no" answer was critical. Maybe Clark might change his answer from "yes" to "no" if pressed, although it was unlikely. A "no" answer would be the last evidence the jury would hear from the defence and be helpful.

Q. You say that he is quite capable of distinguishing right from wrong, subject to his delusions?

A. Subject to his particular delusion, yes.

It was not the answer Fitzpatrick had hoped to hear.

The Crown had hired two medical doctors to respond to the medical team of the defence.

The first was James Wallace, who had been the medical superintendent of the Asylum for the Insane at Hamilton, Ontario, for about the past nine years. The institution had about six hundred patients. Although Wallace had seen Riel for only half an hour in private and had been present during the trial, he had formed an opinion about Riel's sanity.

Q. What is your opinion?

A. I have not discovered any insanity about him, no indication of insanity.

Q. What would you say then in view of the evidence and your examination? Is he of sound mind or is he not?

A. I think he is of sound mind.

Q. And capable of distinguishing right from wrong?

A. I think so.

Q. And know the nature and quality of any act which he would commit?

A. Very acutely.

Osler, having finished his examination-in-chief, quickly sat down. All that Dr. Wallace had said was that in a short, one half hour examination of Riel, he had come to the conclusion that Riel was legally sane. A half hour was hardly enough to assess any patient's condition, and in cross-examination Fitzpatrick went quickly to the amount of time Wallace had spent in examining Riel.

Q. You have no doubt whatever in your mind, from the examination you have made of this man during half an hour and from the evidence which you heard here, that he is of perfectly sound mind?

A. Well, I should qualify, I should qualify my answer to that question. I have only had a limited examination of him, *and in any case of obscure mental disease, it sometimes take a very long time before one can make up their mind;* but from what I have seen of him, I say that I have discovered no symptoms of insanity.

Fitzpatrick drove home this devastating admission with the next question.

Q. So that what you say now, doctor, is purely and simply this, not that he is not insane, but that you have not been able to discover any symptoms of insanity?

A. That is what I say, I say *I have not discovered it.* It would be presumption for me to say that he is not insane, from the opportunities that I have had; *but my opinion is fairly fixed in my mind that he is not insane.*

Q. You are aware that a great many cases exist in which men are found to be perfectly insane without its being possible to discover any trace of insanity, are you not?

A. *Oh, sir, I have had patients in my asylum for weeks sometimes before I found any symptoms of insanity.*

[...]

Q. Therefore you are obliged to say that all you have discovered in this case, or all that you are now in a position to say is that you have not discovered any traces of insanity?

A. That is all my conscience will allow me to say.

Fitzpatrick had received an important admission from Dr. Wallace. All Wallace had said was that after speaking to Riel for a half-hour, he discovered no symptoms of insanity. An experienced cross-examiner would have sat down. He had made his point. He could argue to the jury that Dr. Roy, who knew Riel intimately because of their long-time association when he was a patient of his institution, was in a better position to assess his sanity. Instead, Fitzpatrick made the fatal mistake many inexperienced cross-examiners make when they try to cross swords with an expert in a field they know little about. Fitzpatrick was a lawyer, not a psychiatrist. He decided to delve into the nature of Riel's illness. In particular, he framed his question in a way that allowed Wallace's response to destroy Riel's defence of legal insanity.

Q. You have heard of that particular form of metal disease known as megalomania probably?

A. Yes.

Q. Would you tell me what are the symptoms which are the characteristics of this disease?

A. That is a simple complication. That is a term which is scarcely ever used, and I think it is only used by one writer.

When he tried to get Wallace to agree that megalomania was a disease of the mind, that Riel was suffering from megalomania, and believed he was destined to fulfill his great mission of leading his people to build a new country of diverse cultures, Wallace disagreed. As far as Wallace was concerned, megalomania was not a mental disease but merely a symptom of a mental disease such as paralytic insanity, or gentle paralysis, or other manias. A person with this symptom had no desire to fulfill his destiny, such as to become a king or a great leader or a wealthy person. *He actually believed he already was a king or a great leader or a wealthy person and was living it in his mind.*

But wasn't this exactly the problem with Riel? Riel believed he was a great prophet leading his people to their destiny. He may not have fulfilled his destiny but *was certainly living it in his mind.* Fitzpatrick seemed to have difficulty framing his questions in such a way as to force Wallace to agree that, if Riel believed he was the great prophet that he thought he was, and even if megalomania was only a symptom of a mental disease and not a disease in itself, then his delusions were the symptom of mental disease, rendering him insane. Wallace was intimately familiar with psychiatric terms and definitions; Fitzpatrick was not.

A common method of testing the validity of an expert's evidence is to refer the witness to a book written by an acknowledged and renowned expert on the subject, particularly one under whom the witness has studied, who has expressed an opinion contrary to what the witness has said in the witness box. Fitzpatrick attempted to do this by referring Dr. Wallace to medical textbooks by French doctors Dagoust and Ducelle, who said that megalomania indicated insanity. However, Wallace responded that he had never read Dagoust's book or heard of a book written by Legrand Ducelle on the subject of megalomania, nor of one by any other French author. Fitzpatrick's cross-examination fell flat. "I don't want to hear of any French authors. I never read them," declared Wallace. Such comments would have endeared him to the anglophone Protestant jury.

Dr. Augustus Jukes was called next to comment on Riel's sanity. He was a police surgeon, not a psychiatrist. He had never treated anyone suffering from mental problems in his practice. As he admitted during his testimony, he had never specifically studied the subject of insanity. This admission alone should have disqualified him from giving expert opinion whether Riel was capable of knowing the nature and quality of his actions or of knowing whether they were wrong. Yet he was allowed to do so. The defence made no objection to his evidence and Judge Richardson, as usual, said nothing.

Although he had had no hesitation in declaring Riel's secretary, William Henry Jackson, insane because he held "peculiar ideas on religious matters," Jukes suddenly lost the impartiality he had shown when he gave evidence for Jackson. Jukes testified that he had seen and spoken with Riel almost every day but could find no evidence of insanity.

Q. Have you formed an opinion as to his mental state? I am speaking now of his insanity; sanity or insanity?
A. I have never seen anything during my intercourse with Mr. Riel to leave an impression upon my mind that he was insane.

However, he also admitted that he had never led the conversation in any way to elicit any possible insane delusions. "I have never made any effort to do so, *because my duty was otherwise.*"

An astonishing admission by a doctor who was prepared to swear that he found no evidence of insanity, especially when he also said that he had heard it rumoured "that he had been formerly insane and that he had been confined."

In cross-examination, instead of pressing Jukes about why he made no effort to elicit any possible insane delusions, Fitzpatrick decided to pursue another tack.

Q. You said, Doctor, that you had not made any endeavour to ascertain, during the intercourse you had with Riel, whether or not he suffered from any particular mental disease? Did you notice any form of insanity, or any mental disease, unsoundness of mind?

A. I never specially examined him as a lunatic. I never made a special examination of him as a lunatic.

Q. You never made any special endeavor to discover whether or not he was suffering from any particular form of mental disease?

A. Never any special endeavor, anything beyond ordinary conversation of the day.

Jukes was prepared to admit that there were "forms of insanity which were not discoverable except after considerable endeavours have been made to discover them." When asked by Fitzpatrick if he agreed to that, he said,

A. Yes; it is so, unquestionably, that you may converse with the man continually and not be aware of his insanity until you touch accidentally, or some other person touches accidentally upon the point upon which he insane.

Q. Had you been informed at any time of the particular mental disease from which Riel was supposed to have been suffering?

A. I don't think I ever knew as much of it as I have learned here.

Either Jukes was not telling the truth, or he had been misled by his superiors about Riel's beliefs. Riel's unusual beliefs were well known to almost everyone in the North-West Territories. His examination of Jackson had revealed Riel's beliefs. What is clear is that Dr. Jukes had no desire to see Riel go free, or at least that he wanted Riel to be confined to an institution for the rest of his life. His evasive answers to the questions that followed clearly demonstrated his bias.

Q. So you had never made any endeavor to …?
A. I never did …

This answer was responsive to the question and Jukes should have left it there. But he continued his answer, trying to defend his impartiality as a representative of the Crown. He quickly found it necessary to justify his failure to question Riel about his beliefs.

A. … that is, I never spoke to him specially with regard to what he believed to be his mission, *knowing that many very sane men might be so, and yet a man might be perfectly sane.*

Jukes had betrayed his complete lack of impartiality. If he was not aware of Riel's beliefs, why speak of what Riel believed to be his mission? Neither Robinson nor Fitzpatrick had mentioned anything about a belief by Riel in a mission. There was no need to. Everyone in the North-West Territories knew that Riel believed that he had a mission. Again his bias against Riel was clearly revealed in the answers he gave to further questions by Fitzpatrick, who was attempting to get him to admit that a person who was acting under an insane delusion was not responsible for his actions. This had been the very basis for Jukes's opinion that William Henry Jackson was insane and not even fit to stand trial. But Jukes would concede nothing that might allow Riel to get off so easily.

Q. So that if a man is laboring under an insane delusion the acts which he does while under that insane delusion, *quoad* [with respect to] the particular delusion, he is not responsible for?

172

The question was one that could have been answered with a simple yes. Instead, Jukes obfuscated, ensuring that the suspicion of fraud was never removed from the mind of the jurors. Starting and stopping, he carefully chose his words to ensure that his answer was craftily framed.

A. If a man is clearly — if it can be proved that a man is acting under an insane delusion, then any act I should consider which he performed under the delusion, any act having special relation to his delusion, I should consider that he was not personally responsible for, if it could be shown clearly that the delusion was an insane one, *and that it was not rather a feigned one for a purpose.*

Fitzpatrick's attempts to get Jukes to concede that Riel would not be responsible for his actions if he were labouring under a delusion that he was divinely inspired from God were met with evasion after evasion by Jukes. His bias against Riel was again clear in this answer to Fitzpatrick:

> My opinion is ... in regard to Mr. Riel, if you will allow me to say it, as far as I have been able to judge from my own personal knowledge, that he is a man of great shrewdness and very great depth, and that he might choose, knowing the great influence which he exercised over these people who have a much inferior education to his own, that regarded him in the light of almost a saviour — I have thought that he might have assumed for the purpose of maintaining his influence with them, more than he really believed.

What he was saying was that he didn't believe Riel had false delusions. Riel only pretended to have them, in order to exercise influence over his Métis followers, who were inferior in education. However, with a bit of prompting from Fitzpatrick, Jukes went on to admit that he had no basis for this damaging conclusion.

Q. This is your impression, Doctor?

A. *I have thought that it might be so.* I don't think it is, for I have never heard him speak on that subject, and I gather that knowledge only from a general knowledge of what has taken place, and from personal knowledge which I acquired in speaking with Mr. Riel, *but never on that subject.*

[...]

Q. And you have never spoken to him on the particular subjects with reference to which he is supposed to have his delusions?

A. Name the subject.

Q. On religion, and the mission with reference to the North-West Territories?

A. I have never spoken to him on either.

Dr. Jukes's opinion of Riel's sanity was of no value and should never have been heard by the jury. If the Crown were putting Dr. Jukes forward as an expert on the question of Riel's mental condition, then there was a duty on Jukes to have raised in conversation matters of religion and Riel's mission so that he could provide a fair and unbiased opinion as an expert. If his evidence amounted to no more than "I have never spoken to him on a single subject about which he has spoken irrationally," Richardson should have instructed the jury that Dr. Jukes's evidence was of no value. Richardson not only failed to do so, he never even referred to the medical evidence, presented by both sides, in his charge to the jury.

The next morning, Friday, July 31, the Crown called three lay witnesses as to Riel's sanity, all of whose evidence was clearly inadmissible. No attempt was made to qualify them as experts. Richardson, as usual, did not intervene and Riel's lawyers never challenged their evidence, although it was critical to the defence of insanity.

Captain George Holmes Young was called again, to give his opinion about Riel's sanity, and was allowed to give evidence that was clearly inadmissible. Christopher Robinson asked him the conversations he had had with Riel.

Q. From the first to last of these conversations with you, did you observe anything to arouse suspicion or indicate that he was of unsound mind?

A. None at all, certainly not. I found that I had a mind against my own, and fully equal to it; better educated and much more clever than I was myself. He would stop and evade answering questions with the best possible advantage.

Q. The idea of mental aberration, unsoundness of mind, never occurred to you?

A. *I believe it was for a purpose, what had been given as a reason for insanity.* [A totally improper answer.]

Q. Did he profess to you to have the Spirit of God or the power of prophesy?

A. No, never to me.

Greenshields attempted to salvage the damage the defence had permitted by not objecting to his evidence.

Q. What experience have you had in dealing with people of unsound mind?

A. None at all.

Q. You are only speaking now from the conversations you had with the prisoner?

A. Merely from the nine days I lived with him.

Q. You never had a medical education in that respect?

A. No.

Q. You do not consider yourself in a position to give an opinion as to the sanity?

A. *I could not give a medical opinion, but I consider that during the nine days I was living with him, I would know if I was living with a lunatic.*

The damage had been done. Captain Young, who admitted that he was not qualified to give a medical opinion, had been allowed to give one. Fitzpatrick pressed Young about what Riel had told him about his goal — "to save the people of the North-West from annihilation" — but Young would concede nothing.

> Q. That was [to be] the practical result of his mission, as you gathered in conversation with him?
> A. *He evaded me, he could not come down to particulars.*

General Middleton was also called again and permitted to give opinion as to Riel's sanity, although he was not an expert on mental illness.

> Q. During all your intercourse with him, did you see anything whatever to indicate any suspicion of unsoundness of mind in him?
> A. No, I cannot say I did — on the contrary.

Although it was not improper to ask whether an accused said or did something that indicated the person was of unsound mind, Middleton was not content to answer the question directly. He had to add "on the contrary," meaning that he did see something that indicated that Riel was of sound mind, and so gave his opinion — which was clearly inadmissible.

> Q. Did it occur to you there was any reason to imagine the man was not perfectly sound in mind?
> A. No, I should say on the contrary he was a man of rather acute intellect. He seemed quite able to hold his own upon any argument or topic we happened to touch upon.
> Q. That question never occurred to you?
> A. Of course I had heard constantly before about reports of insanity. I heard for instance one or two of the people that had escaped from him, scouts, half-breeds. One man I remember told me "Oh Riel is mad, he is a fool, he told me what he is doing at Batoche." So that I really had heard it, *but I came to the conclusion he was very far from being mad or a fool.*

Greenshields had just heard an important admission from Middleton, but did not pursue it in cross-examination.

Q. Of course you never had seen Riel previous to his surrender on the 15th?
A. Never.

* * *

Captain Richard Deane of the North-West Mounted Police gave his testimony under examination by George Burbidge, the federal deputy minister of justice. Deane had been put in charge of Riel from May 23 until his trial, and said that he visited Riel frequently.

Q. From the observation you had of him have you seen anything to indicate that he is not of sound mind?
A. Nothing whatever.
Q. Anything to indicate the contrary?
A. Yes, I think so; he always gave me the impression of being very shrewd.

The last witness for the Crown was Joseph Piggott, a corporal in the North-West Mounted Police. He had charge of Riel from May 22. Although he said that he never conversed with Riel, he was allowed to give an opinion of Riel's sanity. Burbidge not only led him into giving an opinion, he also improperly suggested the answer to him.

Q. Have you seen anything in his conduct to show he is not of sound mind?
A. No, sir, I always considered him of sound mind.
Q. You have heard him speak?
A. Often, sir.
Q. *And he speaks with good reason?*
A. With reason and politeness.

CHAPTER 7

The Speech by the Defence

It was now time for the speeches of the lawyers to persuade the jury
to return a verdict in their favour. The speeches were to be followed
by Richardson's charge to the jury — a summing-up of the evidence
presented and an explanation of the law that they were to apply to the
case. Each side had only one opportunity to address the jury. Since the
defence had called witnesses, the law required the defence to go first. If
the defence had not called any witnesses, the law would have required the
Crown to go first. But Riel's lawyers had called witnesses and it meant
that the Crown now had the last word to the jury. It was an important
tactical advantage. The lawyer who went second would have the advantage of hearing all of the arguments presented by Riel's lawyer and be
able to respond to them. Riel's lawyer would have to anticipate what the
Crown's lawyer intended to say and give their response to it. This was not
an easy task.

Criminal lawyers have varying views on the importance of the address to the jury. Canada's greatest criminal lawyer, G. Arthur Martin,
Q.C., had no doubt about its importance.[1] He was convinced after almost thirty years of defending accused that the address to the jury "often
exerts a decisive influence on the outcome of a criminal prosecution."
There is no information what influence the addresses of the lawyers in

the Riel trial had on the jury. There could not be. No one was or is still entitled to know. The jury are not allowed to reveal what takes place in the jury room. It is a crime to do so. Jury secrecy prevents lawyers, the press, and the public — even the judge — from making inquiries.

Riel's lawyers had called three witnesses and the two psychiatrists to testify as to Riel's mental state at the time of the rebellion and had forfeited the right to address the jury last. Only one lawyer was allowed to deliver the address. That task fell to lead counsel Charles Fitzpatrick. There had only been a half-hearted attempt by Riel's lawyers to justify his actions. They knew that there was no justification available in law and the jury would be told this by Richardson. Rebellion, even one that was morally justifiable because of the inaction and indifference of the federal government, was no defence in law to treason, and there had been overwhelming evidence of rebellion. The only way to save Riel from the gallows was to argue that he was insane at the time. Would Riel destroy their efforts to save him by asking the judge to allow him to address the jury after his lawyers had addressed them? If he did, it would be hard for his lawyers to argue that he was insane. His insanity appeared only when he spoke of religious matters. Riel wanted to speak about why he fought the federal government.

If Riel were allowed to address the jury, his lawyers knew that Crown counsel would follow his speech by going straight to the heart of his defence. They would say that Riel had led a rebellion, plain and simple, and rebellion against the legitimate government was treason. They would say that the suggestion that he was legally insane at the time was nonsense. Had he not shown his true colours by demanding $35,000 to abandon the Métis cause? He had only one motive — greed; not to help the Métis people to achieve their rights. Had not one of Riel's own witnesses, Father André, confirmed that he was prepared to sell out the Métis for $35,000 or less?

Fitzpatrick realized that he had to put the historical events leading up to the rebellion in perspective favourable to Riel if he was to convince the jury that they should acquit him. The Canadian government's deliberate indifference in failing to respond to the complaints of the Métis was the real villain, not Riel. Riel had not turned to rebellion because he was an evil, greedy man. He had turned to rebellion because he had been pushed and prodded into it by an uncaring government, neglectful of its responsibilities to those early settlers — the Métis — who had opened up the country.

Fitzpatrick began by praising, in eloquent language typical of the time, the volunteers who had left their homes in the east to quell the rebellion.

> In the month of March last, towards the end of the month, a cry of alarm spread throughout the country, which was flashed with the rapidity of lightning all throughout the Dominion of Canada. A rebellion was supposed to exist in this section of the Dominion. It was said that the country was placed in peril. Men from the north and from the south, and from the east and from the west, men rose and rallied around the flag of their country ready to do or die. Clerks left the stools of their counting houses, mechanics left their shops, and all stood ready to do or die in the defence of their country. In this peaceable, law-abiding country the hum of industry to a certain extent ceased and it was superseded by the tread of armed men, and the sounds and strains of martial music. Men came, as I said, from all parts of the Dominion to this section of the country. War, to a certain extent, prevailed for a short time. Cut-Knife Hill, Fish Creek, Batoche — all those battles were fought — and as a result we find today the prisoner at the bar now stands indicted for high treason.

It was now time to remind the jury about the independent role that they were to play as judges in this case.

> You see now, gentlemen, arrayed on one side all the forces of the Government, and on the other side all the

weaknesses of the rebels at Batoche. You now see the storm raging furiously around this man's head. You now see the waves ready to engulf him, but, gentlemen, if we have but the flint-locks of Batoche in our hands, if we have nothing else at our disposal but our weak talents, when I look around me I see a silver lining to the cloud, and the storm which is rising so furiously around this man, and that silver lining I see there before me in you, good men and true. I say, gentlemen, that, notwithstanding this man may be weak, and not withstanding that the Government has arrayed all its talents against him, I see in that semblance of an English jury, this one grand right that you shall say to the Government, thus far shalt thou go and no further; thou shalt not touch one single hair of this man's head except in justice and in fair play, and not one single hair shall you allow to be touched unless it is in accordance with the well understood principles of law and justice, and of equity, and especially of fair play.

Although they were not really a true British jury — they were only six and not twelve — they still had the power to do justice.

Gentlemen, as I said when I opened this case, what I now have before me is a shred of that proud institution known as a British jury. What I now see before me is but a shred of it, but even a shred of it is sufficient to save a man, when that shred is woven by such material as that that I now see before me. You have but the shred of a jury, but it is sufficient I trust, in this case, to see that justice is done.

He reminded them of what the Crown had to prove in this case and not to be swayed by Osler's anticipated lurid description of the corpses of the government's soldiers lying in the snow.

In this case, you have heard a very brilliant statement made of a case for the prosecution. You have seen, gentlemen of the jury, the very learned counsel who opened the case for the Crown state to you all the events which he intended to prove. You have seen in his hands — and he is truly master of the art — you have seen how in his hands the wounds of our citizen soldiers who died at Duck Lake and at Fish Creek — how they were made to do the duty for the Crown. You have seen how their bloody corpses were made to do duty for the Crown. You have seen how their bloody corpses were appealed to, how the blood-stained snow was brought to your presence — all that has been done.

First, gentlemen, we must limit ourselves to a plain statement of the facts and ask you to bear in mind but two things. In the first place, to what extent, and how was this rebellion carried on as it has been described here? What proof has been given before you by the Crown of the overt acts of treason laid at the door of this man. And, secondly, to what extent is he responsible for those acts?

It was important to remember that the Métis who fought at Duck Lake, Fish Creek, and Batoche were fighting for what they believed was a just cause.

I know, gentlemen, that it would be extremely right for me now here to say a word of praise for those citizen soldiers who at the call of duty left their homes and firesides and came here to fight a battle for what they thought was right — I know gentlemen, that it would be right to say a word about them, but I know, gentlemen that all I can say can never be equal to the task which I see imposed upon myself, for I know that the name of Fish Creek and of Batoche and of Cut Knife Hill shall be inscribed in letters of gold on the annals of the history of our country. I know that the names of those men who died in those battles shall be written on something more durable than marble or stone, that they shall be engraved on the hearts of their grateful countrymen; but gentlemen, in the face of all this, is it possible that no voice shall be heard, no voice shall be heard to say a word in favour of the vanquished? Is it possible that in a country like this, that all men shall cringe to power, that all men shall be on the side of victory, and that no voice shall be heard to plead the cause of the vanquished? Shall we resemble the Romans of old after the fight of the gladiators and say, victory to the victors, life to the victors and death to the vanquished? No, gentlemen, I know that such shall not be the case here, and I know that when I plead for those unfortunate men, for those men who died on the side of the rebels at Duck Lake, Fish Creek and Batoche — I know that I plead for good men and grave, men who died fighting for what they thought was right; men who died for what they thought was fair and just, and if they were misguided, they were none the less brave men and men looked upon as our fellow citizens and to have done honor to our common country.

The Crown had objected when the defence had attempted to lead evidence of what had caused the rebellion and that objection had been sustained by Richardson. Now was his opportunity to raise it in argument. Surely Richardson would not stop him here, although he might later tell the jury that the cause did not justify Riel's actions. It was now time to put the rebellion in perspective and to stress what the defence believed to be the real cause of it.

It is right for me to say, gentlemen, that the Government of Canada had failed wholly in its duty towards these North-West Territories — and here I may as well remark that I speak not with the eye of a politician; when I speak of the Government, all parties are identical and the same in my eyes — I say that the Government of Canada had failed wholly in its duty towards these North-West Territories, and I say, gentlemen, that it is a maxim of political economy that the faults of those whom we have placed in authority necessarily injuriously affect ourselves, and it is thus we are made the guardian of each other's rights. The fact that the Government and the people placed in authority have committed faults towards the North-West to a large extent do not justify rebellion; but, gentlemen, if there had been no rebellion, if there had been no resistance, is there any one of you that can say to-day, is there any one of you that can place his hand on his conscience and honestly say that the evils under which this country has complained would have been remedied?

Fitzpatrick now went on at length tracing the history of how providence had first given the lands to the Indigenous Peoples, how French and English settlers had then taken possession of it, and how England and the government of Canada had treated the conquered Indigenous Peoples not with buckshot and cannonballs but with treaties, all of which must have been wearisome to the six men who sat motionless in their Sunday best in the jury box enduring the oppressive heat of the prairie summer. He reminded them that the Métis had played an important role in the development of the West and had prevented Indigenous wars.

Why is it that this country has not been the scene of so many Indian wars as we have seen ravaging the United States? Why is it that this country here as to its Indian policy, has been such a great success? Why is it that the Indian policy of our Government has been so successful? It is purely and simply because of the fact that the

185

half-breed always stood between the Indian and his fellow white man. The half-breed was the distinctive characteristic intermediary between the two and gentlemen, it is impossible for us to find any better illustration of that principle than has been afforded us by this last unfortunate war. In the whole of this war, what do we find? When find the savage instinct of the Indians roused, when we find them roused up ready to do and commit acts of the utmost brutality, what do we find and standing between him and his fell designs? Where do we find the man that is brave enough and plucky enough to say thus far shalt thou go and no farther? You have found it in the case of the half-breeds. You have found the half-breed always standing between the Indians and the white men.

Fitzpatrick reminded them that after the buffalo had gone, the Métis turned to farming, how grievances arose between them and the government, and when they could not get satisfaction, and being unworldly and ignorant, they

looked around themselves, and the first thing they saw was Manitoba. The first thing they saw was Manitoba, and they said to themselves, why, here in Manitoba, the people were situated as we are, they had about the same rights, the privileges as we had before Canada came into this country, and they said to themselves, why, with those rights, what resulted? What position are they in to-day? What is the difference between their position and ours? They said their position is entirely different from ours, as entirely different as day is from night, they are in full enjoyment of all the privileges of the British constitution. They are in full enjoyment and peaceable possession of their lands. They have been conceded titles. Titles have been conceded by the Government to them by which they have the muniments of titles to the little patch they have tilled. How did they come by all this? How did they acquire it? Then some of the old men of the district began to think far back as 1870 when a difficulty arose there between the Government and the people — a difficulty arose in which there was one man who guided the movement, from which movement a successful issue was obtained, and they said, the man that did so much for the half-breeds there, the man that obtained from them their rights surely will consent to do as much for us, the man who acted in Manitoba and gained for the Manitobans, for our brothers of that district their rights and privileges, will surely do as much for us as he did for them. Then the word goes around and the name of Louis Riel suggests itself to every person ...

Fitzpatrick knew that the Crown would present Riel as a selfish and greedy man, one who had returned to the northwest with one goal in mind — to use the Métis so that he could extract money from the federal government in exchange for leaving the territory. He had to dispel that portrayal at once.

Is this the man who will be represented to you and has been represented to you as a selfish, ambitious man, with no desire in the world but for selfishness and for egotism — this man who has been represented to you as the man who endeavours to seek himself first and everyone else after? Where do they find this man? Not, as I said, rolling in the lap of luxury. No gentlemen of the jury, he occupied the humble position of a village schoolmaster; he was there with his wife, an humble Cree woman, with his little children there in Montana,

endeavouring to earn for them their daily bread by the
sweat of his brow as a schoolmaster; he was there acting
as a schoolmaster among these people and endeavouring to earn his modest pittance, and, gentlemen, he is
asked, and from there he comes up to join this movement — he does not hesitate. He does not, before he
leaves there, stipulate that he shall be paid for his services. He does not tell these men: You want me to leave
my country; you want me to leave this home that I have
made for myself and you want to bring me back there
in the hands of my enemies, to a certain extent. He does
not stipulate for payment. He says: No, you are my
brethren; the same blood that runs through my veins
runs through yours, and any services that I may be able
to give you are free to command, and went with them.

Fitzpatrick turned to the theme of what he was to argue over and over
again. That while it was true that there was a transition from constitutional agitation to open armed rebellion, rebellion was understandable in
the circumstances. Constitutional agitation was acceptable where you have
elected representatives to Parliament who are prepared to take your grievances to Parliament and to present them to other elected representatives for
redress. But the North-West Territories had not been given representatives
in the Parliament of Canada to constitutionally agitate on their behalf.

But when you are in the North-West Territories very
nearly 2,000 miles away from those who make the laws
under which you are governed — very nearly 2,000
miles away from the people who make the laws for you,
and in the making of which laws you have no voice, over
which you have no control, in which representative institutions you have no one to represent you — here you
have those Métis, gentlemen of the jury, you have these
unfortunate Métis of the Saskatchewan 2,000 miles away

from Ottawa, 2,000 miles away from this representative House of Parliament and without one single representative either constitutional or otherwise to represent them, without one single voice to be raised in their favor. You have the fact that this country has been in the hands of the Dominion of Canada for the last fourteen or fifteen years, you have that fact and you have the fact that during all that time those men have not been able to get one single representative, not been able to take any part direct or indirect in the management of their affairs, of their own affairs or the affairs of their country. Now, where is the constitutional agitation? How can you be told on those facts that those men could constitutionally act? Could you be told that on those facts they could have endeavored to obtain a redress of their wrongs by this constitutional agitation? I say, gentlemen of the jury, the situations are entirely different, that which was constitutional agitation in England cannot be considered as constitutional agitation here and what is considered constitutional agitation in Canada, in any other part of the Dominion of Canada, cannot be considered as applying to the North-West Territories, for the situations are entirely different.

It was now time to get to the issue of Riel's sanity. Fitzpatrick had to explain why the defence was attempting to prove Riel was insane when Riel himself was maintaining his sanity.

You have been told how at Prince Albert, at a meeting held there, this man said, let us agitate, let us agitate by constitutional means. We must obtain the redress of our wrongs during five years, but if we do not obtain it at the end of five years, we will agitate for five years more, and probably at the end of ten our voices shall

189

have been able to pierce from the Saskatchewan Valley down to the House at Ottawa; but, gentlemen, at a given moment, in the beginning of March, as I said when I opened, an appeal to arms took place, and here I confess I tread on dangerous ground. Either this man is the lunatic that we his counsel have tried to make him, or he is an entirely sane man in the full possession of all his mental faculties and was responsible in the eyes of God and man for everything that he has done. If he is a lunatic, we, in the exercise of a sound discretion, have done right to endeavor to prove it. If he is a sane man, what humiliation have we passed upon that man, we his counsel endeavoring, despite his orders, despite his desire, despite his instructions, to make him out a fool. If he is a sane man, gentlemen of the jury, if he is the sane man that the Crown will endeavor to represent him, are there any redeeming features in his character and in his conduct of this rebellion? Are there any redeeming features in what he has done in connection with it which necessarily appeal to the sympathies and to the judgment? Here we find this man taking part in this, acting in concert with a naturally excitable population, acting with them in entire sympathy with the movement which began long before he came into the country or had anything to do with it. At a given moment — if he is a sane man — that movement, like all other popular movements, got ahead of him, got beyond his control.

Riel, Fitzpatrick reminded them, did not run away after the hostilities were over. He did not run away from justice, but stood his ground, prepared to accept any punishment if his actions were wrong.

Did he fly and leave women and children to be massacred? And did he fly from the hands of justice, or did

he stand his ground like a man, and did he come before the representatives of Her Majesty and say, if any is
to suffer, let me suffer; if anyone is to be punished, let
me be punished; if any victim is to be found, I am the
victim that is to go upon the scaffold; and I fought for
liberty, and if liberty is not worth fighting for, it is not
worth having?…

But, gentlemen, I have stated those facts to you simply to show you that no matter how you look at the
character of Louis Riel, there are to be found in it redeeming features; but, gentlemen, I still maintain that it
was a wise movement on our part that we were justified
by the facts, that our view has been borne out by the
evidence, and that we were bound in our instructions
as representing this man to say that he is entirely insane
and irresponsible for his acts, and will now proceed to
examine that branch of the case.

Riel, he pointed out, was suffering from megalomania, a characteristic of which is that those who have it "are naturally irritable, excitable,
and will not suffer to be contradicted in any respect." The Crown had
represented Riel as a deep, designing, cunning man with intelligence of
the very highest calibre. If he was as painted by the Crown, was it realistic
to expect that Riel would take on the government of Canada and win?

You have this man represented to you as going coolly
to work for the purpose of obtaining his ambition by
enrolling four or five hundred poor unfortunate Métis,
with flintlocks, with guns, with limited ammunition,
and, as General Middleton said, attacking the whole
power of the Dominion of Canada, with a power of
Britain behind her back…. Oh, gentlemen, I think
I could show you how a deep, designing man would
have achieved his object better than this under those

circumstances; I think I can show you how much more easy, if Riel is the man he is represented to be by the Crown, how he could have achieved his object in a different method from this.

Here is this man brought into the country, this man who had succeeded in Manitoba who had the whole force of the Métis at his back, who had behind him not only the French half-breeds, but also the English half-breeds, you see this man coming into the country, who is the embodiment in person of those deprived of their rights and their privileges, and you see this man doing what? What did he do? What did the ordinary common dictates of reason tell him to do? What did ordinary common sense tell him to do? Why did he not do as he said he wanted to do at Prince Albert, lie low and continue on fomenting this movement, and continue on guiding this movement, and is it possible to expect that in the course of time the North-West is not going to have its rights?... Would that not be the way a reasonable man should have acted? Would that not be the way that you or I or any other man of common sense would have acted.

The only reasonable explanation for Riel's conduct, Fitzpatrick urged the jury to accept, was Riel's delusional belief that he was inspired by God and that he was communicating with the Holy Ghost.

Therefore, gentlemen, you have these facts in evidence, that this man, laboring under the insane delusion that he at some future day would have the whole of the North-West Territories under his control, and being thoroughly convinced that he was called and vested by God, for the purpose of chastising Canada and of creating a new country and a new kingdom here, acting under that insane delusion, what do we find him doing? We find him then taking such steps as would enable him to carry out the object which he then had in view. We find this man believing himself to be inspired by God and believing himself to be in direct communication with the Holy Ghost, believing himself to be an instrument in the hands of the Lord of Hosts. We find him with forty or fifty men going out to do battle with against the forces of Canada. If the man was sane, how is it possible for you to justify such conduct as that? If the man was insane you know it is one of the distinguishing characteristics of his insanity that he could see no opposition of his objects, that he believed himself to be under the guidance of the Lord of Hosts, and natural reason, he could reason naturally, subject to his insane delusion, he reasoned naturally that the All Powerful will necessarily give him the victory no matter what may be the material that may be placed in his hands, no matter how inadequate that material may appear to a sane man, I, knowing that I am inspired by the Almighty, knowing that I am the instrument in the hands of God, I know that I will necessarily gain the victory; and he goes forth and gives battle with these men. Therefore, gentlemen of the jury, you have one illustration of the insanity, of the unsoundness of this man's mind in those very facts.

There was still the nagging piece of evidence that Fitzpatrick would have to explain — that Riel was prepared to go away for $35,000. It was the most powerful piece of evidence that Riel was not insane, and a clear indication that he was prepared to sell out the Métis for forty pieces of silver. How was he to explain it?

Was it for the purpose of putting it into his pocket? Was it for the purpose of leaving Canada and going away and living in the United States in ease and luxury with this money? Was it for the personal gratification and the personal advantages of Louis Riel that he wanted this money? You remember the evidence, and I need not remind you of it. You remember that he said he wanted that money for the purpose of enabling him to carry out his mission, and he wanted to go to the United States to found a newspaper, as he said, and with that newspaper to rouse up the foreign nations to enable him to come in here and take possession of the country. Now, in that fact alone is evidence of his insane delusions, there is evidence that there is the manner which is characteristic of this delusion, of this malady, and which enables men to reason properly and to achieve the object which they have in view, always subject to their insane delusions.

I told you yesterday, I had occasion to put it before to you that those men subject to this malady can reason perfectly, and as Dr. Clark said, subject always to their delusions. He reasoned perfectly. He says: "I want to get this money, I want it to help me in my object and I want to attain that object and I know that I can attain it, and I necessarily will attain it." That is the only interpretation which can be put on it, and that is the only interpretation which can reasonably be put on that demand of $35,000.

Fitzpatrick reminded the jury that both doctors had travelled two thousand miles to give their evidence and had no reason not to tell the truth. Dr. Roy had come two thousand miles at the request of the Crown as well as the defence and had been in constant study of mental diseases for more than fifteen years. Dr. Roy was a "foreigner" (a rather peculiar term used by one Quebecer for another) and endeavoured to give his evidence "so that it could be thoroughly understood." Roy's opinion that Riel was insane was corroborated by Dr. Clark.

You have heard the remark made by Dr Clark that struck me as being peculiarly applicable to this case. You have heard the remark which was made by him, when he said that this man, if this man was sane, he took very insane methods to arrive at his objects, when he began by making the remark of the very purpose which he had in view, by means of which he showed if he was perfectly sane. For instance, he gave to you the illustration, he illustrated his remarks by referring to his religion, and he said that necessarily if he was sane his religious duties would tend to alienate the sympathies of the half-breeds.

What about the expert witnesses for the Crown? The doctors had said that insanity was not always readily apparent. There had been notorious cases in England where an accused had appeared perfectly normal during the court proceedings but was subsequently discovered to be labouring under an insane delusion.

Gentlemen, you must remember this fact, that those men come here and tell you they have a very limited knowledge of this man, that their intercourse with him has been extremely limited, and they will tell you, what? Not that he is sound, they will not on their oath undertake to swear positively this man is not of unsound man, but they will tell you, gentlemen, that all they can tell you is that they have not been able to discover any symptoms of insanity.

What about the letter that the Crown would undoubtedly rely upon that had purportedly been written by Riel to Poundmaker, the famous chief of the Cree Nation inciting the Cree to rebellion? There was no evidence that the letter had been read to Poundmaker, except a bystander who said that he heard something being said to him. If this evidence was true, why was Poundmaker (who was in the custody of the police) not brought before the court to give evidence against Riel, he asked the jury? Why were Big Bear, Chief of the Plains Cree, and the other "Indians" to whom he was alleged to have incited rebellion, not brought to court to testify against Riel? he asked.

> Now, gentlemen, why are those men not examined? Why was the best proof of that criminal act not adduced? Why were those Indians not brought before you here and examined? Why were those that were within a stone's throw of this building not brought here, and men brought from Poundmaker's reserve to prove that fact? What is the reason if that, can you find any justification for it? Can you find any excuse for it? I say you cannot, gentlemen, and I say we have the right to expect that when such a terrible accusation as that is made against a man, the very best possible evidence should be given so that there can be no doubt about it, I say that such a statement as that is of the character to alienate the sympathy of every right-minded man, if he is sane; I say that such a statement as that is of a character to go very far towards putting the rope around this man's neck and putting him to the gallows, and it is of such a nature as to alienate the sympathy of every right-thinking man in the community.

Fitzpatrick was now grasping at straws. There was no obligation on the Crown to produce Poundmaker, or Big Bear, or any of the Indigenous Peoples. The Crown had produced sufficient evidence to establish that Riel had committed treason. The real issue was whether he was insane or not. Fitzpatrick continued to ask these questions, which must have been tedious to the jury. It was now time to sum up his case and to put the best face on it. Riel, he knew, was going to be allowed to address the jury and would undoubtedly harm the defence of insanity.

Now, gentlemen, I say that the conduct of Louis Riel throughout the whole of this affair is entirely inconsistent with any idea of sanity but is entirely consistent with his insanity. As I said to you a moment ago in speaking at the opening of this case, the fact of his delivering himself up is one of the characteristics of a man suffering from the insanity from which he is suffering, because he cannot appreciate the danger in which he is placed. It is impossible for him to appreciate the danger in which he places himself, and he never sees that there is any possibility that any harm can happen to him. If that man was perfectly sane, gentlemen, if that man was perfectly sane in doing as he did do, then you have to say whether or not, as I said before, there are not some redeeming features about this man's character, in the heroic act which he did in delivering himself up to Middleton. On the other hand, if he is insane, as I contend he is, you see then the proof, for any man of ordinary prudence knows that this man could have escaped and could have evaded the officers of the law and the soldiers. Notwithstanding all that, he comes and gives himself over to General Middleton and is prepared to take the consequences, no matter what they are. I say that that is one of the characteristics of his malady, that that is one of the proofs of his insanity and that is one of the characteristics which are laid down in all the books, as being characteristic of the disease of those men who believe themselves to be in constant intercourse with God, because they think God is always around them, that He is constantly taking care of them and that no harm of any kind can befall them.

It was now time for Fitzpatrick to make his final plea. He had spoken for several hours to six local citizens who had sat patiently in the sweltering courtroom. The defence team had done their best to save a man who did not want to be saved. It was a final plea in rhetoric that was common in 20th-century courtrooms, yet seldom heard today.

> Now, gentlemen, my task is at an end. I know I leave this case safely in your hands. This man, gentlemen, the prisoner at the bar, is an alien in race and an alien in religion, so far as you and I are concerned. This man, gentlemen, so far as you are concerned entirely in both, and so far as I am concerned in one; this man, gentleman, as I have stated to you is in your hands, without the provisions of an ordinary trial by jury as understood elsewhere. This man is in your hands without the provisions which the humane laws of England have made for people like him in Manitoba, and in the Province of Quebec, where he would have the right to have one-half people of his own nationality. But, gentlemen, I do not complain of that. I do not complain. I tell this man with confidence that justice will be done him, and I know that when I go home to my country, and when I am asked as to what has taken place here, when I am asked about this country, I will safely be able to say that this is the land, gentlemen, that free men till, that sober suited freedom choose, this is the land that where first with friends or foes a man speak the thing he will, I will tell them that I have come here a stranger myself in a strange place; I will tell them that I have come here to plead the cause of an alien in race and an alien in religion; I will tell them that I spoke to British subjects, that I appealed to British jurors, and that I knew full well that the principles of English liberty have always found a safe resting place in the hearts of English jurors. I know, gentlemen, that right will be done. I know you will do him justice, and that this man shall not be sent to the gallows by you, and that you shall not weave the cord that shall hang and hang him high in the face of

all the world, a poor confirmed lunatic; a victim, gentlemen, of oppression or the victim of fanaticism.

Fitzpatrick had said all that he could on behalf of Riel. It was now
time to sit down and let Riel put the noose around his own neck, if he
chose to speak.

CHAPTER 8

Riel's Speech from the Dock

After Fitzpatrick had completed his address to the jury, Judge Richardson invited Riel to address the jury as the law entitled Riel to do. "Prisoner, have you any remarks to make to the jury? If so, now is your time to speak."

François Lemieux was immediately on his feet. Maybe one last warning to Riel might dissuade him from what he was about to do — destroy his defence of insanity.

> May it please your Honors. At a former stage of the trial you will remember that the prisoner wished to cross-examine the witnesses, we objected at the time, thinking that it was better for the interest of the prisoner that we should do so. The prisoner at this stage is entitled to make any statement he likes to the jury and he has been so warned by your Honor, but I must declare before the court that we must not be considered responsible for any declaration he may make.

Judge Richardson had already decided that he had no choice but to let Riel speak, if he wished to do so, and announced his decision to the disappointed lawyers.

"Certainly, but he is entitled, and I am bound to tell him so."

Today, the right of an accused to step into the witness box and give evidence in one's own defence is considered the natural mark of a civilized society, even though an accused does not have to testify if he does not wish to do so. In fact, an accused need not say a word in his own defence. He can remain silent and thus say to the Crown, "You prove my guilt" — and his silence cannot be used against him. His silence cannot be the subject of comment by either the judge or Crown counsel, or a factor to be considered by the jury in deciding guilt or innocence; although a juror with a bit of common sense may wonder why an innocent man would not be anxious to step into the witness box and declare his innocence to the world.

Unfortunately, that was not the law in 1885 in Canada or in England, nor during the previous six hundred years. The common law of England did not permit an accused to give evidence in his own defence. This harsh rule did not allow anyone who was a party to court proceedings to give evidence, including an accused who might be on trial for his life. On the other hand, a person who claimed to have suffered harm at the hands of the accused was permitted to testify against him because he was not considered a party to the proceedings. A criminal prosecution was a contest between the King (or Queen) and the accused, not between the complainant and the accused. There were other disadvantages facing an accused, such as the fact that it was not until 1640 that an accused charged with a felony could call witnesses on his behalf and, even then, such witnesses were not allowed to give their evidence under oath, because of the belief that if they contradicted the witnesses for the Crown, they would probably be lying. The thought that the accused might be innocent and that the witnesses against him might be lying never seemed to cross the mind of lawmakers.

An accused also suffered from other disadvantages. Today, we take for granted the right to have a lawyer represent us in every aspect of a trial. But it was not until 1760 that an accused's lawyer, if he could afford one, was allowed to cross-examine the witnesses for the Crown, although the lawyer was allowed to argue points of law. Even then the accused's lawyer was not allowed to address the jury. Finally, in 1836, less than 185 years ago (and only fifty years before the trial of Riel), the Prisoners' Counsel Act was passed by the British Parliament, which allowed prisoners accused of felony to make their full defence by counsel but not give sworn evidence. Ironically, this right was opposed by no fewer than twelve out of the fifteen English judges at the time, who threatened to quit if the law were passed. In the end, they never did carry out their threat.

Although an accused was not allowed to testify in his own defence, he was allowed to make a statement from the prisoner's dock after the Crown had presented all of its evidence against him. The statement, however, could not be under oath and therefore did not possess the sanctity of sworn testimony that was considered essential to the dignity of a criminal trial. The statement or speech from the dock was simply that; and his lawyer, if he were able to afford one, was not allowed to ask him questions that might be germane to the issues in the case or even direct him to those matters pertinent to his defence. On the other hand, one advantage was that it saved him from a gruelling cross-examination by Crown counsel or pointed questions from the judge that might spell his doom. Some saw the rule as an advantage to an accused whose lawyer could say to the jury, "If only my client were allowed to enter the witness box and declare his innocence, but alas, his lips are sealed."

A century ago, most prisoners who passed through the courts were poor and illiterate, and could hardly afford the services of an experienced lawyer to defend them. Few could understand the complexities of a criminal trial even if they had a good case; there was the fear that an innocent person, unable to give a good honest-sounding account, would convict himself out of his own mouth. Many lawmakers had little faith in the ability of the average Englishman to withstand the rigours of cross-examination by Crown counsel, even if they were innocent. Eventually, the cries of law reformers won the day. In 1898, the

British Parliament finally passed a law abolishing the rule that disqualified an accused from testifying in his own behalf. Canada, however, had taken the lead five years earlier and had abolished the rule in 1893 for all offences, including treason.

Although the 1893 amendment was eight years too late for Louis Riel to go into the witness box and declare under oath his innocence, his lawyers would have thought of the right to testify as a disadvantage in his case. The evidence of treason led by the Crown was overwhelming. What could he say? If the federal government had not ignored the Métis petitions, there would not have been any rebellion. If Superintendent Lief Crozier had not led ninety Prince Albert Volunteers and North-West Mounted Police to Batoche, the Battle of Duck Lake would have never occurred. None of these excuses explained or justified armed rebellion against a legally constituted and functioning government authority. What Riel wanted to do was explain why he had led the resistance against the government who had treated him shamefully and what he wanted to do for the Métis. Surely, he thought, the jury would understand his motives and acquit him. More importantly, he wanted to convince them that he was not insane as his lawyers claimed. If he was found not guilty by reason of insanity, then the reason for the Métis resistance would have no meaning.

Riel's lawyers saw the situation differently. If Riel was found by the jury to be legally sane, he was guilty of treason and would suffer the maximum penalty. They wanted to save his life, even if it meant that he would be committed to an insane institution for the rest of his life. They must have realized after their discussion with him that if he was allowed to speak before the jury deliberated their verdict, it was unlikely that the jury would find him not guilty by reason of insanity. A speech by Riel, who, according to Dr. François Roy, only demonstrated irrationality when he spoke about religious matters, could dispel any notion that he might be legally insane. Although the right to speak to a jury or to give sworn testimony (after 1893) might be an advantage to a sane accused who had a legally recognized excuse for his conduct, it was not an advantage to Riel. It would only be an unusual and rare case where a defence lawyer who is raising the defence of legal insanity on behalf of an accused would allow the client to address the jury.

Riel's lawyers found themselves at a disadvantage because Riel wanted to speak to the jury. Although the accused was not permitted to give evidence under oath, Richardson said that he would allow Riel to make a speech from the prisoner's dock. Christopher Robinson and B.B. Osler had no objection and told Richardson that the statute entitled Riel to address the jury. They didn't say what statute they were referring to. It was certainly not the 1836 Prisoners' Counsel Act, which had allowed prisoners accused of felony to make their full defence by counsel. Nor was there anything in the 1875 or the 1880 North-West Territories Acts permitting an accused represented by counsel to address the jury. Both Robinson and Osler wanted Riel to address the jury, knowing that he would disavow the defence of insanity. And, of course, Richardson would have deferred to their expertise without asking them what statute they were relying on.

The dismissal of all preliminary attacks on the jurisdiction of the court had left Riel's lawyers with only one defence to save his life — insanity. If his lawyers had ever believed that this defence had any hope of success, that belief began to vanish quickly when Riel rose to give his speech from the dock. Defence counsel also assumed that Richardson was required by law to offer Riel the right to address the jury, but were anxious to dissociate themselves from anything that Riel might say. They asked Richardson to persuade Riel to follow their instructions, but the judge assumed from what Robinson and Osler had said that he had no choice; Riel was entitled to speak. And Riel had made it perfectly clear during the trial that he was not happy that his lawyers were saying that he was insane. Riel did not want to discharge his lawyers, although he was entitled to do so. An accused did not have to be represented by a lawyer if he did not want one.

However, Riel's lawyers, once they agreed to defend him, were not entitled to withdraw from the case unless Riel consented or the judge gave
them permission to do so. Although Riel's lawyers were required to take
their instructions from him (even though they considered him insane),
they did not have to follow those instructions if they believed that they
were not in his best interests.

Understandably, Riel had never wanted to plead insanity. Only a sane
person, fully aware of the legal significance and implications of his actions, would want to advance a defence of insanity to save his life, particularly if it were his only defence. And only an insane person, who did
not appreciate the fact that his actions had legal implications that might
jeopardize his life, would disavow the defence of insanity. The fact that
his speech from the dock was a disavowal of his insanity was probably the
strongest evidence of his insanity.

Riel probably wanted to die as a martyr and the Canadian government was happy to accommodate him. Rejecting his lawyers' attempts
to argue that he was legally insane at the time of the rebellion, he ex-
claimed that "life, without the dignity of an intelligent being, is not
worth having." His life had been certainly one series of failures after
another. The earlier rebellion in Manitoba in 1871 had ended in his
exile, and a life of poverty and ignominy in the United States. He had
fought the Canadian government twice and lost. His dream of creating a separate Métis country had been dashed and it was unlikely that
there would ever be another chance to lead his people. If he died at the
hands of the detested federal government, at least in death he would be
remembered. Why shouldn't he be allowed to die and be remembered
as a hero to his people?

Did Judge Richardson correctly conclude that he had no other alternative but to allow Riel to make a speech to the jury if he wanted?
On the one hand, Richardson knew that if he allowed Riel to speak,
any possibility of a successful defence of insanity would quickly evap-
orate. On the other hand, if he did not allow Riel to speak and he was

convicted, he knew that there would be a public outcry and he would be in for a great deal of public criticism. The safer decision was to allow him to speak.

Riel began with an immediate disavowal of his insanity. It was a rambling speech, following no particular order, seeking to justify his actions. Sometimes, there was a great deal of logic in his comments; other times he seemed to wander aimlessly. It is difficult to determine what influence he had upon the jury from simply reading the cold print.

> Your Honors, gentlemen of the jury: It would be easy for me today to play insanity, because the circumstances are such as to excite any man, and under natural excitement of what is taking place today (I cannot speak English very well, but am trying to do so, because most of those here speak English), under the excitement which my trial causes me would justify me not to appear as usual, but with my mind out of its ordinary condition. I hope with the help of God I will maintain calmness and decorum as suits this honorable court, this honorable jury.

The defence had tried to show that his insanity was manifested in unusual religious fervour. Riel now attempted to explain his actions, not as those of an insane person, but as one who was justified in following the course that he did. He was, in effect, undoing all that his lawyers had tried to do for him.

> You have seen by the papers in the hands of the Crown that I am naturally inclined to think of God at the beginning of my actions. I wish if you — I do it you won't take it as a mark of insanity, that you won't take it as part of a play of insanity. Oh, my God, help me through

Thy grace and the divine influence of Jesus Christ. Oh, my God, bless me, bless this honorable court, bless this honorable jury, bless my good lawyers who have come 700 leagues to try to save my life, bless also the lawyers of the Crown, because they have done, I am sure, what they thought their duty. They have shown me fairness which at first I did not expect from them. Oh, God, bless all those around me through the grace and influence of Jesus Christ our Saviour, change the curiosity of those who are paying attention to me, change that curiosity into sympathy with me. The day of my birth I was helpless and my mother took care of me although she was not able to do it alone, there was someone to help her take care of me and I lived. Today, although a man I am helpless before this court, in the Dominion of Canada and in this world, as I am helpless on the knees of my mother the day of my birth.

One can imagine what went through the minds of Riel's lawyers as they heard Riel, whom they had portrayed as legally insane, disclaim to the jury insanity as the reasons for his actions. Would the jury understand that legal insanity does not demand the language of the raving lunatic? Legal insanity is not characterized by incoherent statements and rambling thoughts. Legal insanity — the inability to appreciate the nature and quality of one's actions or to know that they are morally or legally wrong — is determined by one's beliefs or lack of them. A person who does not understand that what he has done is legally or morally wrong can often argue with cold logic the rightness of his beliefs. In the time it takes to make a speech, Riel could easily convince a jury that he was perfectly sane and appreciated what he had done. Yet to the trained psychiatrist, who would know what questions to ask him, Riel could be legally insane.

When Riel finally turned to explain the reasons for his actions, his lawyers knew that he was about to seal his fate. Riel wanted to tell the jury that he had come to aid his suffering people and to justify the rebellion.

But even if the jury had sympathy for Riel's motives, his lawyers knew that it could not legally justify a verdict of not guilty. Richardson would soon tell the jury that justification was no defence to treason and that they must apply the law.

When I came into the North-West in July, the first of July 1884, I found the Indians suffering. I found the half-breeds eating the rotten pork of the Hudson Bay Company and getting sick and weak every day. Although a half-breed, and having no pretensions to help the whites, I also paid attention to them. I saw they were deprived of responsible government, I saw that they were deprived of their public liberties. I remembered that half-breed meant white and Indian, and while I paid attention to the suffering Indians and the half-breeds I remembered that the greatest part of my heart and blood was white and I have directed my attention to help the Indians, to help the half-breeds and to help the whites to the best of my ability. We have made petitions, I have made petitions with others to the Canadian Government asking it to relieve the condition of this country. We have taken time: we have tried to unite all classes, even if I may speak, all parties. Those who have been in close communication with me know I have suffered, that I have waited for months to bring some of the people of the Saskatchewan to an understanding of certain important points in our petition to the Canadian Government and I have done my duty. I believe I have done my duty. It has been said in this box that I have been egotistic. Perhaps I am egotistic. A man cannot be individuality without paying attention to himself. He cannot generalize himself, though he may be general. I have done all I could to make good petitions with others, and we have sent them to the Canadian Government, and when the Canadian

Government did answer, through the Under Secretary
of State, to the secretary of the joint committee of the
Saskatchewan, then I began to speak of myself, not before; so my particular interests passed after the public
interests. A good deal has been said about the settlement
and division of lands a good deal has been said about
that. I do not think my dignity today here would allow
me to mention the foreign policy, but if I was to explain
to you or if I had been allowed to make the questions
to witnesses, those questions would have appeared in an
altogether different light before the court and jury. I do
not say that my lawyers did not put the right questions.
The observations I had the honor to make to the court
the day before yesterday were good, they were absent of
the situation, they did not know all the small circumstances as I did. I could mention a point, but that point
was leading to so many that I could not have been all
the time suggesting. By it I don't wish it understood that
I do not appreciate the good works of my lawyers, but if
I were to go into all the details of what has taken place, I
think I could safely show you that what Captain Young
said that I am aiming all the time at practical results was
true, and I could have proved it. During my life I have
aimed at practical results, I have writings, and after my
death I hope that my spirit will bring practical results.

It was important to Riel that the jury understand that he was not
insane. God had given him a mission to carry out in the Saskatchewan.
God was on his side and would deliver him from his oppressors. A verdict
of not guilty by reason of insanity would render his mission meaningless.

It is true, gentlemen. I believed for years I had a mission, and when I speak of a mission you will understand
me not as trying to play the role of insane before the

grand jury so as to have a verdict of acquittal upon that ground. I believe that I have a mission, I believe I had a mission at this very time. What encourages me to speak to you with more confidence in all the imperfections of my English way of speaking, it is that I have yet and still that mission, and with the help of God, who is in this box with me, and He is on the side of my lawyers, even with the honorable court, the Crown and the jury, to help me, and to prove by the extraordinary help that there is a Providence to-day in my trial, as there was a Providence in the battles of the Saskatchewan.

Had he not accomplished his mission in Manitoba in spite of the way he had been treated by the Canadian government? Why? Because he was blessed by God, he said, who was protecting him and his family. God had also blessed him when men like General Middleton and Captain Young testified that they found no insanity in him, contrary to what his doctors and lawyers had told the court.

I have not assumed to myself that I had a mission. I was working in Manitoba first, and I did all I could to get free institutions for Manitoba; they have those institutions today in Manitoba, and they try to improve them, while myself, who obtained them, I am forgotten as if I was dead. But after I had obtained, with the help of others, a constitution for Manitoba, when the Government at Ottawa was not willing to inaugurate it at the proper time, I have worked till the inauguration should take place, and that is why I have been banished for five years. I had to rest five years, I was willing to do it. I protested, I said: "Oh, my God, I offer You all my existence for that cause, and please to make of my weakness an instrument to help men in my country." And seeing my intentions, the late Archbishop Bourget said: "Riel has no narrow views, he is a man to accomplish great things," and he wrote that letter of which I hope that the Crown has at least a copy. And in another letter, when I became what doctors believed to be insane, Bishop Bourget wrote again and said: "Be ye blessed by God and man and take patience in your evils." Am I not taking patience? Will I be blessed by man as I have been by God?

I say that I have been blessed by God, and I hope that you will not take that as a presumptuous assertion, it has been a great success for me to come through all the dangers I have in that fifteen years. If I have not succeeded in wearing a fine coat myself I have at the same time the great consolation of seeing that God has maintained my view; that He has maintained my health sufficiently to go through the world, and that he has kept me from bullets, when bullets marked my hat. I am blessed by God. It is this trial that is going to show that I am going to be blessed by man during my existence, the benedictions are a guarantee that I was not wrong when by circumstances I was taken away from adopted land to my native land. When I see British people sitting in the court to try me, remembering that the English people are proud of that word "fair-play," I am confident that I will be blessed by God and by man also.

Riel was convinced that his mission was God's mission and God was in his corner. A finding by the jury that he was not guilty by reason of insanity would undo all that he had been trying to do and would be a blot on his name. He now turned on his lawyers and Dr. Roy for trying to have the jury return a verdict that he was insane.

To-day when I saw the glorious General Middleton bearing testimony that he thought I was not insane, and when Captain Young proved that I am not insane, I felt that God was blessing me, and blotting away from my name the blot resting upon my reputation on account of having been in the lunatic asylum of my good friend Dr. Roy. I have been in an asylum, but I thank the lawyers for the Crown who destroyed the testimony of my good friend Dr. Roy, because I have always believed that I was put in the asylum without reason. Today my pretension is guaranteed, and that is a blessing too in that way. I have also been in the lunatic asylum at Longue Pointe, and I wonder that my friend Dr. Lachapelle, who took care of me charitably, and Dr. Howard are not here. I was there perhaps under my own name.

What was most important to Riel was that he not be found insane by the jury, even if it meant his life. It would destroy his life's work.

Even if I was going to be sentenced by you, gentlemen of the jury, I have this satisfaction if I die — that if I die I will not be reputed by all men as insane, as a lunatic. A good deal has been said by the two reverend fathers, André and Fourmond. I cannot call them my friends, but they made no false testimony. I know that a long time ago they believed me more or less insane. Father Fourmond said that I would pass from great passion to great calmness. That shows great control under contradiction, and according to my opinion and with the help of God I have that control.

Next, Riel turned to the evidence of his cousin Charles Nolin, whom he claimed had testified falsely against him. Nolin had not told the truth when he said that Riel wanted Nolin to give up his contract with the government. He simply did not want Nolin to take the contract, as it would show weakness and compromise their cause. What he told Nolin was to wait to see if the government was going to listen to them. Nolin also wanted him to renounce his American citizenship but he refused because he felt that it would give him better bargaining power on behalf of the Métis. As far as his ambition was concerned, he had none. He had been offered a position on the council but had refused it. "I speak of those things to defend my character, as it has been said that I am egotistical." Riel now turned to a defence of his actions.

> The agitation in the North-West Territories would have been constitutional, and would certainly be constitutional today if, in my opinion, we had not been attacked. Perhaps the Crown has not been able to find out the particulars, that we were attacked, but as we were on the scene it was easy to understand. When we sent petitions to the Government, they used to answer us by sending police, and when the rumors were increasing every day that Riel had been shot there or there, or that Riel was going to be shot by such and such a man, the police would not pay any attention to it. I am glad that I have mentioned the police, because of the testimony that has been given in the box during the examination of many of the witnesses. If I had been allowed to put questions to the witnesses, I would have asked them when it was I said a single word against a single policeman or a single officer. I have respected the policemen, and I do today, and I have respected the officers of the police; the paper that I sent to Major Crozier is a proof it: "We respect you, Major." There are papers which the Crown has in its hands, and which show that demoralization exists among the police, if you will allow me to say it in the court, as I have said it in writing.
> Your Honors, gentlemen of the jury: If I was a man of today perhaps it would be presumptuous to speak in that way, but the truth is good to say, and it is said in a proper manner, and it is without any presumption, it is not because I have been libelled for fifteen years that I

do not believe myself something. I know that through the grace of God I am the founder of Manitoba. I know that though I have no open road for my influence, I have big influence, concentrated as a big amount of vapour in an engine. I believe by what I suffered for fifteen years, by what I have done for Manitoba and the people of the North-West, that my words are worth something. If I give offence, I do not speak to insult. Yes, you are the pioneers of civilization, the whites are the pioneers of civilization, but they bring among the Indians demoralization. Do not be offended, ladies, do not be offended, here are the men who can cure that evil; and if at times I have been strong against my true friends and fathers, the reverend priests of the Saskatchewan, it is because my convictions are strong. There have been witnesses to show that immediately after great passion I could come back to the great respect I have for them.

Riel now turned to the evidence of George Ness who had said that he had called Archbishop Taché a thief. He did not deny that he had, but explained that he had done so because Taché had purchased a piece of land from a widow at a cheap price.

I read in the Gospel: "Ye Pharisees with your long prayers devour the widows." And as Archbishop Taché is my great benefactor, as he is my father, I would say because he has done me an immense deal of good, and because there was no one who had the courage to tell him. I did, because I love him, because I acknowledge all he has done for me. I say that we have been patient a long time, and when we see that mild words only serve as covers for great ones to do wrong, it is time when we are justified in saying that robbery is robbery everywhere, and the guilty ones are bound by the force of public opinion to take notice of it. The one who has the courage to speak out in that way, instead of being an outrageous man, becomes in fact a benefactor to those men themselves, and to society.

Riel explained that he was trying to break from the Church of Rome to avoid the infighting that had been going on for centuries.

As to religion, what is my belief? What is my insanity about that? My insanity, your Honors, gentlemen of the jury, is that I wish to leave Rome aside, inasmuch as it is the cause of division between Catholics and Protestants. I did not wish to force my views, because in Batoche to the half-breeds that followed me I used the word, *carte blanche*. If I have any influence in the new world it is to help in that way and even if it takes 200 years to become practical, then after my death that will bring out practical results, and then my children's children will shake hands with the Protestants of the new world in a friendly manner. I do not wish these evils which exist in Europe to be continued, as much as I can influence it, among the half-breeds. I do not wish that to be repeated in America. That work is not the work of some days or some years, it is the work of hundreds of years.

Riel now started to ramble aimlessly, his thoughts scattering about the fact that the "half-breeds" considered him to be a prophet, how the spirit directed his actions, and that there was nothing unusual about the noises that Nolin said guided his actions since "every half-breed could foretell the future." It must have been painful for his supporters and sympathizers to listen as he desperately tried to justify his actions to the jury.

It is not to be supposed that the half-breeds acknowledged me as a prophet if they had not seen that I could see something into the future. If I am blessed without measure I can see something into the future, we all see into the future more or less. As what kind of prophet I would come, would it be a prophet who would all the time have a stick in his hand, and threatening, a prophet of evil? If the half-breeds had acknowledged me as a prophet, if on the other side priests come and say that I am polite, if there are general officers, good men, come into this box and prove that I am polite, prove that I am decent in my manner, in combining all together you have a decent prophet. An insane man cannot withhold his insanity, if I am insane my heart will tell what is in me.

Last night while I was taking exercise the spirit who guides and assists me and consoles me, told me that to-morrow somebody will come *t'aider*, five English and one French word *t'aider*, that is to help you. I am consoled by that. While I was recurring to my God, to our God, I said, but woe to me if you do not help me, and these words came to me in the morning, in the morning someone will come *t'aider*, that is today. I said that to my two guards and you can go for the two guards. I told them that if the spirit that directs me is the spirit of truth it is today that I expect help....

Mr Nolin came into the box and said that Mr Riel said that he had a noise in his bowels and that I told him that it meant something. I wish that he had said what I said, what I wrote on the paper of which he speaks, perhaps he can yet be put in the box. I said to Nolin, "Do you hear?" Yes, I said there will be trouble in the North-West and was it so or not? Has there been no trouble in the North-West? Besides Nolin knows that among his nationality, which is mine, he knows that the half-breeds as hunters can foretell many things, perhaps some of you have a special knowledge of it. I have seen half-breeds who say, my hand is shaking, this part of my hand is shaking you will see such a thing today, and it happens. Others will say I feel the flesh on my leg move in such a way, it is a sign of such a thing, and it happens. There are men who know that I speak right. If the witness spoke of that fact which he mentioned, to show that I was insane he did not remember that perhaps on that point he is — insane himself, because the half-breed by the movement of the hand, sometimes of his shoulders, sometimes his legs, can have certain knowledge of what will happen....

The half-breeds also knew that I told them that they would be punished, that I did not say it of my own responsibility, but that I said it in the same way as I have told them other things. It was said to me that the nation would be punished. Why? Because she had consented to leave Rome too quick. What was the meaning of that? There was a discussion about too quick; they said that they should do it at once. Too quick does not mean too soon, if we say yes, it shows no consideration to the man. If God wants something, and if we say yes, that is not the way to answer him. He wants the conscience to say: yes, oh my God, I do Thy will; and because the half-breeds quickly separated from Rome, in such a quick manner, it was disagreeable to God and they were punished, and I told them it would happen; fifty of those who are there can prove it. But, you will say, you did not put yourself as a prophet? The 19th century is to be treated in certain ways, and it is probably for that reason I have found the word "exovede," I prefer to be called one of the flock; I am no more than you are, I am simply one of the flock, equal to the rest. If it is any satisfaction to the doctors to know what kind of insanity I have, if they are going to call my pretensions insanity, I say humbly, through the grace of God, I believe I am the prophet of the new world.

It must have suddenly dawned on Riel that his assertion that he was a "prophet of the new world" might be indicative of his insanity because he suddenly turned to the jury and disavowed any such suggestion.

> I wish you to believe that I am not trying to play insanity, there is in the manner, in the standing of a man, the proof that he is sincere, not playing. You will say, what have you got to say? I have to attend to practical results. Is it practical that you be acknowledged as a prophet? It is practical to say it. I think that if the half-breeds have acknowledged me, as a community, to be a prophet, I have reason to believe that it is beginning to become practical. I do not wish, for my satisfaction, the name of prophet, generally that title is accompanied with such a burden, that if there is satisfaction for your vanity, there is a check to it. To set myself up as Pope, no, no, I said I believed that Bishop Bourget had succeeded in spirit and in truth. Why? Because while Rome did not pay attention to us, he, as a bishop, paid attention to us.

Riel realized that he was rambling and had lost the attention of the jury. It was time to put his submissions into some logical order if he expected the jury to reject his lawyers' submissions that he was insane. He slowly turned to the theme presented by his lawyers that the court had no authority to try him for treason.

> You have given me your attention, your Honors; you have given me your attention, gentlemen of the jury, and this great audience, I see that if I go any further on that point I will lose the favor you have granted me up to this time, and as I am aiming all the time at practical results, I will stop here, master of myself, through the help of God. I have only a few more words to say, your Honors. Gentlemen of the jury, my reputation, my liberty, my

life, are at your discretion. So confident am I, that I have not the slightest anxiety, not even the slightest doubt, as to your verdict. The calmness of my mind concerning the favorable decision which I expect, does not come from any unjustifiable presumption upon my part. I simply trust, that through God's help, you will balance everything in a conscientious manner, and that, having heard what I had to say, that you will acquit me. I do respect you, although you are only half a jury, but your number of six does not prevent you from being just and conscientious; your number of six does not prevent me giving you my confidence, which I would grant to another six men. Your Honor, because you appointed these men, do not believe that I disrespect you. It is not by your own choice, you were authorised by those above you, by the authorities in the North-West; you have acted according to your duty, and while it is, in our view, against the guarantees of liberty, I trust the Providence of God will bring out good of what you have done conscientiously.

Although this court has been in existence for the last fifteen years, I thought I had a right to be tried in another court. I do not disrespect this court. I do respect it, and what is called by my learned and good lawyers, the incompetency of the court must not be called in disrespect, because I have all respect.

The only things I would like to call your attention to before you retire to deliberate are: 1st. That the House of Commons, Senate and Ministers of the Dominion, and who make laws for this land and govern it, are no representation whatever of the people of the North-West.

2nd. That the North-West Council generated by the Federal Government has the great defect of its parent.

3rd. The number of members elected for the Council by the people make it only a sham representative legislature and no representative government at all....

The Ministers of an insane and irresponsible Government and its little one — the North-West Council — made up their minds to answer my petitions by surrounding me slyly and by attempting to jump upon me suddenly and upon my people in the Saskatchewan. Happily when they appeared and showed their teeth to devour, I was ready: that is what is called my crime of high treason, and to which they hold me today. Oh, my good jurors, in the name of Jesus Christ, the only one who can save and help me, they have tried to tear me to pieces.

If you take the plea of the defence that I am not responsible for my acts, acquit me completely since I have been quarrelling with an insane and irresponsible Government. If you pronounce in favor of the Crown, which contends that I am responsible, acquit me all the same. You are perfectly justified in declaring that having my reason and sound mind, I have acted reasonably and in self-defence, while the Government, my accuser, being irresponsible, and consequently insane, cannot but have acted wrong, and if high treason there is it must be on its side and not on my part.

When Riel paused for a moment to collect his final thoughts. Judge Richardson, anxious to end it, inquired wearily, "Are you done?"

RIEL: Not yet, if you have the kindness to permit me your attention for a while.
RICHARDSON: Well, proceed.

Riel now decided that he should seek some sympathy from the jury for himself and his wife and children.

For fifteen years I have been neglecting myself. Even one of the most hard witnesses on me said that with all my vanity, I never was particular to my clothing; yes, because I never had much to buy any clothing. The Rev. Father André has often had the kindness to feed my family with a sack of flour, and Father Fourmond. My wife and children are without means, while I am working more than any representative in the North-West. Although I am simply a guest of this country — a guest of the half-breeds of the Saskatchewan — although as a simple guest. I worked to better the condition of the people of the Saskatchewan at the risk of my life, to better the condition of the people of the North-West, I have never had any pay. It has always been my hope to have a fair living one day. It will be for you to pronounce — if you say I was right, you can conscientiously acquit me, as I hope through the help of God you will. You will console those who have been fifteen years around me only partaking in my sufferings. What you will do in justice to me, in justice to my family, in justice to my friends, in justice to the North-West, will be rendered a hundred times to you in this world, and to use a sacred expression, life everlasting in the other.

I thank your Honor for the favor you have granted me in speaking; I thank you for the attention you have given me, gentlemen of the jury, and I thank those who have had the kindness to encourage my imperfect way of speaking the English language by your good attention. I put my speech under the protection of my God, my Saviour, He is the only one who can make it effective. It is possible it should become effective, as it is proposed to good men, to good people, and to good ladies also.

Riel's speech to the jury had sealed his fate. All that was left was for the Crown lawyers to make their submissions and Richardson to deliver his charge to the jury, and to await the inevitable result of their verdict.

CHAPTER 9

The Speech by the Crown

The Crown had the last word. Christopher Robinson, a brilliant orator, had the ability to cut through Fitzpatrick's rhetoric and get down to the nub of the issues in the case. It was no time for emotion. He knew that many of the jurors sympathized with the Métis for the way that they had been treated by Ottawa. It was not a time to parade the banner of loyalty to the Crown. It was a time for cold logic and Robinson had the ability to reduce the most complex issues to simple logic. It was time for the jurors to put aside their personal feelings and do their legal duty without sympathy for the accused, whatever the consequences.

Robinson began by pointing out that nineteen Crown witnesses had given uncontradicted evidence of Riel's involvement in leading and inciting rebellion against the government of Canada. This was no time for sympathy for Riel. Indeed, if anyone needed sympathy, it was the Métis who had been duped into becoming involved in a rebellion they could not win. The villain in this scenario was Riel. His motive was far from altruistic; it was simple greed. He was prepared to sell his flock for $35,000, or even less, if Father André could get it for him.

Louis Riel's trial.

There are two or three reasons peculiar to this case why I shall find it unnecessary to occupy your time at such length as is usual in trials of this description; it will not be necessary to go over the evidence in detail for a reason we seldom find in cases of this kind. As a general rule it is necessary for the representative of the Crown at the conclusion of the case to go over the evidence in detail and compare the different statements which are frequently contradictory. But in this case, gentlemen, there is no contradiction, there is no dispute, there is not a single witness whose word has been doubted, there is not a single fact proved on the part of the Crown which anybody has been called to contradict, and it stands therefore as an admission, and an admission made by counsel for the defence that the case as presented has been made out beyond all question — there can be no doubt about that either on the documentary evidence or the evidence of the witnesses. What I have to do, therefore, in the first place, is to address myself to the only defence which has in reality been set up here, and I have next to show you, because I think it right to show you, that every single allegation of my learned friend's statement made to you in the opening of the case has been proved to the very letter.

Robinson had now laid the groundwork for his address. The Crown had proved the case of treason to the hilt. The defence had attempted to muddy the waters with rhetoric and justification. There could only be one defence left to Riel — insanity. How could there be any basis for this defence, he asked, when Riel's lawyers were also saying that he was justified in urging the Métis to rebellion?

What my learned friend's address amounted to was practically this: they told you in fact that this rebellion was justifiable. My learned friend, Mr. Greenshields, told you that the men responsible for the blood that was shed were the people who had refused the petitions of the half-breeds made under the direction and guidance of the prisoner at the bar. In the next breath he told you that this rebellion was directed and carried on by an irresponsible lunatic.

If the only thing, gentlemen, that can be charged against the persons at the head of affairs, is that they hesitated to accede to the request presented to them through the hands and by the direction of a person whom my learned friends tell you is insane, surely they may be excused for their hesitation.

When my learned friend, Mr. Greenshields, told you that the name of this prisoner would go down to posterity as that of a man who was justified in the action he has taken, he had to tell you in the next breath that he honored and praised the men who risked their lives to put down the rebellion. Gentlemen, is not that the very height of inconsistency? Are you to be told as sensible men that all credit and respect is due to those brave and loyal men who shed their blood and lost their lives to put down this rebellion, and at the same time that that man who organized this rebellion and who is responsible for it is to go down to posterity with an honored name, and as a victim of the wrongs of his country?

My learned friends must make their choice between their defences. They cannot claim for their client what is called a niche in the temple of fame and at the same time assert that he is entitled to a place in a lunatic asylum. I understand perfectly well the defence of insanity; I understand perfectly the defence of patriotism, but I am utterly unable to understand how you can be told in one breath a man is a noble patriot and to be told in the next breath that every guiding motive of his actions, every controlling influence which he is bound by his very nature to give heed to, is that of overweening vanity, a selfish sense of his own importance and an utter disregard to everything but his own insane power. There must be either one defence or the other in this case.

Unfortunately it becomes my duty to show to you, that the case which the Crown believes it has made out is, that this prisoner at the bar is neither a patriot nor a lunatic.

But before I proceed further as to that, I would ask you in all seriousness, as sensible men: do you believe that a defence of insanity could have any conceivable or possible applicability to a case of this description?

Was it possible that Riel could have fooled all of the Métis into believing that he was sane when in fact he was insane, Robinson asked the jury? He had not been in the Métis community for almost a year and addressed the residents on a number of occasions. They had placed their lives and property under his control, and trusted in his judgment, yet had

not heard from any one of them that during all that time there was the smallest suspicion he was affected with any unsoundness of mind whatever.

Now gentlemen, am I speaking reason or am I not speaking reason? Unless all reason and common sense has been banished from the land is it possible that a defence of insanity can be set up in the case of a person of that description? If so, I should like to know what protection there is for society, I should like to know how crimes are to be put down. I should like to know more; I should like to know if the prisoner at the bar is not in law to be held responsible for this crime, who is responsible? He was followed by some six or seven hundred misled and misguided men. Are we to be told that the prisoner at the bar was insane but that his followers were sane? Is there any escape from the one inevitable conclusion either that the prisoner at the bar was perfectly sane and sound in mind or that all the half-breed population of the Saskatchewan were insane? You must have it either one way or the other.

What in reality is the defence set up here: what in reality is the defence which you, as sensible men, are asked to find by your verdict? You are asked to find that six or seven hundred men may get up an armed rebellion with its consequent loss of life, its loss of property, that murder and arson and pillage may be committed by that band of armed men, and we are to be told they are all irresponsible lunatics....

Can you say with any reason that a man who has lived among his fellow-men for eighteen months, probably the most prominent man in the district, that he can live for that length of time without his unsoundness of mind being found out, if his mind is unsound? Can you say that this prisoner can, by any application of law, administered by reasonable men, be held to be irresponsible for his actions? And if he is irresponsible are you to say, or are you not to say to all the men who followed him in his crime "it was your duty, it was your business, living as you did so long with the prisoner, to know more about this man's unsoundness of mind," and his insanity; it was your duty to know more about him than such witnesses as Capt. Young and General Middleton, who have seen him just lately, who can discover nothing unsound about him. Are you to tell these men it was their duty to discover his unsoundness of mind and not to follow him because he was a lunatic? If not then no one is responsible for this rebellion.

Robinson had placed the issues squarely before the jury. It was now time to look carefully at the medical evidence. What had the medical doctors said about insanity? They had said simply that the very essence of an insane impulse is that it is impervious to reason; you cannot reason an insane man out of it. But what if you could reason him out of it? What if the offer of a substantial sum of money could reason him out of the impulse? Would it not then follow logically that the impulse was not insane at all? It was not impervious at all to reason — at least not to money, or the payment of a large sum of money.

The moment you find the impulse which possesses a man yielding to reason, force or any motive, that moment that ceases to be an insane delusion. We hear of poor creatures in asylums who suppose themselves to be possessed of all the wealth of the world. Do you suppose if you went to one of them and offered him $100 in exchange for all the wealth he imagined himself possessed of, and if he accepted that, that you would have a lunatic before you? You might have an impostor, but the lunacy is at an end. Or if you go to the poor creature who thinks herself to be a queen and offer her $100 to give up her throne, and you find her willing to do so, you will no more discover a lunatic here than in the case I have just referred to. The most well known form of mania is what is called homicidal mania. That is a mania of which there are always instances in our asylums. The one idea, the one feeling and thought that possesses the man, is a desire to take human life, and that has more than once been set up as a defence to murder. Do you suppose if you find a man who had been paid $1,000 to commit a murder, or who says he would not commit a murder unless he got $1,000, and who then sets up as a defence this homicidal mania, do you think any jury would listen to him for a moment?

Robinson now turned to the issue that was to haunt Riel's lawyers for the rest of the trial and into the court of appeal. How could it be said that a man who claims to be legally insane — who does not know the nature and quality of his actions, or if he did know, did not know that what he was doing what was wrong — is prepared to abandon his people for a bribe from the federal government.

Now, what are the facts here? We are told that this man's controlling mania was a sense of his own importance and power; that he was so possessed with over-weening vanity and insane ambition that the one thing which he was unable to resist, which in his own mind justified all crimes, and was an atonement for all guilt, was his own sense of greatness and position and his own power. Well, gentlemen, is it not a fact that he expressly said that if he could get a certain sum of money he would give up this power and this ambition and go away. Now,

229

my learned friend, Mr. Fitzpatrick, has said to you all that can be said upon that head. He says he made that offer through Nolin, that what he desired to do with the money was to go to a foreign country and work out some schemes of conquest there. Gentlemen, did he say that to Father André, or to Mr. Jackson? Am I right or am I wrong in suggesting to you that the prisoner at the bar was capable of adopting his arguments, his convictions to the men with whom he had to reason? He tells Nolin that he wished the money to go to a foreign country and work out his schemes, and why? Because he was one of his own people, one whom he believed to be in sympathy with his own schemes. Did he tell Father André anything of the kind? When he wanted Father André to get this money for him what was it he said to him? He said, if I get the $35,000 I will go, I will leave the country. Did he tell Father André he was going on any absurd schemes of conquest, that he was going to return with his army and devastate Manitoba? No, gentlemen, that was not said, and the reason why it was not said was because he knew it would ruin all his chances with Father André.

And in the same way he reasoned with Mr. Jackson. Jackson is an Englishman, and the prisoner knew if he had told Jackson any of these absurd ideas it would have had no influence whatever with him.

Fitzpatrick had said that this was "a land where a man may speak the thing he will, what seems right to him." The answer to that submission, Robinson pointed out, was simple.

Gentlemen, I wish the prisoner at the bar had confined himself to speaking what he thought to be right. It is not for what he spoke that he is in this situation; it is entirely for the acts he did, and the crimes he committed that throws upon us the painful duty of trying him here. If he had only considered this was a free land and a land where free speech will always get a man his rights, there would have been no difficulty or trouble in the matter. It was just because he was not contented with constitutional agitation, just because he desired to carry on armed rebellion, to have his own way, just because he was not contented with that constitutional agitation which others are satisfied to follow; it was for this reason that he occupies the unhappy position in which he finds himself today.

Although Fitzpatrick had said that Riel had started with no intention, expectation, or desire of anything beyond constitutional agitation, and that he had been overtaken by the speed of events that had taken place, Robinson pointed out that Riel's actions leading up to the first skirmish were consistent only with rebellion, not constitutional agitation. Had Riel not spoken of taking up arms in December months before?

Now, what does the evidence show in that respect? You will remember in the first place, according to the evidence of Nolin, he spoke of taking up arms as long ago as December....

On the 3rd of March the prisoner at the bar is accompanied by sixty armed half-breeds to the Halcro settlement, and there he made use of the expression, "They talk to us about the police, but here are our police," pointing to the armed men. The next thing we find is that on the 5th of March and on the 6th, he told Nolin that he had decided to take up arms, that that was his view of the proper course. We hear Nolin dissented from that, and we hear that they disagreed. (And you must remember that they are isolated people and their ways are not in some respects our ways.) They agreed I say that it was better to have a novena or nine days' prayer in order to avert the trouble and agitation which was in the settlement. Riel, the prisoner, seems to have said it was too long a time, but the novena was carried against him.

Gentlemen, if in all he had done he was sincere and truthful, would not the prisoner at the bar heartily have joined in that prayer? What would his conduct have been? Would he not have attended this nine days' prayer and earnestly addressed his thoughts to avert from this country the bloodshed which he foresaw was coming upon it? What did he do? That novena was appointed at his suggestion to begin on the 9th of March and end on the 19th, and what was his course in the meantime? If Nolin's evidence is to be believed the prisoner did what he could to prevent the people from going to the church where these prayers were being said: and we find that before the 19th of March came under his direction and guidance armed rebellion had broken out, and Nolin was taken prisoner and in custody in his hands....

The next thing we find is that on the 18th and 19th, a week before hostilities broke out, and on the 18th more especially, speaking to Dr. Willoughby, he told him that in one week from that day the police would be wiped out of existence. He told Dr. Willoughby he would let him know who would do the killing in this country. He said: "You know Louis Riel's history." ... He told him the last rebellion would be nothing to this one. He said the time had now come when he was to rule this country or perish in the attempt. Well, gentlemen, is that the talk of a man whom the situation has overwhelmed, or the talk of a man who was the creature of circumstances?

The next thing we find is that on the 18th pillage and robbery is committed on inoffensive citizens. We find two stores are robbed, Walters' & Baker's and another,

Kerr's. We find both these stores looted and pillaged. We find the prisoner coming to the nearest of these stores and demanding arms and ammunition. Can we fancy anything more premeditated and designed? We find the preparations made for war just as patiently and quietly as they are in the case of two nations who have declared war against each other. On the 18th he told Mr. Lash that the rebellion had commenced and that they intended to fight until the whole Saskatchewan valley was in their hands. He told him on the 26th he had sent an armed body to capture the Lieutenant Governor, that he had waited fifteen years and at last his opportunity had arrived.

The witness Tompkins tells you that, being arrested on the 19th of April, he heard the prisoner at the bar address his followers in these words: "What is Carlton; what is Prince Albert? March on my brave army!"

We find on the 21st he took the most deliberate step which could be taken, not in words but in writing. This which I have in my hand is a document in the prisoner's own handwriting. On the 21st he addresses Major Crozier, then commandant of the Mounted Police at Carlton, this summons: "The councillors of the provisional government of the Saskatchewan have the honor to communicate to you the following conditions of surrender: You will be required to give up completely the situation which the Canadian Government have placed you in at Carlton and Battleford, together with all Government properties. In case of non-acceptance we intend to attack you when to-morrow, the Lord's Day, is over, and to commence without delay a war of extermination upon all those who have shown themselves hostile to our rights."

Can you fancy anything more deliberate, or more prepared, anything carried out with more plain intention and preparation?

Nor was it a rebellion started out of mistaken motives, as Fitzpatrick had urged the jury to consider. No, Robinson stated, it was a rebellion actuated by Riel for selfish motives.

> You have heard the evidence of Astley, who tells you that at the battle of Batoche the prisoner wanted him to go and see the general and contrive some means by which he could be introduced to him, that he might then explain to him that he was the founder of this new religion, and that the councillors were responsible for the war, and he said to Astley, "you know I have never borne arms." Astley points to the contrary, that he had borne arms. Now, if he did say that, was that the act of an honest man, a brave man, or a true man? Was it right in him as an honest and a brave man to get it represented not that he but his followers were responsible for the rebellion, and that his share in the business was religious only? You have further the evidence of Astley, who tells you that in his conversation with the prisoner at Batoche the principal thing in the prisoner's mind seemed to be his own grievances. Jackson tells you the same story, and Nolin confirms it and so does Father André.

Fitzpatrick had said that throughout the entire series of events, Riel had shown no desire to shed blood. Not so, Robinson, pointed out.

> His treatment of McKay, does that bear out this assertion or not? McKay went with great self risk, and incurred great danger, to the enemy's camp, among a band of armed men, saying that he did not come as a spy, but as one of Her Majesty's soldiers, and he came to warn them against their criminal measures....
> Gentlemen, what do we find with regard to the treatment of Mr. McKay? He was tried for his life

because he had attempted to teach reason and sense to his fellow half-breeds. We find the prisoner at the bar brought the charge against him, and said it was his blood they wanted, and McKay having spoken for himself that Champagne got up and said: "We want no blood here: we want only our rights," and the prisoner then left the room and went away.

Fitzpatrick had said that there was no real proof that Riel had attempted to incite the Indigenous Peoples to rebellion. Robinson quickly disposed of that argument.

Gentlemen, is there any foundation for that statement of my learned friend that there is no proof that the documents we find in his handwriting were ever made use of?

Do you think, gentlemen, that men at a time of that sort would write out statements which they do not entertain? Do you think they put in writing and sign with their own names plans which they don't intend to carry out, or do you think that these words which I find in that document, No. 112, in the handwriting of the prisoner, signed by himself, and in which I find these expressions, are without intent:

"Take all the ammunition you can in whatever store they may be; murmur, growl and threaten; raise up the Indians; do all you can to put the police in an impossible position."

Do you think the letters to Poundmaker, found in his camp, which it is shown was sent to him by a half-breed, in Riel's own handwriting, telling him of the victory over the police at Duck Lake, and thanking God for their success: "If it is possible, and you have not yet taken Battleford, destroy it; take all the provisions and come to us; your number is such that you can send us

a detachment of forty or fifty men." Do you think that
that, sent as it was to an Indian chief, was not intended
to raise him to take up arms and go on the warpath and
assist in this rebellion?

Robinson then quickly answered Fitzpatrick's submission that the
Crown should have called Poundmaker to state whether he had received
the letter from Riel inciting him to rebellion. Why did the Crown not
call him? If the Crown had done so, Robinson said, it would have been
in breach of Poundmaker's right to remain silent and would have incriminated him at his own trial.

It was because we did understand fair play, because it
would have been improper to have called Poundmaker
to swear to that, that we did not call him. If we had
attempted to put Poundmaker in the box to prove the
receipt of this document we should have been asking Poundmaker to declare on his oath his own complicity in this rebellion and Poundmaker would have
to say to us "I decline to answer your questions," and
any judge would have said to those who acted for the
Crown, "gentlemen, you had no business to put a man
in that position." ... It was because we respect the law,
because we wanted fair play that we didn't attempt to
call anyone here except the one person who is free from
any charge of complicity in this rebellion, and who was
bound to prove the taking of that letter to Poundmaker.

Robinson, who was now almost at the end of his speech, reminded
the jury of the duty imposed upon Crown counsel.

Now, gentlemen, the Crown in this case has a double
duty to perform. In the first place, to see that the prisoner has had every impartiality and fair play and every

consideration which it was in their power to give him, and which the law afforded him. Let there be no mistake about that. If this fair play has not been granted, if this trial has not been impartial, if we have omitted any part of our duty, all I can say is that the prisoner's life has been in our hands quite as much as in the hands of the learned gentlemen for the defence.

But, gentlemen we have another duty to perform; we have the cause of public justice entrusted to our hands; we have the duty of seeing that the cause of public justice is properly served, that justice is done.

I will leave this case with confidence in your hands.

The Crown asks only what is just, and the Crown believes justice will be done. That is all the public and all the community have ever asked, and to that the public and the community are fully entitled and that they believe they will receive.

CHAPTER 10

The Judge's Charge to the Jury

I t was now time for Judge Richardson to charge the jury. As trial judge, it was his responsibility to provide assistance to the jury in reaching a proper verdict. To do so, he had to review the evidence that had been presented by each side, explain the law of treason, and then fairly and impartially instruct the jury on the defence raised by Riel and his lawyers and the evidence to support it. The judge was also required to tell the jury that although they were the sole judges of the facts, they must accept the law as he had defined it for them. The length and complexity of his charge would depend on the length and complexity of the case.

The judge will tell the jury that he will review with them the evidence that has been heard, but if their recollection of what a witness has said differs, they must rely on their own recollection, and not his. This simple statement is not as straightforward or lacking subtlety of persuasion as it seems. Attached to it is a pernicious practice that has existed since 1166 when Henry II first began to send out circuit judges to try cases with knights or ordinary freemen as a jury — the triers of fact — as opposed to trial by ordeal, trial by compurgation, or trial by battle, all of which were appeals to God to smite the guilty. It permits a judge to express his opinion to the jury about the credibility of each witness who has testified. Its coercive intent was to ensure that persons who posed any threat to the Crown were not permitted to escape the gallows by jurors who might have misgivings about the credibility of the Crown's witnesses or the fairness of the prosecution. In order to protect the King's peace — peace in the realm — the juries were subjected to overbearing directions by the judges to reach a particular verdict — usually one of guilty as charged — under penalty of fine or imprisonment. The practice reached its apogee during the Bloody Assizes, allowing Judge George Jeffreys to bully juries into guilty verdicts against innocent victims after the Monmouth Rebellion. It was not until Bushell's case in 1670 that it was finally established that a jury was allowed to return a verdict without fear of imprisonment or bankruptcy by excessive fines, even if their decision was not one the Crown wanted. Even the Libel Act (also known as the Fox Act) passed by the British Parliament in 1792, which finally authorized juries to return their own verdict in seditious libel prosecutions, was quick to ensure that judges were entitled to express their opinion about evidence. The practice existed in 1885. Unfortunately, it still exists today.

Understandably, a judge will have formed an opinion during the course of the trial as to who should or should not be believed. The right to comment on the credibility of a witness is justified on the absurd assumption that so long as the judge also tells the jury that they are entitled to totally disregard his opinion if they disagree with it and make their own findings of credibility of the witnesses, the jury will exercise their independence and not be influenced by the judge's opinion. What the rule fails to recognize and acknowledge is the important and persuasive role that a judge plays in a trial. Lloyd Paul Stryker, in his biography of Thomas Erskine, the famous 18th-century barrister and later lord chancellor of England, eloquently (and with some exaggeration) described the influential role that a judge sitting with a jury plays in the dynamics of a trial.[1]

Physically elevated above all others in the courtroom, elevated by the aloof dignity of his position, elevated also by the robes of his office, every circumstance is present to impress upon his hearers the picture of the judge's inviolable impartiality. The quiet and measured tone, the calm expression of a placid impassivity, contrasting strangely with the fire of advocacy, all tend to give the man upon the bench an intellectual dominion over juries. He has great power. Here, say the jurors to themselves, is at least one man unswayed by prejudice or passion, unmoved by any motive save that of seeing justice done. Such power entails correlative responsibility. A judge who embraces his high opportunity to force or even influence a verdict in accordance with his own caprice departs from the great role in which he has been cast. His use of his peculiar seat of power for his own ends is treason to his trust. It is nonetheless a violation because he has embraced his opportunity to accomplish that which in good conscience he thinks ought to be done. It is a crime if he is moved by fear of power or quest of popular acclaim.

* * *

For Judge Richardson, his charge to the jury was the highlight of a mediocre legal career. He must have realized that it was unlikely that he would ever have another chance to be at the centre of an important trial. He knew that whatever he told the jury would be subject to minute inspection for errors by a court of appeal if Riel were convicted. Newspapers would be reporting to the curious public every word he said and whether he had been fair to Riel in his charge. But more importantly, he was hoping to become one of the new superior court judges when it came time for the federal government to appoint judges for the North-West Territories. As a judge of the superior court, he would have reached the pinnacle of his legal career. With security of tenure and a pension for life, he could no longer be removed from office for failing to do the bidding of the federal government.

It has been said by some writers that Richardson's conduct of the trial was fair, although none have explained what is meant by "fair." If they meant that he did not interfere in the conduct of the defence and show open hostility to Riel or his lawyers, that comment is true. But the time of judicial bullying had long since passed, and by the mid-19th century, superior court judges had enjoyed security of tenure for over 150 years and were no longer required to toady to the Crown or risk losing their job, although the stipend of magistrates depended upon it. If fairness meant that he was silent during the trial — as he was — silence has never been the *sine qua non* of a fair judge. In a jury trial, the judge has the duty to ensure that there is a proper balance between the Crown and defence, remaining silent but jumping into the fray when either side attempts to improperly influence the jury. Richardson's silence during the trial when the Crown improperly led damaging evidence and his pro-Crown charge to the jury can hardly be considered fair.

Late on Friday afternoon, the thirty-first day of July, 1885, Richardson began delivering his charge by reminding the jury of the importance of the case and the seriousness of the charge of treason. He then told them what treason was in law as defined by the specific charge in the case — "levying war against Her Majesty in her realms in these territories" — and read out the specific section from the statute of Edward III:

> To constitute high treason by levying war, there must be insurrection, there must be force accompanying that insurrection, and it must be for the accomplishment of an object of a general nature. And if all these circumstances are found to concur in any individual case that is brought under investigation, that is quite sufficient to constitute a levying of war.

He reminded them that the burden of proof was upon the Crown and that before they could find Riel guilty, they had to be satisfied conclusively of his guilt.

> Having refreshed your memory as to the evidence which was supplied on the part of the Crown, and which you have heard on the part of the defence, it will be your duty to say whether that has been proved or not. If it has not been proved, if the evidence has not brought it home conclusively to this man, he should be acquitted. If it has been brought home to the prisoner, then another question turns up which you have most seriously to consider, is he answerable?

Richardson explained to the jury that he was going to read his notes of the evidence to them and to make certain observations about the evidence. Although the judge was and still is the master of the law, the jury are the absolute masters of the facts and must be told that. Since Bushell's case in 1670, juries have had the absolute right to reach their own independent conclusion on the evidence. Even so, judges have not quite let go of the right to try to influence the jury in their deliberations. Richardson could not refrain from exercising that right. He told the jury that the first thing they must decide — be satisfied about — was whether there was a rebellion, and then added, "*as I think you must be.*" Then they had to decide whether it was "brought home conclusively ... that the prisoner at the bar was implicated." He had no doubt that it had been and immediately turned to what he thought was the real defence to the case — that Riel was insane at the time. It was his duty to instruct the jury how they were to treat that defence and to explain the evidence introduced by the defence and the prosecution. First, he explained the onus of proof where the defence of insanity was raised:

> If you are satisfied that he was implicated in the acts in which he is said to have been implicated, *he must as*

completely satisfy you that he is not answerable by reason
of unsoundness of mind.

"He must as completely satisfy you that he is not answerable" could
only have one meaning. Richardson was telling the jury that Riel had the
burden of satisfying them *beyond a reasonable doubt* that he was legally
insane at the time of the rebellion. While that explanation of the law was
believed to be correct in 1885, it was eventually recognized by 1912 that
it was wrong and would have entitled Riel to a new trial.

Richardson then spent the rest of the afternoon reading to the
jury his personal notes of what each witness had said when they testified. Unfortunately, they do not appear to have been transcribed by
the court reporter, nor is there any indication of what, if anything,
he said about the testimony of the medical doctors who testified for
and against Riel. He told the jury that what he had put before them
were "any salient points that struck me as important." In that hot,
stuffy, airless August courtroom, the minutes must have seemed like
unendurable hours to the jury as they listened patiently to Richardson
reading in a dry matter-of-fact way what he had written down in his
notebook, what each witness had said. At 6:00 p.m., he adjourned
court for the day.

At 10:00 a.m. the following morning, court resumed and Richardson
reminded the jury that

> in my opening remarks to you yesterday afternoon, I
> explained to you that an important duty devolved upon
> us, one share of it upon myself and the other upon
> yourselves. My part of that duty being to see that you
> recollect the evidence placed before you, *and any salient
> points that struck me as important, and might assist you in
> your deliberation*, are brought to your notice …

Richardson then continued reading his notes of the evidence of each
witness for the rest of the morning. When he had completed, he again

repeated that they were to acquit Riel unless the Crown had satisfied them as to his guilt. Then, for some unexplained reason, he decided to explain the objections that had been raised by the defence at the beginning of the proceedings to the jurisdiction of the court to try Riel, and why he had dismissed those objections. The record doesn't say if the jury was present during the argument, which they should not have been. It was not something that concerned them. It was a legal issue, and, as he pointed out, "With that we have really nothing to do." It was to be decided by him and not by the jury. Finally, Richardson turned to the defence of insanity:

> Then has anything been shown here to relieve him from responsibility? His counsel urged that at the time he committed the acts charged, he was of unsound mind, that he did not know what he was doing, and for that reason he should be acquitted.

As the trial judge, it was his legal responsibility to review the expert evidence of all of the psychiatrists and to explain to the jury how that evidence should be considered by them. However, Richardson failed to do so, and we must ask why? Was it because he did not understand the evidence? Was it because he did not understand the law? Was it because he did not believe insanity should excuse criminal conduct? Or was it because he felt that there was very little merit to this defence? It was probably a combination of all of these things. Certainly, he did not think much of a defence of insanity and made sure to let the jury know it as he rambled on about how this "question of unsoundness of mind has given rise in former years to a very great deal of consideration."

> I heard a case referred to yesterday which resulted in a great scandal in Great Britain. That was not the only case, it was followed some years afterwards by a case involving still greater scandal. The law has been put in such a shape now that when the question was set up,

judges may be able to tell the jury fixedly in words what their duties are in regard to responsibility for crime when insanity is set up as a defence. As to insanity, as you saw yesterday, doctors differ as do lawyers. Month by month I may say, week by week, additions are made to classes of mania, new terms are used, branches which were under the simple category of mania come out with new names. I heard a name given in evidence yesterday that I never heard before, megalomania, but it seems to be accepted as a symptom or as a fixed branch of insanity, but *it is not every man who is pronounced insane by the doctors and who from charity or kindness should be placed under restraint and be put in one of the asylums; it is not I say, every one of them that is to be held free from being called upon to answer for offences he may commit against the criminal law.*

His first comment indicated that he did not understand the M'Naghten rule:

His counsel urged that at the time he committed the acts charged he was of unsound mind, that he did not know what he was doing, and for that reason he should be acquitted.

That was not the M'Naghten rule. The question posed by the rule was not whether the accused was insane but whether at the time of the committing of the act, the accused was labouring under such a defect of reason, from disease of mind, as not to know the nature and quality of the act he was doing; or if he did know it, that he did not know what he was doing was wrong. Whether the two were the same was not the issue. What was important was whether Riel's mental state at the time of the rebellion fell within the rule. Repeating that it resulted "in great scandal" had nothing to do with the case, but was an attack on the law.

His next comment was clearly unnecessary and had nothing to do with the case. It was a suggestion that the insanity defence depended upon which doctor was giving evidence — an attempt at disparaging the expert testimony. Finally, although Richardson was correct that "not every man pronounced insane by the doctors" was necessarily insane under the law, it was a misleading statement unless he also explained what was meant by legal insanity. However, Richardson decided not to do so, or simply did not understand that he was required to do so. As far as he was concerned, Riel could not be insane — lacking in reasoning power — when he was prepared to abandon the Métis' cause if the federal government would give him $35,000. Didn't the fact that both Nolin and Father André had said that Riel wanted $35,000 from the federal government clearly demonstrate that Riel had reasoning power; and, if he had reasoning power, Riel had to be sane even though Dr. Roy and Dr. Clark had given evidence to the contrary? Roy and Clark, who understood the workings of the mind far better than Richardson, had said that Riel was legally insane. Instead of carrying out his legal responsibility of impartially reviewing their medical evidence, Richardson decided to disparage it by simply ignoring it.

> The line is drawn very distinctly, and where the line is drawn, I will tell you shortly. Before doing so, and to assist you in your deliberations, let me draw your attention to some points suggested to my mind by the evidence. You recollect the statements as to the prisoner's appropriating property, and making prisoners of others simply because they, to his idea, opposed him in his movements. It has been suggested by the Crown, in reference to the $35,000, that it tends to show that this was all a scheme of the prisoner's to put money in his own pocket. Be that as it may, one of the witnesses, Nolin, speaks distinctly as to the $35,000, and *on that branch of his evidence we have his corroborated by the priest Father André,* and further by Jackson.

Captain Young and other witnesses had said that Riel had not shown any symptoms of insanity in their conversations. To Richardson, this was indicative of reasoning power, and reasoning power meant that Riel must be sane even though Dr. Roy and Dr. Clark had said reasoning power on matters that did not involve religion did not mean that he was sane. To Richardson, laymen such as Captain Young and the other witnesses were far better judges of whether Riel was insane than the two experts.

> Then you have heard the evidence given by Captain Young as to the conversations he had with the prisoner. Witness after witness gave evidence as to what occurred in March at the time of the commencement of this rebellion. Some of them speak of the prisoner being very irritable when the subject of religion was brought up. It appears, however, that his irritability had passed away when he was coming down with Captain Young, as we do not hear anything of it then. Does this show reasoning power?

Richardson continued to hammer home to the jury over and over again why they should reject the defence of insanity in the case of Riel.

> Then at what date can you fix this insanity as having commenced? The theory of the defence fixes the insanity as having commenced only in March, but threats of what he intended to do began in December. Admitting that the insanity only commenced about the time of the breaking out of the rebellion, what does seem strange to me is that these people who were about him, if they had an insane man in their midst, that some of them had not the charity to go before a magistrate and lay an information setting forth that there was an insane man amongst them, and that a breach of the peace was liable to occur at any moment, and that he should be

taken care of. *I only suggest that to you, not that you are to take it as law, I merely suggest it to you as turning upon the evidence.*

Riel's lawyers had never said that Riel's insanity commenced only in March. Dr. François Roy had said that Riel's condition had existed for some time, at least since he was a patient at Beauport many years before. Dr. Daniel Clark had not said anything about Riel's insanity having commenced in March. Richardson was so convinced that Riel was sane that he was going to ensure that the jury would not allow Riel to escape the gallows. The jury were to hear his reasons why the defence of insanity should not succeed, not the doctors who were far more qualified than he was to judge Riel's mental state.

Having scoffed at the medical evidence of Riel's mental condition by simply ignoring it, Richardson repeated that the onus of proof was upon the defence.

Having made the remarks I have, I am simply called upon to tell you what is legal insanity, insanity in the eye of the law, so far as crime is concerned. The Crown must in all cases, particularly such as this, bring home conclusively the crime charged to the prisoner. If the Crown has done that, on the prisoner rests the responsibility of relieving himself from the consequences of his acts. The law directs me to tell you that every man is presumable to be sane and to possess a sufficient degree of reason to be responsible for his crimes until the contrary is proved to your satisfaction. And that to establish a defence on the ground of insanity, *it must be clearly proved* that at the time he committed the act, the party accused was laboring under such defective reasoning from a diseased mind as not to know the nature and quality of the act he was committing, or that if he did know it, that he did not know that he was doing wrong.

That I propound to you as the law.

Richardson finished his charge by appealing to their responsibilities as citizens of Canada to ensure that crime was punished. But what he failed to tell them as well was that it was a citizen's role to ensure that everyone accused of crime received a fair trial, and that the jury stood between the state and the individual to guarantee that justice be done.

I think I have reduced my remarks within the smallest possible compass. You have been kept close at this case since Tuesday morning, and I cannot conceive that any further remarks would be of any assistance to you. On you rests the responsibility of pronouncing upon the guilt or innocence of the prisoner at the bar. Not only must you think of the man in the dock, but you must think of society at large, you are not called upon to think of the Government at Ottawa simply as a Government, you have to think of the homes and of the people who live in this country, you have to ask yourselves, can such things be permitted? There was one point I intended to have mentioned but which has escaped me. You will bear in mind that the law of the land under which this trial is held was objected to on behalf of the prisoner, and he has a perfect right to object to it, but the law of the land was in existence years before he came into this country three years ago, that Act came into force in 1875, and the law which he is said to have broken has been in existence for centuries, and I think I may fairly say to you that *if a man chooses to come into the country, he shall not say, I will do as I like and no laws can touch me.* A person coming into the country is supposed to know the law, it is his duty. We have the law given to us and we are called upon to administer it. I, under the oath that I have taken, and you, under the oath administered to you on Tuesday morning, are to pass between this man and the Crown.

> If therefore the Crown has not conclusively brought guilt
> home to the prisoner, say so, say that you acquit him sim-
> ply by reason of that.

What Richardson was asking the jury to do was indefensible. He was appealing to the passions of the jury to convict Riel in order to protect their homes and families. Today, such instructions to the jury would be considered reversible error and result in a new trial.

Burdens of proof have always been difficult for a jury to understand. In a criminal case, it is well known that the onus lies upon the Crown to prove the accused's guilt and the standard of proof that the Crown must meet is proof beyond a reasonable doubt. Proof beyond a reasonable doubt does not mean to a standard of absolute certainty. If the standard were absolute certainty, then nobody would ever be convicted. Reasonable doubt simply means that any doubt about the accused's guilt must be based on reason and common sense. In charging the jury, Richardson had never used the words "beyond a reasonable doubt." He had instructed the jury that they had to be "satisfied" that Riel was implicated in the rebellion. On the issue of Riel's sanity or insanity, he had used the same words. The defence had to clearly prove that Riel was insane at the time of his treasonable actions.

> To establish a defence on the ground of insanity, *it must
> be clearly proved* that at the time of committing the act
> the accused was labouring under such a defect of reason
> from disease of the mind as not to know the nature and
> quality of the act he was doing, or if he did know it that
> he did not know he was doing what was wrong.

He stressed again and again that it was up to Riel to clearly prove his insanity.

If you are conclusively convinced that the prisoner was im-plicated, then has anything been shown here to relieve him from responsibility?...

If you are satisfied that he was implicated in the acts in which he is said to have been implicated, he must as completely satisfy you that he is not answerable by reason of unsoundness of mind.

"*It must be clearly proved.*" "*He must as completely satisfy you.*" Was this a correct interpretation of the law? Was there an obligation upon the defence to clearly prove Riel was insane at the time? In the M'Naghten case, the English judges had used the same word. They had said that

the jury ought to be told in all cases that every man is presumed to be sane, and to possess a sufficient degree of reason to be responsible for his crimes, *until the contrary is proved to their satisfaction.*

Under the law "every man is presumed to be sane, and to possess a sufficient degree of reason to be responsible for his crimes." In other words, although the onus was upon the Crown to prove beyond a reasonable doubt that Riel had committed treason and that he intended to do so, the Crown did not have to prove that Riel was also sane at the time that he committed it. The law presumed that everyone was rationally responsible for his own conduct. The onus was upon Riel to prove that he was suffering from a disease of the mind that should excuse him in law for his conduct.

Such a rule, long embedded in the common law of England, was eminently sensible. How could the Crown be expected to prove that Riel was sane? How could the Crown be expected to probe the mind of every person accused of a crime to prove that he or she was capable of understanding the nature or consequences of their action, or if he did, or that if he did know it, that he did not know that he was doing wrong? Any other rule would bring the justice system to a complete halt.

Once the Crown had satisfied that onus of proving that Riel had committed treason, the onus shifted to the accused to prove that he was insane. For the defence to succeed, it had to be "proven" to the "satisfaction" of the jury that the accused was insane. But what did "proven to the satisfaction of the jury" mean? Did it mean proof beyond a reasonable doubt or simply on a balance of probabilities? If it meant balance of probabilities, then all that the defence had to do was to tip the scales in favour of Riel. But if it meant proof beyond a reasonable doubt, it was an impossible burden for the defence to meet. How could an accused ever prove he was legally insane if all the Crown had to do was to call a single doctor to say that in his or her opinion the accused was sane? No matter how many witnesses, expert or otherwise, said the accused was legally insane, a jury could never be satisfied beyond a reasonable doubt of the accused's legal insanity so long as one expert witness said he was legally sane. Richardson had imposed an impossible burden upon Riel's lawyers, which could never have been satisfied.

Judge Richardson interpreted the law to mean "proof beyond a reasonable doubt," not simply "on a balance of probabilities." He had also imposed an additional burden on the defence by telling them that Riel's lawyers had to "clearly" prove Riel's insanity, although the judges in the M'Naghten case had said "*proved to their satisfaction*," not "*clearly proved to their satisfaction*." Although he had charged the jury on what he considered was the law at the time, it turned out later to be a misstatement of the law. Unfortunately, it took another thirty-six years for the Supreme Court of Canada to declare that it was a misstatement: too late to save Riel from the gallows.

On March 11, 1921, the Supreme Court of Canada reversed the conviction of a man for murder after the trial judge had told the jury that they ought to convict the accused unless he was able to establish that he was insane at the time of the murder *beyond a reasonable doubt*. In *Clark v. The King*,[2] the trial judge had instructed the jury that "if you entertain any reasonable doubts as to the sanity of the prisoner at the time he committed the act, why then it is your duty to convict." Clark's conviction was set aside and a new trial was ordered. The Supreme Court judges asked themselves, "how can a man rightly be adjudged guilty of a crime if upon all of the evidence there is a reasonable doubt whether he was capable in law of committing crime." The onus of proof upon the defence, the court said, had to be proof on a balance of probabilities and not proof beyond a reasonable doubt.

Unfortunately for Riel, the distinction between the two burdens of proof was fatal to his defence. It was also compounded by Richardson's imposing the additional burden of having to *clearly* prove his insanity to the jury's satisfaction. Two doctors called by the defence had said that he was insane at the time; and two called by the Crown had said he was not. In order for the jury to be *clearly* satisfied beyond a reasonable doubt that Riel was insane, they would have had to completely reject the evidence of the two Crown doctors. They would also have had to reject all the opinion evidence of all the other non-expert witnesses that Richardson had improperly allowed the Crown to introduce. If the test had been proof on a balance of probabilities — a mere tipping of the scales in his favour as the Supreme Court said it was — they would have only had to prefer the evidence of Riel's doctors to the Crown's doctors, even if ever so slightly.

Although Richardson may be forgiven for instructing the jury that they were to find Riel guilty unless he *proved to their satisfaction* that he was insane, as the law stated at the time, he cannot be forgiven for adding the word "clearly." To succeed on this charge, the jury would have had to be satisfied that the evidence of Dr. François Roy and Dr. Daniel Clark was so far superior to that of the Crown's doctors that it could leave them in no reasonable doubt of Riel's insanity. The expectation that a jury of six laymen would be able to ever draw that conclusion was simply an impossible burden for the defence to meet.

CHAPTER 11

The Verdict of the Jury

At 2:15 p.m. on August 1, 1885, the jury retired to consider their verdict. They were not very long. After only an hour, they returned with a verdict, an ominous sign for Riel. The clerk of the court rose to address them.

> Q: Gentlemen are you agreed upon your verdict? How say you, is the prisoner guilty or not guilty.
> A: Guilty.
> Q: Gentlemen of the jury, hearken to your verdict as the court records it, "You find the prisoner, Louis Riel, guilty, so say you all."
> A: Guilty.

Technically the foreman should have been asked to give a verdict with respect to each count in the indictment. After all, Riel was facing six charges, and each required a separate and distinct verdict. The proper procedure did not seem to matter to Judge Richardson. All of the charges amounted to a verdict of treason and there was only one sentence that he could pass.

The jury obviously had some difficulty reaching a common consensus because Francis Cosgrove, the foreman, had one more thing to say:

> Your Honors, I have been asked by my brother jurors
> to recommend the prisoner to the mercy of the Crown.

The jury must have realized that a guilty verdict could only result in a sentence of death. By adding their recommendation "to the mercy of the Crown" to the verdict, they must have believed that the sentence of death that usually followed a conviction for treason would be commuted by the government to a sentence of life imprisonment. If there were only one sentence for treason, then the unanimous recommendation of clemency must have been made because the jurors were reluctant to send the prisoner to his death. As far as all were concerned, they did not believe he should suffer the ultimate penalty. Was it because they had some doubts about whether Riel was legally insane at the time and Richardson's instructions left them with no room for an insanity verdict? Had there been any suggestion made during the course of the trial that a verdict of guilty with a recommendation of mercy would automatically result in commutation of the death sentence? There was nothing in the record of the proceedings to suggest that the judge or the prosecutors had made such an offer. If the jurors were reluctant to send him to his death, could it have been that some of the jurors felt that he might be legally insane but were not brave enough to hold out for such a verdict? Or was it simply that they felt that the government had brought on the rebellion itself by the way that the Métis had been treated? What is clear is that all six jurors believed that he should spend the rest of his life in prison rather than be executed. If the law had permitted the jury to impose the sentence, or at least recommend whether the prisoner should live or die, there is little doubt that they would have voted unanimously for life imprisonment.

History can never record what went on in the jury room. What were the six men thinking when they made a unanimous recommendation of mercy? How the members of the jury deliberated and voted has been subject to absolute secrecy since the 17th century when judges were no

Members of Riel's jury.

longer allowed to meddle in the deliberations of the jury. After a long struggle with the Crown, jurors finally achieved their independence from judges who attempted to coerce a jury to reach a particular desired verdict. Without secrecy, free and frank discussions among jurors would never take place. Not even today can a judge force a juror to reveal what happened in the jury room unless an investigation is conducted into jury tampering or jury misbehaviour. Secrecy also insulates the jury from losing litigants' attempting to overturn their verdict by questioning jurors after the trial to find out whether there was some basis to overturn it.

What the jury did not know is that the government was not required to comply with their recommendation of mercy. Until 1905, when Britain finally created a Court of Criminal Appeal, it had been the practice of the British government to give a recommendation of mercy by the jury serious consideration to ensure that no innocent or insane accused might be wrongfully executed. Was the jury influenced by the British practice or had they been misinformed somehow? If the jury had known that the government would not honour their recommendation, would their verdict have been "not guilty by reason of insanity"? The secrecy rule meant that no one could ever find out what was behind their recommendation. Judge Richardson responded with the customary answer to such recommendations:

I may say in answer to you that the recommendation which you have given will be forwarded in proper manner to the proper authorities.

Richardson then asked Riel the usual question put to a convicted person before sentencing — whether he had anything to say before sentence was passed upon him. Riel said that he did and then went on to address the court again for three hours, attempting to justify his life of revolution. After he had spoken, Judge Richardson proceeded to pass the only sentence allowed to him under the law:

Louis Riel, after a long consideration of your case, in which you were defended with as great ability as I think counsel could have defended you with, you have been found by a jury who have shown, I might almost say, unexampled patience, guilty of a crime the most pernicious and greatest that man can commit. You have been found guilty of high treason. You have been proved to have let loose the flood-gates of rapine and bloodshed, you have, with such assistance as you had in the Saskatchewan country, managed to arouse the Indians and have brought ruin and misery to many families whom if you had simply left alone were in comfort, and many of them were on the road to affluence.

For what you did, the remarks you have made form no excuse whatever. For what you have done the law requires to you answer. It is true that the jury in merciful consideration have asked Her Majesty to give your case such merciful consideration as she can bestow upon it. I had almost forgotten that those who are defending you have placed in my hands a notice that the objection which they raised at the opening of the court must not be forgotten from the record, in order that if they see fit they may raise the question in the proper place. That has been done. But in spite of that, I cannot hold out any hope to you that you will succeed in getting entirely free, or that Her Majesty will, after what you have been the cause of doing, open her hand of clemency to you.

For me, I have only one more duty to perform, that is, to tell you what the sentence of the law is upon you. I have, as I must, given time to enable your case to be heard. All I can suggest or advise you is to prepare to meet your end, that is all the advice or suggestion I can offer. It is now my painful duty to pass the sentence of the court upon you, and that is, that you be taken from here to the police guard-room at Regina, which is the gaol and the place from whence you came, and that you be kept there till the 18th of September next, that on the 18th of September next you be taken to the place appointed for your execution, and there be hanged by the neck till you are dead, and may God have mercy on your soul.

CHAPTER 12

The Appeals

R iel was not hanged on September 18 as ordered by Judge Richardson. His lawyers had filed an appeal of the verdict, and a reprieve was automatically granted while his appeal was being heard. Normally, an appeal would be heard by the court of appeal of the province (or the territory) where the trial had been held. In the late 19th century, the court of appeal of a province usually consisted of three judges of the superior court of the province called the Court of Queen's Bench (or King's Bench, depending upon the gender of the British monarch) who were chosen by the chief justice of that province to hear the appeal. The chief justice presided over the appeal, particularly if the case was an important one. However, the Parliament of Canada had not exercised its powers under section 96 of the British North America Act to create a superior court for the North-West Territories when it had passed the North-West Territories Act of 1880. It had transferred the authority to hear appeals from the trial courts of the North-West Territories to the superior court of its neighbour, the Manitoba Queen's Bench, but only where the death penalty had been imposed. Moreover, the appeal court only had the authority to confirm the conviction, or to order a new trial. It had no power, as provincial courts of appeal have today, of setting aside the conviction, acquitting Riel, and sending him to a mental institution, probably for life, if the appeal judges were convinced that he was insane at the time that the offence was committed.

Riel's lawyers had originally wanted him to be tried in Manitoba because an accused in that province was entitled to have a judge of the Queen's Bench sitting with a mixed jury of twelve English- and French-speaking jurors, but he had been denied that right. Now a panel of judges of the Manitoba Court of Queen's Bench was about to hear his appeal. His lawyers were not so sure this was necessarily a good thing, and their concerns had merit.

At the time, there were four members of the Manitoba Court of Queen's Bench. One of the judges, Joseph Dubuc, had been a friend of Riel years before. He decided, quite properly, that he should absent himself from the court by conveniently attending an alumni reunion at the Collège de Montréal. The appeal was argued before the remaining three judges: Chief Justice Lewis Wallbridge, Mr. Justice Thomas Wardlaw Taylor, and Mr. Justice Albert Clements Killam.

Chief Justice Wallbridge was born in Belleville, Ontario, and had been called to the bar of Ontario in 1839. After practising in Bellville for nineteen years, he was elected to the Legislative Assembly of Canada in 1858 and appointed solicitor general for Canada West in 1863. In 1882, he was appointed chief justice of Manitoba at the age of sixty-six. Mr. Justice Taylor was born in Scotland and called to the bar of Ontario in 1858. He was appointed to the Manitoba Court of Queen's Bench in 1883 at the age of fifty and succeeded Wallbridge as chief justice in 1887 on Wallbridge's death. Mr. Justice Killam was born in Nova Scotia and was called to the Ontario bar in 1877. He practised law in Windsor until 1879 when he moved to Winnipeg. In 1883, he was elected to the House of Commons as a Liberal member for Winnipeg South, but sat for only two years until he was appointed to the Manitoba Queen's Bench on February 3, 1885. He eventually succeeded Taylor as chief justice upon Taylor's death in 1899. On August 8, 1903, he was appointed to the Supreme Court of Canada but left that appointment fifteen months later to become Chief Commissioner of the Board of Railway Commissioners.

John Skirving Ewart, Q.C., a leading barrister in Winnipeg, had been retained by the defence to present the appeal on behalf of Riel. He was assisted by Riel's trial counsel, François-Xavier Lemieux and Charles Fitzpatrick. Christopher Robinson, Q.C., and Britton Bath Osler, Q.C., were again retained by the federal government to respond to the appeal. A third counsel, J.A.M. Aikins, Q.C., a leading barrister in Manitoba, was also retained by the Crown to assist Robinson and Osler.

Although the prime minister had ordered Riel to be tried in Regina, Robinson and Osler had been concerned that a treason trial proceeding before a magistrate with a six-member jury in Regina was illegal. English common law required a person accused of treason to be tried by a judge of the superior court presiding over a jury of twelve members of the community. The only tribunal set up to try criminal cases under the North-West Territories Act of 1880 was a "Magistrate with a Justice of the Peace and a jury of six." If Riel were sent to Manitoba, he could be tried by a judge of the Manitoba Court of Queen's Bench, a superior court, with a jury of twelve. However, Riel was still a hero in Manitoba and the prime minister was concerned that it might be difficult to get a conviction. Sir Alexander Campbell, the federal justice minister, had received a letter from Chief Justice Wallbridge advising that a trial in Winnipeg might create some difficulty because "the jury in Winnipeg would be composed of twelve, of whom the prisoner might insist that a moiety be half-breeds." In Regina, Riel would not be entitled to a mixed jury. It would have to be all white men and only six of them.

One way of getting around the problem was for Parliament to appoint a special commission, presided over by a superior court judge with a jury, a procedure well known to English law, to conduct the trial. Another problem was the grand jury. English common law required the Crown to present a bill of indictment before a grand jury made up of twelve local citizens who had the absolute authority to decide whether a British subject should be forced to stand trial at all. The grand jury institution traced its origin to the Assize of Clarendon in 1164 and was older than trial by jury, which had been introduced in 1215 by Henry II after trial by ordeal had been abolished. All of the other provinces had introduced the grand jury institution into their justice system. No one could be indicted under British law and tried for treason unless the grand jury consented. But the North-West Territories Act of 1880 was silent on whether a grand jury was required to give its consent to a criminal prosecution. Robinson and Osler were concerned that if they bypassed a grand jury and went directly to a Regina magistrate, there was the risk that a conviction might be overturned by a court of appeal. Neither lawyer was prepared to take responsibility for such a procedural disaster that might hurt their reputation.

Sir John A. Macdonald had been adamant that Riel was to be tried by Magistrate Richardson in Regina. This meant that a court of appeal had to first decide whether the consent of a grand jury was necessary. At the time, there was a case pending before the Manitoba Court of Appeal that involved this very question, *R. v. Connor.*[1] John Connor had been tried in Regina for murder three months earlier by a court composed of Magistrate Richardson and two justices of the peace with a six-man jury. He had been convicted and sentenced to death. His lawyers — J.S. Ewart, Q.C., and T.C. Johnstone, later on Riel's legal team — had appealed to the Manitoba Court of Appeal, arguing that Connor's trial was illegal because the Crown had not presented an indictment to a grand jury and obtained their consent to prosecute. Osler had been retained by the Crown so that he could argue the case before Chief Justice Wallbridge, who would be presiding with his colleagues, Mr. Justice Taylor and Mr. Justice Dubuc. If the court declared that it had not been necessary to obtain the consent of a grand jury to prosecute John Connor, the Crown could proceed to prosecute Riel in Regina without a grand jury's consent.

Ewart's submission on behalf of Connor was simple and straightforward. At common law, no one could be tried for an indictable offence unless the Crown presented a bill of indictment to a grand jury of twelve members of the community that set out the specific accusation against the accused and obtained their consent to prosecute. It was a screening device by members of the community for prosecutions lacking evidence; there was no appeal from their decision. If they decided that there was sufficient evidence to put an accused on trial they would write "true bill" on the indictment. If they were not satisfied, they would write "no bill" on the indictment, which meant the Crown had no authority to proceed with the trial. The consent of a grand jury to a criminal prosecution was a fundamental right of every British subject unless *specifically* denied by law. The North-West Territories Act of 1880 had not specifically denied an accused the right to have his prosecution first approved by a grand jury. The act was simply silent on the issue.

Led by Chief Justice Wallbridge, the court quickly dismissed the argument that it was necessary for a grand jury to decide whether an accused should be put on trial. The North-West Territories Act had never established a grand jury institution to screen prosecutions.

> British subjects going to an uninhabited country are said to take the Common law with them. *Although the grand jury may exist at common law, it is an institution, and not the law itself.* I can find it nowhere laid down, that this institution more than any other institution existing from time memorial accompanies the subject, but I find it laid down that such colonists carry with them only so much of the English law that is applicable to their own situation and the condition of the infant colony, which slate is applicable to the present position of the North West Territories, or at least they have been so treated by the Parliament of Canada.

What the judges were saying was that although British subjects took the common law with them wherever they settled new territory, the grand jury institution — the right at common law to have all charges screened by a grand jury — was not one of the fundamental rights enjoyed by British subjects at common law. It was merely an institution that could be dispensed with if it was not "applicable to their own situation and the condition of the infant colony." There was no need to *specifically* abolish it. If Parliament had not established a grand jury in any province or territory, that was enough. It was not necessary to submit an indictment to them for their approval before a prosecution could proceed.[2]

Could such logic also be extended to trial by jury? If Parliament had not established trial by jury in the North-West Territories, did that mean that trial by jury did not exist? The problem with that reasoning was that both the grand jury and trial by jury — born in 11th- and 12th-century England — had developed together and been nourished by the common law. They were an integral part of the criminal law process. If the grand jury was merely an institution and not a fundamental right, the same could be said of trial by jury. If trial by jury was not applicable to the situation and the condition of the inhabitants of the North-West Territories, it would mean that the inhabitants would not have been entitled to trial by jury if Parliament had remained silent and not introduced it.[3]

The Manitoba Court of Appeal had spoken and there was no longer any impediment to proceeding with Riel's trial before Magistrate Richardson without the consent of a grand jury. The suggestion that there should be a special commission to try Riel was quickly buried. The theme that the Parliament of Canada was supreme in passing (or not passing) laws affecting the North-West Territories would later come up again in Riel's trial and haunt his lawyers.

Riel's lawyers' main argument before the Manitoba Court of Appeal was that the overwhelming weight of psychiatric evidence showed that he was insane at the time of the rebellion. However, Chief Justice Wallbridge was not impressed with the medical evidence. As far as he was concerned, the jury could not reasonably have come to any other conclusion than Riel was legally sane.

> Taking the definitions of this disease, as given by the experts, and how does his conduct comport therewith. The maniac imagines his delusions real, they are fixed and determinate, the bare contradiction cause irritability.

Father André's evidence of Riel's claim of compensation from the Canadian government for $35,000 and his response, "If I am satisfied with that, the half-breeds will be," came back again to haunt the defence. How could the defence say that Riel did not know the nature and quality of his actions, or, if he did know, that what he was doing was wrong, if he was prepared to leave Canada and the Métis cause for $35,000, the chief justice asked.

> He was willing and quite capable of departing with this supposed delusion, if he got the $35,000. A delusion must be fixed, acted upon, and believed in as real, overcome and dominate in the mind of the insane person. An insanity that can be put on and off at the will of the insane person, according to the medical testimony, is not insanity at all, in the sense of mania.

Mr. Justice Killam was also contemptuous of the claim that Riel was insane at the time of the rebellion, but not because Riel was really looking for compensation from the government for past grievances. He could not understand how someone who believes that the laws of God justify his actions could be said to be insane:

> A man who leads an armed insurrection does so from a desire for murder, rapine, robbery, or for personal gain or advantage of some kind, or does so in the belief that he has a righteous cause, grievances which he is entitled to take up arms to have redressed. In the latter case, if sincere, he believes it to be right to do so, that the laws of God permit, nay even calls upon him, to do so; and to adjudge a man insane on that ground, would be to open the door to an acquittal in every case in which a man with an honest belief in his wrongs, and that they were sufficiently grievous to warrant any means to secure their redress, should take up arms against the constituted authority of

the land. His action was exceedingly rash and foolhardy, but he reasoned that he could achieve a sufficient success to extort something from the Government, whether for himself or his followers. His actions were based on reason and not insane delusion.

Mr. Justice Taylor was less critical of the psychiatric evidence but found it impossible, on the evidence, to come to any other conclusion than that reached by the jury.

> The appellant is, beyond all doubt, a man of inordinate vanity, excitable, irritable, and impatient contradiction. He seems to have at times acted in an extraordinary manner; to have said many strange things, and to have entertained, or at least professed to entertain, absurd views on religious and political subjects. But it all stops short of establishing such unsoundness of mind as would render him irresponsible, not accountable for his actions.

When Riel's lawyers found no sympathy for their argument that Riel was insane, they turned to their main argument — that he had not been legally tried in accordance with the laws regarding treason. All of the British statutes, they said, relating to treason starting from the earliest, the statute of Edward III, down to the last in the reign of George III, defined what constituted treason, and provided for the mode in which an accused was to be tried, including the qualification of jurors, their number, and the method of choosing them. These laws, they said, had been in force in the North-West Territories since the time of the first settlers. When the Dominion Parliament passed legislation affecting the people of the North-West Territories, it was only exercising powers that had been delegated to them by the British Parliament. Powers that are delegated, they argued, had to be strictly construed and could not be exercised to deprive the people of the rights and protection that had been secured to them as British subjects by Magna Carta, or to alter in any way the treason statutes to their prejudice.

Again, the court was not sympathetic. Parliament was supreme and could do whatever it wanted. This was 1885 and Canada had no Charter of Rights entrenching fundamental rights in a constitution that could not be changed willy-nilly by Parliament. Parliament then, representing the will of the people, could change the law whenever it pleased. Mr. Justice Taylor answered the argument thus:

> That these rights and privileges, wrested by the people from tyrannical sovereigns many centuries ago, were and are valuable, there can be no question. Were the sovereign at present day endeavouring to deprive the people of any of these, for the purposes of oppression, it would speedily be found that the love of liberty is as strong in the hearts of British subjects today as it was in the hearts of their forefathers, and they would do their utmost to uphold and defend rights and privileges purchased by the blood of their ancestors. But it is a very different thing when the legislature, composed of the representatives of the people, chosen by them to express their will, deem it expedient to make a change in the law, even though the change may be the surrender of some of these old rights and privileges.

When it was pointed out to him that the people of the North-West Territories were not represented in Parliament to cast a vote either against or for the legislation that had deprived them of the fundamental rights that citizens should have, Taylor was still not impressed. It didn't matter that the people of the North-West Territories did not have a voice in electing members of Parliament to speak for them in the House and to vote on the laws that affected them. They were still represented by Parliament even if they had not been given the right to vote for their own representatives. Although laws to provide a legislative structure for the territories must "precede their being directly represented there," this did not answer the question why Parliament found it necessary to deny the people of the territories the fundamental right of trial by a jury of twelve citizens of the community, particularly in a treason trial, presided over by a judge of the superior court, a right enjoyed by the citizens of neighbouring provinces. If the citizens of the North-West Territories were to have their common law rights as British subjects taken away from them, surely they should have been allowed to elect representatives to Parliament to vote on the issue. Taylor did not seem to understand this distinction.

The real answer of course, which the court was not prepared to admit, was expediency. It would have been difficult, and probably very expensive, to assemble the usual panel of fifty to a hundred members of the community from which a jury of twelve could be chosen. In fact, the provision for a six-member jury instead of the usual twelve was to remain in Saskatchewan, Alberta, and in the Northwest and Yukon Territories for almost another one hundred years, being ruled unconstitutional only after the Charter of Rights and Freedoms was passed in April 1982.

Riel's lawyers then referred to American cases where the courts had said that the legislature was not supreme, that the sovereign power is vested in the people, and that the legislature has only a limited portion of that sovereign power, which the people had specifically delegated to it. Those common law rights that had not been delegated to the legislature were still retained by the people, they argued. Not so, said Taylor. In Canada, the sovereign power was vested in the Dominion Parliament, not the people, "though it cannot do anything beyond the limits which circumscribe these powers."

In desperation, Riel's lawyers raised a technical argument attacking the validity of the trial itself. Section 76(7) of the North-West Territories Act of 1880, they said, required Richardson to take down in writing full notes of the evidence and other proceedings, and he had not done so. Under the section, the "Stipendary Magistrate shall, upon every such trial, take or cause to be taken, in writing full notes of the evidence and other proceedings thereat." The section had been passed to ensure that there was an accurate record of all of the proceedings in the event of an appeal or if the federal government was asked to consider clemency.

Richardson had not personally taken down full notes of the evidence and the proceedings. His shorthand reporter had done so and probably more accurately than he could have done. The court had little patience with this argument. The section did not require Richardson personally to take the notes, the judges said. He only had to "cause (the notes) to be taken" and had caused them to be done by directing the reporter to do so.

Based on the evidence presented at trial, it was doubtful whether the Manitoba Court of Appeal could have come to any other conclusion. If there was to be any criticism of the court, it had to be levelled at Chief Justice Wallbridge. His involvement in steering Riel's trial before Magistrate Richardson and then sitting on the appeal of his conviction was a sad day for the administration of justice of Canada. Less than fifty years later, Lord Hewart, chief justice of England, had to remind judges that they must never involve themselves in the affairs of government. In 1924 in the *Sussex Justices* case, he pronounced his now famous statement,

> It is of fundamental importance that justice should not only be done but should manifestly and undoubtedly be seen to be done.

* * *

The dismissal of Riel's appeal by the Manitoba Court of Appeal was not the last chance to save his life. He had the right to apply for leave to appeal his conviction to the Supreme Court of Canada. If unsuccessful, there was still the chance that the Judicial Committee of the Privy Council in London, the final court of appeal from the colonies, might grant leave to hear his appeal. Riel's lawyers decided to bypass the Supreme Court and go directly to London and seek leave to appeal from the Judicial Committee. The federal government would now have to grant Riel another reprieve from execution of his death sentence to allow his lawyers to prepare their case and take a boat to England. The trip, in those days, could take a couple of weeks. A reprieve was granted initially to October 16 and then to November 10.

On October 21, Riel's lawyers began their appeal. Bingham, Q.C., a British barrister, had been retained to argue the appeal because one of the lawyers had to be a member of the British bar, and Fitzpatrick appeared with him. The government of Canada was represented by no less than the attorney general of England, Sir Richard Webster, Q.C., and two junior counsel. Sitting on the Judicial Committee were six Law Lords, the chancellor being Lord Halsbury, whose name had been lent to well-known legal texts on the laws of England.

No attempt was made to argue that Riel was justified in launching a rebellion or that he was insane at the time. The main argument had to be to the jurisdiction of Richardson, a magistrate, to try Riel for treason. There were also procedural arguments, such as the fact that no indictment had been preferred before a grand jury, there was no coroner's inquisition, and the evidence was not taken down in writing by the judge as required by section 76(7).

Lord Halsbury, who delivered the decision of the Judicial Committee, did not even consider that the arguments merited calling upon Sir Richard Webster to respond, and leave to appeal was summarily refused. He pointed out that it was the usual rule of the committee not to grant leave in criminal cases, except where some clear departure from the requirements of justice had taken place.

There were only two arguments "capable of plausible or, indeed, intelligible expression," in other words, worthy of comment.

The suggestion that any laws passed by Parliament respecting the procedure in criminal matters that conflicted with British law were ultra vires (beyond the law) and beyond the competence of the Canadian Parliament to enact without merit, because similar laws had been authorized under the criminal procedure of India and

> forms of procedure unknown to the English common law have there been established and acted upon, and to throw the least doubt upon the validity of powers conveyed by those words would be of widely mischievous consequence.

In other words, British subjects living in the colonies were not entitled to the same legal rights as those living in Great Britain or in other provinces of Canada.

The second argument, that section 76(7) of the North-West Territories Act required the magistrate to "take *or cause to be taken* in writing full notes of the evidence" *himself,* was also summarily dismissed. Richardson had not taken the notes himself but had a shorthand reporter do it for him. The statute had been literally complied with. Richardson had *caused* the notes to be taken when he directed the shorthand reporter to take them. There was no requirement that he do so personally.

> Their Lordships will, therefore, humbly advise Her Majesty that leave should not be granted to prosecute this appeal.

The Judicial Committee's decision was Riel's last judicial avenue to save his life. It would now be up to Prime Minister Macdonald and his cabinet to decide whether or not Riel would hang.

CHAPTER 13

The Medical Commission

S ir John A. Macdonald was obviously disturbed by the jury's recommendation of mercy. Did they have some concern about Riel's
sanity? Had there been some offer or suggestion to the jury that a
recommendation of mercy would be automatically acted upon by the
federal government? If Riel was indeed insane, it would be inhumane to
hang him. Riel was not simply a common criminal. He was a founder of
the province of Manitoba, a leader of the Métis of the Canadian prairies,
and, more importantly, a symbol of the Métis aspirations in the west.
If it turned out later that he was, in fact, insane, hanging Riel would
split the country. Pressure had been mounting on the cabinet for three
months to set up a commission to look into the matter. There had been
petitions from Quebec demanding clemency and petitions from Ontario
demanding that the sentence of death be carried out. Macdonald's government was in a dilemma. If it commuted Riel's sentence of death,
Orange Ontario would in an uproar, because they were demanding his
execution as the punishment for his execution of Thomas Scott in 1870.
If the government simply let justice take its course and did not interfere,
Quebec would be up in arms.

The prime minister was also faced with the possibility that his
Quebec supporters might defect if Riel were executed. The French

Canadian members of his cabinet, particularly J.A. Chapleau and Hector Langevin, had to be placated somehow. A solution appeared when François Lemieux submitted a petition to have Riel's mental state further examined. Macdonald decided to appoint a commission to conduct a medical inquiry into Riel's present sanity. If he were insane now, regardless of his mental condition at the time of the rebellion, it would be inhumane to hang him. A finding by a medical commission that Riel was insane would give Macdonald an excuse to exercise the royal prerogative of mercy and placate Quebec and, hopefully, Ontario. If the commission concluded that Riel was sane, then he could let the law take its course.

On October 31, 1885, Macdonald appointed two medical men to examine Riel. Dr. Michael Lavell, who had been appointed warden of Kingston Penitentiary in 1885, was suggested to him. Lavell, a devout Methodist and staunch Conservative, had been professor of obstetrics at Queen's University and the first dean of the Women's Medical College in Kingston. He would easily satisfy Orange Ontario. But if Quebec were to be appeased, Lavell would have to be balanced by a French Canadian. Thirty-eight-year-old Dr. François-Xavier Valade, who had been born in Montreal but had set up a medical practice in Ottawa, was chosen to fill that role. Valade had been appointed the previous year as public analyst for the Department of Inland Revenue to test food samples for adulteration. However, neither Lavell nor Valade had any special expertise in insanity. Moreover, Macdonald had written letters of instruction to each of them to the effect that they were to determine whether Riel was capable of telling the difference between right and wrong — the M'Naghten test — not whether he was medically insane.

In his formal letters to the two doctors, the prime minister made his intentions quite clear:[1]

> I need scarcely point out to you that the Enquiry is not whether Riel is subject to illusions or delusions, but whether he is so bereft of his reason as not to know right from wrong and is not an accountable being.

In a private letter to Dr. Lavell, the prime minister made his intentions clearer and more explicit. Lavell was directed to speak with the men who had testified as to Riel's sanity at his trial and to consult with Dr. Augustus Jukes. Macdonald also stressed that

> a man may have his mind so unhinged as to warrant
> two medical men to certify his insanity so as to send
> him to an asylum for curative purposes and yet be open
> to the penalties of the law for a breach of such law.[2]

Lavell and Valade immediately left for Regina by separate trains and checked into their hotels under assumed names. On November 7, they spoke with those who had been in charge of Riel over the previous four months — NWMP officers; Father André, his spiritual director; and Dr. Jukes, who was also asked to submit an opinion. A day earlier, Jukes had written a ten-page report to Macdonald in which he indicated that although Riel was holding unusual views and was subject to hallucinations, he was legally accountable for his actions.[3]

> I cannot escape the conviction, that except upon certain
> questions of a purely religious and private nature, hav-
> ing relation to what may be called Divine mysteries, he
> is perfectly sane and accountable for his actions.
>
> That Riel differs systematically from the large ma-
> jority of mankind in the views he entertains respecting
> certain questions relating to religious subjects or rather
> to certain spiritual phenomena such as inspiration, and
> prophetic vision in relation thereto, must be admitted.
> On these subjects he cherishes illusions or hallucinations
> which vary materially in intensity under varying physical
> and mental conditions; but diversities of opinion and be-
> lief upon these and kindred subjects do not properly con-
> stitute insanity, nor do they ... interfere with or obscure
> in the slightest degree a clear perception of duty, or the

difference between moral right and wrong ... or render his judgment less sound in the affairs of every-day life.

Both alone and together, Lavell and Valade spoke with Riel without revealing their identities, telling him that they were travellers who wished to make his acquaintance. They met the next day to try to thrash out their report. Lavell wrote that Valade was at first strong for reporting Riel as of insane mind on account of his foolish expressions.[4]

> I contested this with him until the last moment, pointed out as strongly as I could the defects in his conclusions, and even got admission that even in his delusions he was not really insane. But I am morally certain he [Valade] was too much in the company of Pére André, and to some extent influenced. He said he could not give a report that would be decidedly adverse.

On November 8, 1885, the two doctors wrote out separate short statements for Lieutenant Governor Dewdney, who immediately telegraphed them to the prime minister. Lavell reported as follows:[5]

> I have the honour to report that having given conscientious consideration to the case of Louis Riel, now confined under sentence of death, and fully appreciating the trust committed to me, and the consequences involved, I am of opinion that the said Louis Riel, although holding and expressing foolish and peculiar views concerning visions as to religion and general government, is an accountable being and knows right from wrong.

Dr. Valade's original report read:[6]

> After having examined carefully Riel in private conversation with him and by testimony of persons who take

care of him, *I have come to the conclusion that he is not an accountable being, that he is unable to distinguish between right and wrong on political and religious subjects which I consider well marked typical forms of a kind of insanity under which he undoubtedly suffers,* but on other points I believe him to be quite sensible and can distinguish right from wrong.

However, Valade's original report was later edited so that his official report omitted that Riel was "not an accountable being." It now read:[7]

> Sir, after having examined Riel carefully in private conversation with him and by the testimony of persons who took care of him, I have come to the conclusion that he suffers under an hallucination on political and religious subjects, but on other points I believe him to be quite sensible and able to distinguish right from wrong.

Dewdney sent a telegram incorporating the text of both opinions, and then immediately mailed the originals to Macdonald together with his own assessment that the difference between the reports was only "a little difficulty about the phraseology between the two doctors," although in fact Lavell and Valade had come to exactly opposite conclusions. In other words, although the two doctors agreed that Riel's mind was strangely divided, and that he was completely normal on all topics except politics and religion, they disagreed on the essential question of whether he was an "accountable being."

Before leaving Regina, Dr. Lavell wrote Macdonald a long letter recounting his experiences, adding at the end, "I will have to meet Dr. Valade at all events, to try to be able to present a joint report." Apparently both men considered their telegraphed reports to be only preliminary statements, and wished to produce a more finished document, with agreement on the wording if possible. Macdonald, however, was content with the telegram he had received from Dewdney giving the opinion of Jukes and the two doctors. Without waiting for their final joint report, he prepared a memo that included the text of his original letters to Lavell and Valade (but not his private instructions to Lavell) and Dewdney's telegrams, which he presented to his cabinet. On November 12, his cabinet, without seeing the original letters of Lavell and Valade, or their considered report, or a letter from Dr. Jukes recommending further study of Riel's writings, voted in favour of going ahead with Riel's execution. It has been suggested that "Macdonald manipulated them to stiffen the resolve of his wavering French ministers."[8]

When the House opened in February 1886, the critics of Riel's execution were ready to press the government for disclosure of the medical reports on his accountability. On March 1, the prime minister was asked if he would lay the reports before the House. Sir John, aware of what was coming, agreed and the documents were tabled on March 9. There was a short excerpt from Dr. Jukes's letter, without his description of Riel's unusual remarks; Dr. Lavell's telegram of November 8; and Dr. Valade's telegram with the missing diagnosis. The opposition members, aware that there were missing documents, pressed for the production of the originals. On March 15, 1886, Sir John Thompson, minister of justice, rose to explain that the cabinet had acted on the original documents that had been sent by Lavell and Valade. The opposition could do nothing in the absence of the missing documents and neither doctor came forward to explain his report. Dr. Valade said nothing further but did write a lengthy memorandum that was later given by his family to the Public Archives of Canada. In it, he wrote:[9]

> We have observed and discovered in the conversation and conduct of the prisoner Riel the evidence of fixed delusions, the expressions of which could by no logical sequence be linked on to ideas previously expressed. It is of no consequence that he manifested lucid intervals, and that he could even talk like a philosopher; nor is it of any importance that taking his fixed delusion as a starting point, he could reason logically in that direction; this would only go to prove that the reasoning faculty was not entirely destroyed.

In conclusion we may state that for the advocates of partial responsibility there exists in the monomaniac two distinct personalities, the one sane, the other insane: now the latter alone is not answerable for his acts, since he has been pushed to commit them by a hallucination, a delirious conception or a delusion. I have stated that Louis Riel was suffering from political-religious hallucinations but on all other matters, he was responsible for his acts, and could distinguish right from wrong. All this means and meant very clearly that in the sphere of the fixed delusions which were constantly occupying his mind and which were the one theme of his writings, speeches, and conversations, he was not fit to perceive the crime of High Treason of which he had been guilty; and that when I examined him he could not in my humble opinion, distinguish between right and wrong on politico-religious questions.

* * *

If they thought that Riel's death was to obliterate his memory from the consciousness of Canadians, Macdonald and his government were seriously mistaken. As Dr. Daniel Clark observed two years after Riel's execution, "A living lunatic in an asylum would have been forgotten but a dead Riel had roused to unwanted activity influences which will not be easily allayed."[10] But Macdonald was determined to hang Riel. He is quoted as saying, "He shall die though every dog in Quebec bark in his favour."[11]

CHAPTER 14

The Aftermath

Although the trial of Louis Riel took place a little over 130 years ago, the guilty verdict and his execution continue to fascinate, anger, and trouble many Canadians today. We continue to ask ourselves — was he really guilty of treason? Was he insane? Was he justified in leading a rebellion because of government indifference to the plight of the Métis and the Indigenous Peoples? Should he have been tried in Winnipeg, where he would have been entitled to a mixed jury of twelve French- and English-speaking members, instead of in Regina with only six English-speaking jurors? Was it the goal of Sir John A. Macdonald's government to rid itself, at any cost, of Riel's presence from the Canadian political scene? Should the government have prosecuted him for felony treason under the act of 1848 instead of the 1352 Statute of Treason and thus prevented the automatic sentence of death if he were found guilty? Should the government have accepted the recommendation of mercy sent by the jury and commuted his sentence to one of life imprisonment? Or should the government have had him committed to an insane asylum? Probably the most disturbing question is whether the government doctored the report of Dr. Valade to read that he found Riel to be sane when in fact he had doubts on that point?

The first question that must be asked is whether Riel had committed acts of treason. Six white Protestant males who made up the jury that tried Riel concluded that he had, and it took them only an hour to reach that conclusion. There was certainly more than enough evidence of treasonable conduct on Riel's part for the jury to return their guilty verdict. Yet it is also important to ask why the jury recommended mercy when they must have known that hanging was the only sentence the judge could impose. Was their recommendation an indication that they had some uncertainty about his sanity, or a reflection that they felt he should not have to pay the ultimate price for defending the Métis cause? We will never know. A jury is not required to give reasons for their decision. A clue to the jury's recommendation may lie in the evidence at the trial.

There can be little doubt of the sufficiency of the evidence presented by the government to establish that Riel's actions during the rebellion amounted to treason. Although, as Riel pointed out in his speech to the jury, the government had ignored petition after petition from the Métis, a resort to arms to remedy even the most egregious injustices was no defence to treason. The usual and customary remedy for government neglect and indifference in a democratic society is an electoral one — to throw out the government of the day at the next election. Here, this was impossible. The federal government had not passed legislation that would allow the people of the northwest to elect members of Parliament to represent them in 1885.

It has been argued that Riel's lawyers should have pleaded that the Métis were only acting in self-defence at Duck Lake and the bloodshed was initiated by the actions of Superintendent Crozier.[1] Others have suggested that the incident at Duck Lake on March 26, 1885, would have never happened if Crozier had not ordered his troops to fire on the Métis. Even so, there was no defence to the confrontations at Fish Creek and Batoche. What these arguments fail to recognize is that the Métis had no business confronting Crozier in the first place. The Métis had already committed acts of treason and the law of self-defence does not allow an aggressor to claim self-defence, unless it is necessary to save his own life. Riel and the Métis had no right to confront Crozier and his men after committing acts of treason and then to claim self-defence because a skirmish occurred. Moreover, even if it could be said that Crozier ordered his soldiers to fire first, his actions amounted to self-defence against the aggression of the Métis. Crozier had every right to fear, after McKay shot Assiyiwan, that the Métis would soon fire on them.[2]

The law of self-defence does not require a person who is or who reasonably believes he is about to be assaulted to weigh to a nicety the exact measure of defensive action he must take; nor is that person expected to stop and reflect upon the risk of deadly consequences that may result from taking justifiable defensive action. Crozier was responsible for the safety of his men. Not to have fired first, considering the confrontational situation in which Crozier found himself and his men, would have exposed his men to unnecessary danger.

It must be remembered that it was not the events at Duck Lake that were Riel's first acts of treason. Eight days earlier, on March 18, Riel and his followers had seized several government offices and had cut the telegraph lines to Prince Albert. The next day, they formed a provisional government and twenty men were named to serve on the governmental council, with Gabriel Dumont as head of the army and Pierre Parenteau, an old Red River settler, as president of the council. Although Riel was not elected to any post on the council, it was not felt necessary, because he was considered to be the acknowledged leader of the movement. Such actions in themselves amounted to treason under the Statute of Treasons of 1352.

Another act of treason was the fact that three days after the formation of a provisional government, Riel had sent a message to Superintendent Crozier demanding that he surrender Fort Carlton, otherwise the Métis would attack the fort "when tomorrow, the Lord's day, is over, and to commence without delay a war of extermination upon all those who have shown themselves hostile to our rights." This message itself amounted to treason and Crozier had no other choice but to lead a force to Batoche to quell the uprising. The incident at Duck Creek occurred when Gabriel Dumont led a large group of Métis to confront the police who were on their way to Batoche. Whatever precipitated the confrontation between Assiyiwan and McKay, there would have been no battle if Dumont had stayed in Batoche.

* * *

Was Riel competently defended by his lawyers? A critic has suggested that they failed to defend him properly because they had not delved into the reasons that prompted the settlers to seek out Riel in Montana, and into the maladministration and neglect of the federal government.[3] However, Riel's lawyers did, indeed, attempt to bring out evidence from the Crown witnesses as to the reasons why the settlers sought out Riel and that his intention in coming to the North-West was to *peacefully* agitate for the Métis, and the fact that until March of 1885, agitation by Riel was peaceful until he realized that the federal government was not going to address his demands. However, the Crown objected to such evidence being introduced at trial since maladministration and neglect by government was no defence to rebellion. Justification has never been, in law, a defence to treason.

Other attacks on Riel's lawyers, such as their failure to procure the attendance of two federal deputy ministers as witnesses and to procure relevant documents, have little merit and are misguided. Evidence of maladministration and neglect by the government may have created sympathy for Riel and his cause but it would have been ruled inadmissible as irrelevant. Also without merit is the complaint of incompetence in failing to apply for a commission to take evidence in Montana of Dumont, Dumas, and Nault that would "prove that Mr. Riel if he had been listened to, not one drop of blood would have been shed ... that the alleged rebellion was commenced and conducted under the direction of a council of fourteen persons, of which council the prisoner was not a member; that he did not participate in any engagement or permit or countenance any overt act of treason." It is unlikely that Richardson, clothed temporarily with the powers of a superior court judge, would have ordered a commission if requested to do so. The order would be discretionary and would have delayed the trial for months; it must be remembered that Richardson had been directed by the government to proceed with Riel's trial with haste. He had refused to grant defence lawyers more than a week's adjournment to prepare Riel's defence, even though they had just travelled over fifteen hundred miles from Quebec

City to Regina, arriving only five days before Riel's arraignment. In the absence of a Crown grant of immunity to Dumont, Dumas, or Nault, it was unlikely that they would have left the safety of Montana to come to Canada to give evidence for Riel, only to be arrested and have a noose hung around their necks.

Although in retrospect it is easy to be critical of Riel's lawyers, it must be remembered how little time they had to prepare an adequate defence. A week was certainly not enough to interview witnesses, particularly Doctors Roy and Clark. Clark's evidence, instead of helpful to the defence, was damaging. Extensive pretrial interviews by Riel's lawyers, if they ever conducted them, would have revealed the weakness of the medical evidence, particularly that of Dr. Clark on the legal test of insanity. Clark's evidence in the end was the final nail in Riel's coffin when he said that the insane know what they are doing. No rational jury could have found Riel not guilty based on such evidence.

Prosecutions in 1885, and for many years after, were trials by ambush by the Crown. Disclosure of the Crown's case was rare; in the North-West Territories the absence of a preliminary inquiry made it impossible for the defence to fully explore the case for the Crown and to properly prepare a defence. The Crown was not required to show the defence the statements of their witnesses, nor even to tell the defence what they expected the witnesses to say. Although the Crown was required by the English Treason Trials Act of 1695 to finally provide the accused with a copy of the indictment against him, it did not require the Crown to disclose the names of witnesses to be called. Even if it had, it would have been impossible for Riel's lawyers to have interviewed them in the week they had been granted to prepare for trial, even if the witnesses could have been located. Knowing what a witness will say is critical to the preparation for cross-examination and how to defend a prosecution. The Crown had all of the advantages; the defence, none. Riel was to be given no quarter by the prime minister.

However, the suggestion by some writers that Riel was ably defended, even under the difficulties facing his lawyers, does not hold up to closer scrutiny. There was no justification for their failure to object to the way the Crown bullied the judge and improperly led evidence from their witnesses. It should have been evident from the first unsuccessful skirmishes that Richardson was going to do nothing that would skewer a successful prosecution. Riel's lawyers also seemed to be in awe of Crown counsel, particularly George Burbidge, who continually breached evidentiary rule after rule. It is inexplicable why they remained silent in the face of the way Burbidge improperly put incriminating evidence in the mouth of the Crown's witnesses, as if he were giving the evidence himself. If they were relying upon Richardson to intervene and stop him, they were sadly mistaken. They should have recognized early in the trial that Richardson was not prepared to prevent the Crown from leading inadmissible evidence, either because he did not understand what constituted inadmissible evidence or improper questioning by the Crown, or because of bias against Riel, or because it might harm the Crown's case.

Probably the greatest error on their part was to call Father André to describe Riel's mental instability. It must have been obvious to Riel's lawyers by the end of the Crown's case that the prosecution lawyers would stress to the jury Charles Nolin's evidence that Riel was prepared to abandon the Métis cause for a payment of $35,000 from the Canadian government. Such evidence would surely destroy any sympathy the jury might have for Riel, who had been portrayed as the saviour of the Métis. Nolin, who had once been a part of the rebellion, obviously had a grudge against his cousin. His evidence could have been easily brushed aside by Riel's lawyers as unreliable because he had a good reason to lie. He had been offered immunity from prosecution in exchange for his testimony against Riel.

There was no need for the defence to call any witnesses, particularly Father André, to repeat what had already been said by the Crown witnesses about Riel's unusual religious views. Evidence of Riel's unusual conduct after March 17 and his plans for the west had been described in great detail by a number of the Crown witnesses and was well known to all. Doctors Roy and Clark, who were in court and heard their testimony, would explain that this peculiar conduct was evidence of and consistent with Riel's insanity. Father André was probably the most highly respected French Canadian religious leader in the northwest. Their decision to call him opened the door to his devastating cross-examination by the Crown about

Riel's request for $35,000 from the federal government, and confirmed Nolin's evidence. Father André's evidence brought credibility to Nolin's evidence that Riel was prepared to abandon the Métis for money. Christopher Robinson hammered home this fact in his address to the jury as to why Riel should not be considered insane. Judge Richardson made a particular point of stressing it as well in his charge to the jury. The judges of the Manitoba Court of Appeal who heard Riel's appeal were also persuaded that Riel was not insane because he was prepared to accept $35,000 to leave the northwest. It was critical to their reasoning why the appeal should be dismissed. There is little doubt that Father André's evidence, instead of helping Riel, was fatal to the defence of insanity and put the noose around his neck.

Was the prosecution conducted fairly? A famous judge of the Supreme Court of Canada, Mr. Justice Ivan Cleveland Rand, wrote over fifty years ago that

> it cannot be over-emphasized that the purpose of a criminal prosecution is not to obtain a conviction; it is to lay before a jury what the Crown considers to be credible evidence relevant to what is alleged to be a crime. Counsel has a duty to see that all available legal proof of the facts is presented: it should be done firmly and pressed to its legitimate strength, *but it must be done fairly. The role of the prosecutor excludes any notion of winning or losing; his function is a matter of public duty that which in civil life there can be none charged with greater personal responsibility.* It is to be efficiently performed with an ingrained sense of the dignity, the seriousness, and the justness of judicial proceedings.[4]

The lawyers for the Crown failed to adhere to these principles from the very beginning of the trial, starting with their objection to an adjournment of the trial and then their gratuitous consent to an adjournment for only one week, knowing full well that this was not adequate time to prepare a proper defence. Crown counsel knew that Richardson relied upon their reputations and was a weak judge. It was Richardson's responsibility, not Crown counsel's, to decide whether an adjournment should be granted, and if so, for how long. In refusing to adjourn for no longer than a week, Richardson revealed that he was not acting independently. He was being directed by the government in Ottawa, who wanted a speedy trial and a predictable guilty verdict. A week was hardly enough time to prepare for a trial as important as this one, when the lawyers had come from the other side of Canada and the witnesses, especially the psychiatrists, would require some time to prepare their defence to a capital crime.

The attack by B.B. Osler on the evidence of Dr. Roy demonstrated the worst kind of anti-French bias that permeated every aspect of the trial. His abuse of Roy, who would not give him the answers that he wanted, to demonstrate that Riel's fixed idea could be changed by the offer of $35,000, followed by the comments that "if the man wants to *hide himself* under the French he can do so," and "it will be for the jury to say whether he is making the change at his own suggestion or at that of counsel on the other side," was disgraceful and unworthy of a lawyer of his stature.

But the bullying tactics of George Burbidge throughout the trial deserve the strongest censure. As deputy minister of justice, it was his duty to set the tone for fairness toward a man who was on trial for his life, and he failed miserably. Although it was the responsibility of the defence to object to his tactics of putting words in the mouths of witnesses and for Richardson to admonish him when he did, Burbidge knew better. He had undoubtedly been sent to ensure that Riel's trial was conducted as quickly as possible to a successful conclusion for the federal government and ignored his obligation to the justice system.

One wonders why it was necessary for the Crown to prosecute Riel so relentlessly to conviction and sentence when the evidence of treason against him was overwhelming. His conviction was a predictable certainty. It was not necessary to do so to prevent any further uprising in the northwest. The Métis rebellion had been crushed, and it was unlikely that another leader of Riel's stature would suddenly appear. Apart from the evidence, we must ask ourselves — did Riel receive a fair trial?

* * *

The role of a trial judge has been described as that of a fair and impartial arbiter, raised above the biases of the crowd, ensuring that due process is done. Fairness, impartiality, and competence in a trial judge are critical to a fair trial and due process, particularly where the prisoner at the bar is fighting for his life. Although some authors have said that Richardson's conduct of the trial was fair and impartial, his role in the trial of Louis Riel hardly fits within the definition of a fair and impartial arbiter.

It is true that Richardson was no Chief Justice George Jeffreys conducting the Bloody Assize. He did not intervene as Jeffreys had done two hundred years earlier, denigrating witnesses and bullying the jury into returning a guilty verdict so that he could revel in imposing the death penalty. In 1685, a judge's tenure depended upon his obsequiousness and obedience to the King. The Act of Settlement, only fifteen years later, finally put an end to judicial dependency. The act, which provided that superior court judges were to hold office during good behaviour subject to a power of removal for cause only upon an address from both Houses of Parliament, put an end to the Crown's control of the courts. Magistrates were not given the same protection. Their tenure depended upon how well they did the King's bidding.

Richardson's problem was that he was simply unsuited to conduct such an important trial. Although he had been a Crown attorney, he did not seem to understand the basic rules of evidence and was obviously awed by the importance and reputation of the Crown lawyers, particularly George Burbidge. He did not seem to understand that he, not the lawyers for the Crown, was the judge. It was his responsibility to intervene when Crown lawyers were improperly suggesting to their witnesses the answers they wanted to hear. Instead, he kept silent and let the prosecutors run the show. It was also his duty when a serious question arose as to the admissibility of certain evidence to remove the jury from the courtroom and rule on the admissibility in their absence. A flagrant example was when he allowed Burbidge to introduce incriminating statements allegedly made by Riel without requiring Burbidge to lay a proper foundation for the admission of the statements. It is most likely that he failed to do so simply because he did not know or understand that it was his duty to do so. As he stated when Riel sought to question Nolin, "If it were an ordinary criminal case, I should not hesitate, but this is beyond the ordinary run of cases that I have had to do within my whole career." Sitting as a magistrate, he probably found his docket filled with petty thievery, assaults, and drunkenness. As a superior court judge, it was his responsibility to take an active role in superintending the trial, ensuring that inadmissible evidence was excluded from the ears of the jury, that the lawyers conducted themselves fairly and properly, and that the jury were properly instructed. The transcript of the evidence reveals that Richardson failed in exercising that responsibility because he did not understand that it was his duty to do so.

Richardson's refusal to grant Riel's lawyers more than a week's adjournment can hardly be considered an act of fairness or of concern for Riel's right to a fair trial. He was not obliged to accede to the Crown's opposition to an adjournment, nor to the Crown's eventual concession that they would consent to a week's adjournment. He was the judge, not Burbidge, or Osler, or Robinson. His decision should have been an independent exercise of his discretion. His decision how long to grant the adjournment should have been governed by only one overriding consideration — the interests of justice — and it was certainly not in the interests of justice to rush to judgment, giving Riel's lawyers little time to prepare for his defence.

Not only did Richardson fail to intervene to prevent Burbidge from improperly bulldozing the evidence, more important was the manner in which he charged the jury to reject the evidence of insanity and convict Riel. It was Richardson's responsibility to review the medical evidence fairly and impartially, so that the jury could appreciate the value and effect of that evidence. Instead he took great pains to disparage the psychiatric evidence of Riel's alleged insanity, focusing on the fact that Riel was prepared to abandon the Métis for $35,000. Those comments, coming from the mouth of the trial judge, whose presence is expected to be the best assurance of neutrality, must have had an overriding influence on the jury.

Richardson's participation at the meeting with police, government, and Hudson's Bay Company officials on March 12, 1885, that concluded that Riel and his supporters should not be permitted to continue their agitation, was another example of his bias against Riel. Having attended that meeting, it was his duty to disqualify himself from presiding over Riel's trial — to ensure that justice should not only be done but should manifestly and undoubtedly be seen to be done — a fundamental principle that he did not seem to understand and justice demanded.

There has been justifiable criticism of the role of Chief Justice Wallbridge in presiding over the appeal. He should have recused himself or have been prevented by the justice minister from sitting in judgment of Riel. His letter to Sir Alexander Campbell, the federal minister of justice, warning him that the "jury in Winnipeg would be composed of 12, of whom the prisoner might insist that a moiety be half-breeds," would have automatically disqualified him from sitting on Riel's appeal trial had the defence been made aware of it. Although it may have been the practice at the time for chief justices to give confidential advice to the government, it did not mean that this practice entitled Wallbridge to sit on the appeal. The fact that the other members of his court concurred in dismissing the appeal does not excuse his failure to disqualify himself, since it is not known what influence he may have had on their decisions. Nor does the fact that the Judicial Committee of the Privy Council agreed with the decision of the Manitoba Court remove the taint of bias. Justice has to be seen to be done and in the case of Riel it was neither seen nor done.

The motives of Sir John A. Macdonald and his government cannot escape criticism. Macdonald was driven by his promise to British Columbia of building a railroad to the province before the American settlers in the west were able to convince their government to annex the North-West Territories — an expression of their belief in manifest destiny — and nobody was going to get in his way. As far as he was concerned, the meddling Métis Riel was not going to succeed this time as he had in the Red

River area. His comment that "He [Riel] shall die though every dog in Quebec bark in his favour" reflected his determination.

Minister of Justice Sir John Thompson's speech in Parliament about why the government acted as it did was an astonishing admission that Macdonald's government would not allow Riel to interfere at any price. In a long, rambling speech in which he reviewed the evidence at trial and defended the government's decision to go ahead with Riel's execution, Thompson, who subsequently became prime minister in 1892 and was instrumental in introducing Canada's first Criminal Code, was straightforward in his reasons.

> With regard to what might have been done in this case, I would like to invite the reflection of the House for a moment as to what might have followed if Executive clemency might have been exercised. One section of hon. gentlemen opposite say that this man ought to have been condemned to imprisonment as a criminal, a great criminal, although not so great as to be outside the Executive clemency; another class on the other side say no, he was totally mad, and he simply should have been put into an asylum. *Had either course been taken, how long would his confinement have lasted?* If the Executive ought to have acted on the broad principle that this was only a political offence, and that therefore the Executive clemency should have been extended to it, it would have been inconsistent with the view that Riel should have been long detained in prison. If he were confined in a lunatic prison, how long, I ask, with the power the evidence showed he had during the outbreak of controlling his own conduct and of getting possession of his senses when he wanted them — with the power of controlling his action and of recovering his balance when he wanted it — how long would it have been deemed just by the humane sentiment of the country to keep him in confinement? He would have been set at liberty,

under the report that he was cured and no longer mad, and he could have established a cure whenever he chose; and what then would have been the security of life and property in the North-West? I think that Louis Riel's next exclamation would have been, not that the rebellion of 1869–70 was not a patch upon that of 1885 but that both together would not be a patch on the rebellion he would raise the next time.[5]

Riel had to be put to death, Thompson was saying, not because there may have been reasons to grant executive clemency, but to prevent the possibility that he might be eventually released from a lunatic asylum or a penitentiary and incite further rebellion. The fact that the rebellion was born of the neglect and indifference of the Canadian government (which the government was not prepared to admit) was irrelevant. Even the fact that the jury that found Riel guilty had recommended mercy was irrelevant. The thorn in Macdonald's side had to be crushed to avoid any further dissent by western Métis and the Indigenous Peoples. Justice and compassion were secondary. Canadian security was overriding.

The next day, Sir Wilfrid Laurier, the member from Quebec East, rose in the House to respond to Thompson's speech, passionately expressing the injustice Quebecers felt about the hanging of Riel by comparing Riel's treatment to that of William Joseph Jackson.

Will it be pretended by any man that if Riel had been in his senses, if he had a sane and discerning mind, he would have accepted an insane man as his chief adviser?... One of the things which we in Lower Canada have felt as deeply as we have ever felt anything, is that we have believed that the measure of justice which was extended to Louis Riel was not the same measure of justice which was extended to William Joseph Jackson. Jackson was put upon his trial, and I am bound to say this, in duty to the Crown prosecutors, that upon that occasion they did their duty. They acknowledged at once the insanity of the prisoner and directed an acquittal … Is it not a fact that these two men were deluded on the same subjects? Jackson spoke rationally, but he had hallucinations, just as Riel had; and yet one of these men is acquitted, is sent to an asylum, and is allowed to escape, while Riel is sent to the gallows. Jackson is free today, and Riel is in his grave. I therefore cannot come to any other conclusion that upon this occasion the same measure of justice which was extended to one man was not extended to the other.

* * *

One writer has argued that Riel's trial was "'fair' in the only meaningful sense of that term," namely, that the trial was "impartially conducted under the prevailing rules of criminal procedure."[6] This suggests that there is a standard of impartially that varies with the times and background leading to the prosecution; that in times of civil unrest, the strictness of the rules of criminal procedure should be relaxed to ensure that troublemakers are punished inexorably to conviction and punishment at any cost, and that the national interest must take precedence over justice.

Although the fairness of a trial is often measured by the temper of the times, there are norms of what constitute a fair trial that are valid in any age. No guilty verdict can claim legitimacy where the prosecution has not ensured that all of the constitutional rights of an accused have been respected and protected. Included in those constitutional rights is the recognition that prosecutors, as ministers of the Crown, have no interest in procuring a conviction. "It is an investigation that should be conducted without feeling or animus on the part of the prosecution, with the single view of determining the truth."[7] Even the most heinous offender is entitled to the protection of his constitutional rights. This is the price that must be paid by a just society.

The fairness of a prosecution is a reflection of the importance that a society places on its justice system and on individual liberty. The rules of criminal procedure have not changed since 1885. Their goal was the same then as it is today: fairness of the prosecution, competence and impartiality of the trial judge, conviction only after the presentation of compelling evidence of guilt, and proof beyond a reasonable doubt. It is a single and unwavering standard that does not change in times of civil unrest. Indeed, in times of civil unrest, the Crown and judges have a greater duty to be particularly vigilant to ensure that the rules of criminal procedure are strictly observed. Over forty years ago, one of Canada's most eminent jurists, Mr. Justice Bora Laskin, chose to dissent from his colleagues in a case where the evidence of the accused's guilt was overwhelming, but the guilty verdict had been rendered by a biased judge. He wrote, "Over and above the question whether the evidence supports the conviction is the question whether the trial is being conducted by an unprejudiced judge who understands the limits of the judicial function and understands his sworn duty to conduct the case within the limits of its issues."[8]

What is clear is that over and above the question of whether the evidence against Riel supported his guilt is the disturbing failure of the Crown and the judge to conduct the trial in accordance with these fundamental principles.

Appendix

EXHIBIT NO. 1

Batoche, 12th May 1885

If you massacre our familes we are going to massacre the Indian agent and others, prisoners.

LOUIS "DAVID" RIEL, Exovede
Per J.W. Astley, bearer

Endorsement on Exhibit No. 1

12th May 1885

Mr. Riel: I am anxious to avoid killing women and children, and have done my best to avoid doing so. Put your women and children in one place, and let us know where it is and no shot shall be fired on them. I trust to your honor not to put men with them.

FRED MIDDLETON, Comdg. N.W. Field Forces

EXHIBIT NO. 2

Batoche, 12th May 1885

Sir: If you massacre our families we will begin by Indian Lash and other prisoners.

LOUIS "DAVID" RIEL, Exovede
Per F.E. Jackson, bearer

EXHIBIT NO. 3

Batoche, 12th May 1885

Major General Middleton: General, your prompt answer to my note shows that I was right in mentioning to you the cause of humanity. We will gather our families in one place, and as soon as it is done we will let you know.

I have the honor to be, General, your humble servant,
LOUIS "DAVID" RIEL

EXHIBIT NO. 4

I do not like war, and if you do not retreat and refuse an interview, the question remaining the same the prisoners.

EXHIBIT NO. 5

St Anthony, 21st March 1885

To Major Crozier, Commandant of the Police Force at Carlton and Battleford

Major: The councillors of the provisional government of the Saskatchewan have the honor to communicate to you the following conditions of surrender: You will be required to give up completely the situation which the Canadian Government have placed you in, at Carlton and Battleford, together with all government properties.

In case of acceptance, you and your men will be set free, on your parole of honor to keep the peace. And those who will choose to leave the country will be furnished with teams and provisions to reach Qu' Appelle.

In case of non-acceptance, we intend to attack you, when tomorrow, the Lord's Day, is over; and to commence without delay a war of extermination upon all those who have shown themselves hostile to our rights.

Messrs. Charles and Maxime Lepine are the gentlemen with whom you will have to treat.

Major, we respect you. Let the cause of humanity be a consolation to you for the reverses which the governmental misconduct has brought upon you.

LOUIS "DAVID" RIEL, Exovede
Rene Parenteau, chairman
Jean-Baptiste Parenteau
Chas. Nolin
Pierre Henry
Gab. Dumont
Albert Delorme
Morse Ouellette
Dum. Carriere
Albert Monkman
Maxime Lepine
Bte. Boyer
Bte. Boucher
Donald Ross
David Tourond
Amb. Jobin
Ph. Garnot, secretary

St Anthony, 21st March 1885

To Messrs. Charles Nolin and Maxime Lepine

Gentlemen: If Major Crozier accedes to the conditions of surrender, let him use the following formula, and no other: "Because I love my neighbor as myself, for the sake of God, and to prevent bloodshed, and principally the war of extermination which threatens the country, I agree to the above conditions of surrender."

If the Major uses this formula and signs it, inform him that we will receive him and his men, Monday.

Yours,
LOUIS "DAVID" RIEL, Exovede

EXHIBIT NO. 6

A calamity has fallen upon the country yesterday. You are responsible for it before God and man.

Your men cannot claim that their intentions were peaceable since they were bringing along cannons. And they fired many shots first.

God has pleased to grant us the victory, and as our movement is to say our rights our victory is good; and we offer it to the Almighty.

Major, we are Christians in war as in peace. We write you in the name of God and of humanity to come and take away your dead, whom we respect. Come and take them tomorrow before noon.

We enclose herein copy of a resolution adopted today by the representatives of the French half-breeds.

True copy, Ph. G.

EXHIBIT NO. 7

Aux Métis du Lac Qu'Appelle

Dear Relatives: We have the pleasure to let you know that on the 26th of last month, God has given us a victory over the mounted police.

Thirty half-breeds and five Cree Indians have met 130 policemen and volunteers. Thanks to God, we have defeated them. Yourselves, dear relatives, be courageous; do what you can. If it is not done yet, take the stores, the provisions, the ammunitions.

[Then follow two or three lines not intelligible.]

EXHIBIT NO. 8 (TRANSLATION)

God has always taken care of the half-breeds. He fed them for many days in the desert. Providence enriched our prairie with the buffalo. The plenty in which our fathers lived was as wonderful as the heavenly manna. But we were not sufficiently grateful to God, our good Father, hence it is that we have allowed ourselves to fall into the hands of a Government which only thinks of us to pillage us. Had he only understood what God did for us before Confederation, we should have been sorry to see it coming. And the half-breeds of the North-West would have made conditions of a nature to preserve for our children that liberty, that possession of the soil, without which there is no happiness for anyone; but fifteen years of suffering, impoverishment and underhand, malignant persecution have opened our eyes; and the sight of the abyss of demoralization into which the Dominion is daily plunging us deeper and deeper every day, has suddenly, by God's mercy as it were, stricken us with horror. And the half-breed people are more afraid of the hell into which the Mounted Police and their Government are openly seeking to drive us, than of their firearms, which, after all, can only kill our bodies. Our alarmed conscience have shouted out to us: Justice commands us take up arms. Dear relatives and friends, we advise you to pay attention. Be ready for everything. Take the Indians with you. Gather them from every side. Take all the ammunition you can, whatsoever storehouses it may be in. Murmur, growl, and threaten. Stir up the Indians. Render the police of Fort Pitt and Battleford powerless. We pray God to open to us a way to go up. And when we get there, as we hope, we shall help you to take Battleford and Fort Pitt. Have confidence in Jesus Christ. Place yourselves under the protection of the Blessed Virgin. Implore St. Joseph, for he is powerful with God. Commend yourselves to the powerful intercession of St. John the Baptist, the glorious patron of the Canadians and half-breeds. Be at peace with God. Keep His commandments. We pray Him to be with you all and to make you succeed.

Try and give to the half-breeds and Indians of Fort Pitt, as quickly as possible, the news we send you.

EXHIBIT NO. 9 (TRANSLATION)

To the Indians; to the half-breeds
The half-breeds and Indians of Battleford, and environs

Dear Brothers and Relatives: Since we wrote to you, important events have taken place. The police have attacked us; we met them and God gave us the victory; 30 half-breeds and 5 Indians fought against 120 men, and after 35 or 40 minutes, they took to flight. Bless God with us for the success he has kindly granted us. Rise; face the enemy, and if you can do so, take Battleford — destroy it — save all the goods and provisions, and come to us. With your numbers, you can perhaps send us a detachment of 40 or 50 men. All you do, do it for the love of God, and in the protection of Jesus Christ, the Blessed Virgin, St Joseph and St John the Baptist, and be certain that faith does wonders.

LOUIS "DAVID" RIEL, Exovede [in pencil] signed by the members of council

EXHIBIT NO. 10 (TRANSLATION)

To our brothers, the English and French half-breeds of Lake Qu'Appelle and environs

Dear Relatives and Friends: If you do not know it already, we shall tell you the reasons that induced us to take up arms. You know that time out of mind our fathers have defended, at peril of their lives, this land which was theirs and is ours. The Ottawa Government took possession of our country. For 15 years they have made sport of our rights, and offended God by overwhelming us with acts of injustice of every kind. The officials commit every species of crime. The men of the Mounted Police are the scandal of the whole country, by their bad language and their bad actions. They are so corrupt that our wives and daughters are no longer safe in their neighborhood. The laws of decency are to them a subject for pleasantry. Oh, my brothers and friends, we should at all times have confidence in God; but now that evil is at its height, we specially require to commend ourselves to our Lord. Perhaps you will see things as we see them. They steal our country from us, and then they govern it so badly, that if we let things go on it would soon be impossible for us to be saved. The English half-breeds of the Saskatchewan are with us heart and soul. The Indians are coming in and joining us from all sides. Buy all the ammunition you can; go and get it, if necessary, on the other side of the line. Be ready. Do not listen to the offers the Ottawa Government make you. Those offers are robbers' offers. Sign no papers or petitions. Let your trust be in God.

[translation] St Anthony, 25th March 1885

To Our Relatives: Thanks for the good news you have taken the trouble to send us. Since you are willing to help us, may God bless you. Justice commands us to take up arms. And if you see the police passing, attack them, destroy them [and written across the first part of this letter, in English, afterwards:] "Notify the Wood Indians not to be taken."

EXHIBIT NO. 11 (TRANSLATION)

I will not begin to work before twelve hours.

Our Relatives: Thanks for the good news you have taken the trouble to send us. Since you are willing to help, God bless you. And if you see the police passing, stop them, disarm them. Justice commands us to take up arms. Then warn the Wood Indians not to let themselves be surprised, but rather to be on their guard; to take ammunition from all the posts of the company, at Lac des Noisettes and Fish Lake.

Mr F. X., Batoche

The French half-breeds have taken up arms to a man. Not one of our people is against us. Tell our relatives, the Indians, to be ready to come and help us, if needed. Take all the ammunition of the company.

EXHIBIT NO. 12 (TRANSLATION)

Trust in God and the circumstances which Providence is now producing in the Saskatchewan. We shall not forget you. If promises are made to you, you will say that the time for promises is past. A time has come when we must have proof for everything. Pray. Be good, keep the commandments of God and you shall want for nothing.

EXHIBIT NO. 13

Dear Relative: We thank you for the good news that you took the trouble to send us. Since you are willing to help us, may God bless you in all what is to be done for our common salvation.

Justice commands to take-up arms. And if you see the police passing by, stop it and take away their arms.

Afterwards notify the Wood Indians that they might be surprised; let them be ready to all events, in being calm and courageous, to take all the powder, the shot, the lead, the posts and the cartridges from the Hudson's Bay store, at Nut Lake and Fishing Lake. Do not kill anybody. No, not molest nor ill-treat anybody. Fear not, but take away the arms.

LOUIS "DAVID" RIEL

EXHIBIT NO. 14

Gentlemen: The councillors of the half-breeds now under arms at St Anthony have received your message of the 22nd of March 1885.

They thank you for the sympathy with which you honor them even in this crisis, and of which you have given ample proof before.

Situated as you are it is difficult for you to approve (immediately) of our bold but just uprising, and you have been wise in your course.

Canada (Ottawa) has followed with us neither the principles of right nor constitutional methods of government. They have been arbitrary in their doings. They have usurped the title of the aboriginal half-breeds to the soil. And they dispose of it at condition opposed to honesty. Their administration of our lands, is which are already weighing altogether false — and which are already weighing very hard on all classes of the North-West people. They deprive their own immigrants of their franchises, of their liberties, not only political but even civil, and as they respect no right, we are justified before God and man to arm ourselves to try and defend our existence, rather than to see it crushed.

As to the Indians, you know, gentlemen, that the half-breeds have great influence over them. If the bad management of Indian affairs by the Canadian Government has been fifteen years without resulting in an outbreak, it is due only to the half-breeds who have up to this time persuaded to keep quiet. But now that the Indians, now that we ourselves are compelled to resort to arms, how can we tell them to keep quiet? We are sure that if the English and French half-breeds unite well in this time of crisis, not only can we control the Indians, but we will also have their weight on our side in the balance.

Gentlemen, please do not remain neutral. For the love of God help us to save the Saskatchewan. We sent to-day a number of men with Mr Monkman to help and support (under as it is just) the cause of the aboriginal half-breeds. Public necessity means no offence. Let us join willingly. The aboriginal half-breeds will understand that if we do we do so much for their interests we are entitled to their most hearty response.

You have acted admirably in sending copy of your resolutions to Carlton as well as to St Anthony. We consider that we have only two enemies in.

The French half-breeds believe that they are only two enemies, Coshen and Carlton. Dear brethren in Jesus Christ, let us avoid the mistakes of the past.

We consider it an admirable act of it has been an admirable act of prudence that you should have sent copies of your resolutions to the police in Carlton and to the men of St Anthony.

We dear brothers in Jesus Christ, let us avoid the mistakes of the past, let us work for us and our children, as true Christians.

LOUIS "DAVID" RIEL, Exovede

If we are well united the police will surrender and come out of Carlton as the hen's heat causes the chicken to come out of the shell. A strong union between the French and English half-breeds is the only guarantee that there will be no bloodshed.

EXHIBIT NO. 15

Resolved first that, when England gave that country to the Hudson Bay Company two hundred years ago, the North-West belonged to France as history shows it.

And when the Treaty of Paris ceded Canada to England no mention of any kind was made of the North-West.

As the American English colonies helped England to conquer Canada they ought to have a share of conquest, and that share ought to be the North-West, since commercially and politically the United States Government have done more for the North-West than ever England did, we ought to have.

Resolved, first, that our union is, and always will be most respectuous towards the American Government, their policy, their interest and towards the territorial Government of Montana as well.

2nd That our union will carefully avoid causing any difficulty whatever to the United States and will not conflict in any way with the constitution and laws of the Government. It is doubtful whether England really owns the North-West, because the first act of government that England ever accomplished over that North-West was to give it as a prey to the sordid monopoly of the Hudson Bay Company, two hundred years ago.

Her second act of government of any importance over that country was to give it in 1870 as a prey to the Canadians.

Our union is, and always will be most respectful towards the American annexation, against England and Rome, Manitoba French-Canadians.

EXHIBIT NO. 16

The French half-breed, members of the provisional government of the Saskatchewan, have separated from Rome and the great mass of the people have done the same.

If our priests were willing to help us, and up to this time our priests have shown themselves unwilling to leave Rome. They wish to govern us in a manner opposed to our interest and they wish to continue and govern us according to the dictates of Leo XIII.

Dear brothers in Jesus Christ, for the sake of God come and help us so that the enterprise against Rome may be a success and in return we will do all in our power to secure our political rights.

EXHIBIT NO. 17

Dear Relatives: We have the pleasure to let you know that on the 26th of last month God has given us a victory over the Mounted Police.

Thirty-five half-breeds and some five and six Cree Indians have met hundred and twenty policemen and volunteers.

Thank God, we have defeated them. Yourselves, dear relatives, be courageous. Do what you can. If it is not done, take the stores, the provisions and the munitions. And without delay come this way, as many as it is possible. Send us news.

LOUIS "DAVID" RIEL, Exovede
Morse Ouellette
Damas Carriere
J. Baptiste Boucher
Emmanuel Champagne
Donald Ross
Pierre Henry
Baptiste Parenteau

Pierre Garriepy
Maxime Lepine
Albert Monkman
Charles Trottier
Ambrose Jobin

The Mounted Police are making preparations for an attack; they are gathering themselves in one force, and no delay should exercise; come and reinforce us.

EXHIBIT NO. 18 (TRANSLATION)

To the Half-breeds and Indians of Battleford and environs

Since we wrote you, important matters have occurred. The police came and attacked us. We met them. God gave us the victory. Thirty half-breeds and five Crees fought against one hundred and twenty men. After a fight of thirty-five or forty minutes, the enemy took to flight.

Bless God with us for the success He has kindly granted us. Rise. Face the police. If you possibly can, if the thing is not already done, take Fort Battleford. Destroy it. Save all the goods and provisions and come to us. With your numbers you can send us a detachment of forty to fifty men.

All that you do, do it for the love of God under the protection of Jesus Christ, of the Blessed Virgin of St Joseph, and of St John the Baptist.

Be certain that faith works wonders.

LOUIS "DAVID" RIEL, Exovede
Pierre Parenteau
Donald Ross
Charles Trottier
Pierre Garriepy
Bte. Boucher
Damas Carriere
Pierre Henry
Antoine Jobin

EXHIBIT NO. 19

15th May 1885

Major General Fred. Middleton

General: I have received only to-day yours of the 13th instant. My council are dispersed. I wish you would let them go quiet and free. I hear that presently you are absent. Would I go to Batoche, who is going to receive me? I will go to fulfil God's will.

LOUIS "DAVID" RIEL, Exovede

EXHIBIT NO. 20

Duck Lake, 27th March 1885

To Major Crozier, Commanding Officer, Fort Carleton

Sir: A calamity has fallen upon the country yesterday, you are responsible for it before God and man.

Your men cannot claim that their intentions were peaceable, since they were bringing along cannons. And they fired many shots first.

God has been pleased to grant us the victory, and as our movement is to save our lives, our victory is good, and we offer it to the Almighty.

Major, we are Christians in war as in peace. We write in the name of God and of humanity to come and take away your dead, whom we respect. Come and take them to-morrow before noon.

We enclose herein a copy of a resolution adopted to-day by the representatives of the French half-breeds.

LOUIS "DAVID" RIEL, Exovede
Albert Monkman
J. Bte. Boucher
Gabriel Dumont
Damos Carriere
Norbert Delorme
Bte. Parenteau

Pierre Garriepy
Pierre Parenteau
Donald Ross
Amt. Jobin
Moise Ouellete
David Tourond
Maxime Lepine P.
Garnot, secretary

[copy of minute]

That a prisoner be liberated and given a letter to the commanding officer at Carlton, inviting him in the name of God and of humanity to come and take away the bodies of the unfortunate who fell yesterday on his side in the combat; that far from being molested he will be accompanied by our condolences in the fulfilment of that sorrowful duty, that we will wait till to-morrow noon. Moved by Mr. Monkman, seconded by Mr Jean Baptiste Boucher, and unanimously carried.

Dated 27th March 1885

Notes

CHAPTER 1: INTRODUCTION

1.   Although commonly known as the Northwest Territories, the British
     North America Act (now the Constitution Act) of 1867 called it the
     North-Western Territory. The territory's name first became official in
     1859 with the British Indian Territories Act, which established British
     jurisdiction over land not in Rupert's Land or British Columbia,
     calling it the North-Western Territory. This included all of what is
     now the Yukon Territory, the provinces of Alberta, Saskatchewan,
     and parts of Manitoba. In 1868 the Canadian Parliament passed
     the Rupert's Land Act, which authorized the acquisition of Rupert's
     Land and the North-Western Territory from the HBC for the sum
     of £300,000. On June 23, 1870, an Imperial order-in-council
     transferred Rupert's Land and the North-Western Territory to
     Canada, at which time it was renamed the North-West Territories.
     In 1905 Alberta and Saskatchewan were created from the southern
     portions of the North-West Territories.

CHAPTER 3: THE REBELLION

1. Blair Stonechild and Bill Waiser, *Loyal till Death: Indians and the North-West Rebellion* (Calgary: Fifth House, 1997), 53–55.
2. Volume 9 (1881–1890) of the *Dictionary of Canadian Biography* reports that

> although Clarke consistently denied this charge, modern historians agree that it was probably well founded. The second rumour suggested that it was largely due to his urgings that Superintendent Lief Newry Fitzroy Crozier marched on Duck Lake on 26 March without awaiting the arrival of Colonel Acheson Gosford Irvine with NWMP reinforcements. Clarke never commented on this charge. He was present during the first stages of the ensuing confrontation but fled precipitately when the fighting broke out. His health collapsed immediately thereafter, and though he was appointed a supply officer of the Canadian expedition to suppress the rebellion, he was unable to fulfil his duties.

3. Paul Wahl and Don Toppel, *The Gatling Gun* (New York: Arco Publishing, 1971).
4. Emmott, N.W., "The Devils Watering Pot," *Proceedings* (United States Naval Institute), September 1972, 70.

CHAPTER 4: THE PLAYERS

1. Sir James Stephen, *History of the Criminal Law of England*, vol. 2 (New York: Burt Franklin) 241–80.
2. See note 1 in chapter 1.
3. *Regina v. Punch* (1985), 48 C.R. (3d) 374 (N.T.S.C.). Although section 11(f) of the charter guarantees the right to trial by jury where the maximum punishment for the offence is imprisonment for five

years or a more severe punishment, it does not specifically guarantee trial by a jury of twelve. However, 631(5) of the Criminal Code requires a jury of twelve to be empanelled before a jury trial may begin. It is unlikely today that Parliament would ever dare reduce the jury to less than twelve.

CHAPTER 5: THE EVIDENCE OF TREASON

1. *Stinchcombe,* [1991] 3 S.C.R. 326.

CHAPTER 6: THE DEFENCE OF INSANITY

1. M'Naghten's Case, (1843) 10 Cl. & Finn 200.
2. (1935) 25 Cr.App.R. 109.
3. The purpose of scrip was to extinguish the Indigenous title of the Métis by awarding a certificate redeemable for land or money — the choice was the applicant's — of either 160 or 240 acres or dollars, depending on their age and status.

CHAPTER 7: THE SPEECH BY THE DEFENCE

1. G.A. Martin, "Closing Argument to the Jury for the Defense in Criminal Cases," *Journal of Criminal Law and Criminology* 58, no. 1 (1967): 2–17, scholarlycommons.law.northwestern.edu/cgi/viewcontent.cgi?article=5424&context=jclc.

CHAPTER 10: THE JUDGE'S CHARGE TO THE JURY

1. Lloyd Paul Stryker, *For the Defense: Thomas Erskine, The Most Enlightened Liberal of His Times, 1750–1823* (Toronto: Doubleday, 1947), 129.
2. *Clark v. The King,* [1921] 35 C.C.C. 261 (S.C.C.).

CHAPTER 12: THE APPEALS

1. *Regina v. Connor*, [1885–86] 2 Man. L.R. 235.
2. The British Parliament specifically abolished the grand jury in 1933. The last province to specifically abolish the grand jury in Canada was Nova Scotia in 1984.
3. Section 76(5) of the North-West Territories Act of 1880 specifically provided for trial by jury.

CHAPTER 13: THE MEDICAL COMMISSION

1. Macdonald to Lavell, 31 October 1885, Library and Archives Canada.
2. Cyril Greenland, "The Life and Death of Louis Riel," *Canadian Psychiatric Association Journal* 10, no. 4 (August 1965): 258.
3. Jukes to Macdonald, 6 November 1885, Library and Archives Canada.
4. Lavell to Macdonald, 9 November 1885, Library and Archives Canada.
5. Greenland, "Life and Death," 258.
6. Greenland, "Life and Death," 258.
7. Greenland, "Life and Death," 258.
8. Thomas Flanagan, *Riel and the Rebellion: 1885 Reconsidered* (Saskatoon: Western Producer Prairie Books, 1983), 140.
9. Flanagan, *Riel and the Rebellion*, 144n29.
10. Daniel Clark, "A Psycho-Medical History of Louis Riel," *American Journal of Insanity* (July 1887): 51.
11. W. Stewart Wallace, ed., "North-West Rebellion," *The Encyclopedia of Canada*, vol. 5 (Toronto: University Associates of Canada, 1948), 19–22, quoted in Claude Bélanger, "North-West Rebellion," in *L'Encyclopédie de l'histoire du Québec / The Quebec History Encyclopedia*, faculty.marianopolis.edu/c.belanger/quebechistory/encyclopedia/North-WestRebellion-CanadianHistory.htm.

CHAPTER 14: THE AFTERMATH

1. George Goulet, *The Trial of Louis Riel: Justice and Mercy Denied* (Victoria: Telwell Publising, 1999). See also J.M. Bumsted, *The Making of a Rebel* (Winnipeg: Great Plains Publications, 2001).
2. Frank W. Anderson, *Riel's Saskatchewan Rebellion* (Humboldt, SK: Gopher Books, 1999). See also Rosemary Neering, *Louis Riel* (Toronto: Fitzhenry & Whiteside, 1977).
3. Goulet, *Trial of Louis Riel*.
4. *Boucher v. The Queen*, [1955] S.C.R. 16.
5. John S.D. Thompson, "The Execution of Louis Riel," Speech of the Hon. John S. D. Thompson, Minister of Justice, delivered March 22, 1886, *Hansard Parliamentary Debates*, Commons. Thompson was minister of justice from September 26, 1885, to June 6, 1891.
6. Flanagan, *Riel and the Rebellion*.
7. Mr. Justice Riddell in *R. v. Chamandy*, [1934] 61 C.C.C. (Ont.C.A.).
8. *R. v Bevacqua and Palmieri*, [1970] 2 O.R.786 (C.A).

Bibliography

ARTICLES AND TEXTS

Anderson, Frank W. *Riel's Saskatchewan Rebellion*. Gopher Books 9. Humboldt, SK: Gopher Books, 1999.

Archer, John H. *Saskatchewan: A History*. Saskatoon: Western Producer Prairie Books, 1980.

Berger, Thomas R. *Fragile Freedoms: Human Rights and Dissent in Canada*. Toronto: Irwin, 1982.

Bliss, Michael, ed. *The Queen v Louis Riel*. Transcript. Toronto: University of Toronto Press, 1974.

Bowsfield, Hartwell. *Louis Riel: The Rebel and the Hero*. Don Mills, ON: Oxford University Press, 1971.

Brode, Patrick. "Osler, Britton Bath." In *Dictionary of Canadian Biography*. Vol. 13. University of Toronto/Université Laval, 2003–. Accessed August 23, 2019. biographi.ca/en/bio/osler_britton_bath_13E.html.

Brode, Patrick. "Robinson, Christopher (1828–1905)." In *Dictionary of Canadian Biography*. Vol. 13. University of Toronto/Université Laval, 2003–. Accessed August 23, 2019. biographi.ca/en/bio/robinson_christopher_1828_1905_13E.html.

Brooke, John. "Insanity." *Law Society of Upper Canada Special Lectures* (1959).

Bumsted, J.M. *Louis Riel v. Canada: The Making of a Rebel.* Winnipeg: Great Plains Publications, 2001.

Castonguay, René. "Chase-Casgrain, Thomas." In *Dictionary of Canadian Biography*. Vol. 14. University of Toronto/Université Laval, 2003–. Accessed August 24, 2019. biographi.ca/en/bio/ chase_casgrain_thomas_14E.html.

Clark, Daniel. "A Psycho-Medical History of Louis Riel." *American Journal of Insanity* 44 (1887/88): 157–69.

Creighton, Donald. *Canada's First Century: 1867–1967.* Toronto: Macmillan, 1970.

Désilets, Andrée. "Lemieux, François-Xavier." In *Dictionary of Canadian Biography*. Vol. 9. University of Toronto/Université Laval, 2003–. Accessed August 24, 2019. biographi.ca/en/bio/lemieux_francois_ xavier_9E.html.

Flanagan, Thomas, "Richardson, Hugh (1826–1913)." In *Dictionary of Canadian Biography*. Vol. 14. University of Toronto/Université Laval, 2003–. Accessed August 23, 2019. biographi.ca/en/bio/ richardson_hugh_1826_1913_14E.html.

Flanagan, Thomas. *Riel and the Rebellion: 1885 Reconsidered.* Saskatoon: Western Producer Prairie Books, 1983.

Gordon, Irene Ternier. *Marie-Anne Lagimodière: The Incredible Story of Louis Riel's Grandmother.* Canmore, AB: Altitude, 2004.

Goulet, George. *The Trial of Louis Riel: Justice and Mercy Denied.* Victoria, BC: Tellwell Publishing, 1999.

Hardy, W.G. *From Sea unto Sea: The Road to Nationhood, 1850–1910.* Canadian History Series 4. Toronto: Doubleday, 1969.

Knox, Olive. "The Question of Louis Riel's Insanity." *Manitoba Historical Society Transactions 3*, no. 6 (1949–50). mhs.mb.ca/docs/ transactions/3/rielinsanity.shtml.

Martin, G. Arthur. "Closing Argument to the Jury for the Defense in Criminal Cases." *Journal of Criminal Law, Criminology and Police Science 58*, no. 1 (1967): 2–17.

Morton, W.L. *The Kingdom of Canada: A General History from Earliest Times.* Toronto: McClelland and Stewart, 1963.

Olesky, Ronald. "Louis Riel and the Crown letters." *Canadian Lawyer* (February 1998): 12–15.

Siggins, Maggie. *Riel: A Life of Revolution.* Toronto: HarperCollins, 1994.

Smith, Donald B. *Destinies: Canadian History Since Confederation.* Toronto: Nelson, 1988.

Stanley, George F.G. *Louis Riel.* Toronto: Ryerson, 1963.

Stonechild, Blair, and Bill Waiser. *Loyal Till Death: Indians and the North-West Rebellion.* Calgary: Fifth House, 1997.

Stryker, Lloyd Paul. *For the Defense: Thomas Erskine, The Most Enlightened Liberal of His Times, 1750–1823.* Toronto: Doubleday, 1947.

Thompson, John S.D. "The Execution of Louis Riel." Speech of the Hon. John S. D. Thompson, Minister of Justice, delivered March 22, 1886. *Hansard Parliamentary Debates*, Commons.

Valade, F.-W. "Report on the Mental Condition of Louis Riel, 1885," MG 27 IJ8.

Wallace, W. Stewart, ed. "North-West Rebellion." In *The Encyclopedia of Canada.* Vol. 5, 19–22. Toronto: University Associates of Canada, 1948. Quoted in Claude Bélanger. "North-West Rebellion." *L'Encyclopédie de l'histoire du Québec / The Quebec History Encyclopedia* (website). Marianopolis College, 2007. faculty.marianopolis.edu/c.belanger/quebechistory/encyclopedia/North-WestRebellion-CanadianHistory.htm.

LETTERS

Macdonald, Sir John A., to Drs. Lavell & Valade. October 31st, 1885. Library and Archives Canada.

Macdonald, Sir John A., to Dr. Michael Lavell. Printed in Douglas Library Notes (Queen's University, Kingston) 12, no. 2 (Spring 1963):16.

CASE LAW

Boucher v. The Queen, [1955] S.C.R. 16.

Clark v. The King, [1921] 35 C.C.C. 261 (S.C.C.).

The Queen v. Louis Riel, [1885] Man. L.R. 321.

Regina v. Bevacqua and Palmieri, [1970] 2 O.R.(2) 786.

Regina v. Punch, [1985] 48 C.R.(3d) 374 (N.T.S.C.).

Regina v. Sugarman, [1935] 25 Cr. App. R. 109.

Rex v. Sussex Justices, [1924] 1 K.B. 256.

Riel v. The Queen, [1885] 10 H.L. 675.

R v. Connor, [1885–86] 2 Man.L.R. 235.

R v. M'Naghten, [1843] 10 Cl. & Finn 200.

Image Credits

I wish to acknowledge and thank the Provincial Archives of Saskatchewan and the Glenbow Archives for providing me with a number of photographs of Louis Riel and his trial that were used in this publication.

54 (top)	Provincial Archives of Saskatchewan R-B2498 (1)-(2)
54 (bottom)	Provincial Archives of Saskatchewan R-B2060
57 (top)	Provincial Archives of Saskatchewan GM-PH-2177
57 (bottom)	Provincial Archives of Saskatchewan R-D1777
61	Provincial Archives of Saskatchewan R-A8843
62 (top)	Glenbow Archives NA-4140-9
62 (bottom)	Glenbow Archives NA-4140-2
66	Provincial Archives of Saskatchewan R-B709 (1)-(2)
67	Provincial Archives of Saskatchewan R-B709-2
91	Provincial Archives of Saskatchewan R-B4528
224	Glenbow Archives NA-4140
257	Provincial Archives of Saskatchewan R-B278

Index

André, Alexis (Father)
  Riel's spiritual advisor, 7–10
  witness at Riel's trial, 143–46
Assiyiwan, 41–42
Astley, John
  delivers Riel's message, 50
  evidence against Riel, 94–97

Batoche, battle of, 46–51
Beauport Asylum, 22, 149, 152–53
Big Bear (Cree chief)
  involvement in rebellion, 42
  refusal to withdraw to reserve, 36
British North America Act 1867, 17–18,
  55–56, 71–73
Burbidge, George Wheelock, Q.C.
  background, 59–60
  conduct at trial, 86
  criticism, 289
  evidence of treason, 91–133

Chapleau, S.E. (sheriff), 8–9,
Clark, Daniel
  criticism of evidence, 287
  evidence for Riel, 162–67

medical background, 161
Clarke, Lawrence
  chief factor RBC, 38
  urges Crozier to attack Métis, 39
coroner's jury, 9–11
Cosgrove, Francis
  jury foreman, 2
  jury recommendation, 2
Crozier, Leif (superintendent)
  battle of Duck Lake, 39–41
  telegraph to Ottawa, 38–39

Dodd, Henry (coroner), 10
Douglas, Thomas (earl of Selkirk)
  background, 18
  relationship with HBC, 19–20
Duck Lake, battle of, 39–43
Dumont, Gabriel
  battle of Batoche, 46–51
  battle of Duck Lake, 39–43
  battle of Fish Creek, 44–46
  escape to U.S., 51
  military strategy, 44
  visits Riel in Montana, 29

Fish Creek, battle of, 44–46
Fitzpatrick, Charles
    background, 63
    counsel for Riel, 63, 71–72
    criticism, 288–89
    speech to jury, 179–99
    submissions as to jurisdiction, 70–72
Fourmond, Vital (Father)
    evidence at trial, 147–49
    letter from Riel, 7–8
fur trade wars, 19

Gatling gun, 47–48
Gibson (deputy sheriff), 9

Halsbury, Lord (chancellor of England),
    4, 271–73
Hudson's Bay Company (HBC)
    administers Red River Settlement, 14
    history, 14
    relationship to Métis, 13–14
    sale of Rupert's Land, 17–18

Indigenous Peoples
    dissatisfaction with government, 35
    famine, 33–34
    relationship with Métis, 34, 36
    involvement in the North–West
        Rebellion, 36
insanity, legal
    defined, 138–39
    history, 136–38
    M'Naghten rules, 137

Jackson, William Joseph (Honoré Jaxon)
    jury directed to acquit, 142
    escape to the U.S., 142
    relationship with Riel, 141
    trial for treason felony, 140–42
Jukes, Augustus
    assessment of Jackson, 141–42
    criticism of evidence, 170
    evidence against Riel, 170–73
    letter to Macdonald, 277–78

post-mortem report, 9–10
jury, trial of Louis Riel
    deliberations, 255–57
    recommendation, 2, 256
    verdict, 2, 255

Killam, Albert Clements (justice)
    appointment, 4, 262
    decision, 267–68

Lagimodière, Marie-Anne, 22
Laurier, Wilfrid
    speech in House of Commons,
        295–96
Lavall, Michael
    appointment, 5, 276
    interviews Riel, 6, 277
    letter to Macdonald, 6
    official report, 6, 278–79
Lemieux, François-Xavier
    background, 61
    counsel for Riel, 69
    criticism, 288–89
Lepine, Ambroise
    associate of Riel, 26–27
    death sentence commuted, 27
    tried for murder of Thomas Scott,
        25–26

Macdonald, John A.
    appointment of medical men, 5
    appointment of prosecutors, 53
    criticism, 293–94
    decision to try Riel with treason, 53–55
    famous quote, 7
    instructions to Dr. Lavelle, 6, 276–77
    instructions to Dr. Valade, 6, 276
    letter from Jukes, 277–78
    prime minister, 4
magistrate, courts, 65–69
Manitoba Court of Appeal
    appointed to hear Riel appeal, 4
McKay, Joe, 40–41
McWilliams, Charles (Father), 9–10

Métis
grievances, 30–34
history, 13–16
loss of the buffalo, 29
move to Saskatchewan, 28–29
relationship with Indigenous Peoples,
15–16
Middleton, Frederick Dobson (major
general)
battle of Batoche, 46–52
battle of Fish Creek, 44–46
command of the Canadian militia,
43–46
evidence against Riel, 174–76

Nolin, Charles
deserts Duck Lake battle, 41,
evidence against Riel, 120–30
involvement in the North-West rebellion, 37–38
makes deal with Crown, 42
Riel's cousin, 36
North West Company (NWC)
clashes with the HBC, 20–21
history, 14
North-West Territories Act (1880), 64,
67, 70–72

Osler, Britton Bath, Q.C.
background, 59
criticism, 289
evidence of treason, 91–133
opening statement, 88–90
prosecution of Riel, 59, 91–133

pemmican
incident with Métis, 19–20
Proclamation (1814), 19
Poundmaker (chief), 42
Privy Council, Judicial Committee, 4

Regina
pile of bones, 58
place of trial, 1

Richardson, Hugh (judge)
background, 64–65, 69
charge to the jury, 1, 242–52
criticism, 291–93
sentence of death, 3–4, 258–59
Riel, Jean-Louis (father of Louis Riel)
childhood, 21–22
death, 23
leader in forcing free trade, 23
support of Guillaume Sayer, 21
Riel, Louis David
American citizenship, 27
ancestry, 23
childhood, 13, 20–23
convalescence in Beauport, 27
disavowal of insanity, 207–8
education in Montreal, 20
elected to House of Commons, 26
execution, 1–10
letter to Father Fourmand, 7–8
organized a National Committee, 24
reconciliation with Catholic Church,
7–8
role in history, 11–12
Scott's execution, 25
sentence of death, 3–4, 258–59
speech to the jury, 3, 207–22
statutory holiday, 11–12
visions, 27
wife, Marguerite, 7, 35
Robinson, Christopher, Q.C.
background, 59
criticism, 289
evidence of treason, 91–133
prosecution of Riel, 59
speech to the jury, 223–37
submissions on jurisdiction, 72–73
Roy, Francois
evidence for Riel, 149–61
medical background, 149

Saint Boniface, 13
Schultz, John Christian
leader of Canada First Movement, 24

opposition to Riel, 24–25
Scott, Thomas
   hero in Ontario, 26
   trial and execution, 25
Statute of Treasons (1352), 55

Taché, Bishop Alexandre
   relationship with Riel, 25–26
Taylor, Thomas Wardlaw (justice)
   appointment, 4, 262
   decision, 268–69
Thompson, John
   criticism, 294–95
   decision to execute Riel, 294
   speech to the House of Commons,
      294–95
treason, high, 83
treason felony, 83

Valade, François–Xavier
   appointment, 5, 276
   interviews Riel, 6, 277
   letter to Macdonald, 279
   memorandum, 280–81
   official report, 6, 278–79

Wallace, James
   evidence for the Crown, 167–70
   medical background, 167
Wallbridge, Lewis (chief justice)
   appointment, 4, 262
   criticism, 293
   decision, 265–67

Young, George Holmes (captain)
   escorts Riel to Regina, 52
   evidence against Louis Riel, 174–76